GODS AND GUITARS

GODS AND GUITARS

Seeking the Sacred in Post-1960s Popular Music

Michael J. Gilmour

BAYLOR UNIVERSITY PRESS

Scripture quotations, where not the author's own translation, are from the New Revised Standard Version Bible, copyright 1989, Division of Christian Education of the National Council of the Churches of Christ in the United States of America. Used by permission. All rights reserved.

Cover Design by Dustin Steller, Five Loaves Creative
Cover Image: Flaming Guitar by Mikhail Bakunovich © 2009 iStockphoto. Used by permission.
Book Design by Diane Smith

Library of Congress Cataloging-in-Publication Data

Gilmour, Michael J.
  Gods and guitars : seeking the sacred in post-1960s popular music / Michael J. Gilmour.
      p. cm.
  Includes bibliographical references (p.   ) and index.
  ISBN 978-1-60258-139-5 (pbk. : alk. paper)
  1. Popular music--Religious aspects. I. Title.
  ML3921.8.P67G45 2009
  781.64'112--dc22
                                        2009020945

CONTENTS

ACKNOWLEDGMENTS

I am grateful to Casey Blaine of Baylor University Press for her infectious enthusiasm and good humor. She saw this project through from initial inquiry to index with efficiency and sharp editorial sense. I also extend thanks to my friends Gary Conway, Richard Pepper, and Joey Royal for reading earlier drafts of this material and offering numerous ideas for improvement. Students at Providence College and Theological Seminary (Manitoba, Canada) endured some of this material in dribs and drabs, and I am indebted to them for their collective knowledge about the subjects examined and their patience with an old guy fixated on such ancient music (which for many of them is pretty much anything before 2009). I usually listen to music with Kyla by my side, and for this reason, I have never enjoyed writing so much. In the words of the prophets, "Without your love I'd be nowhere at all."

OPENING NOTES

. . . I stopped going to churches and got myself into a different kind of religion. Don't laugh, that's what being in a rock 'n' roll band is, not pseudo-religion either . . . Show-business is Shamanism: Music is Worship; whether it's worship of women or their designer, the world or its destroyer, whether it comes from that ancient place we call soul or simply the spinal cortex, whether the prayers are on fire with a dumb rage or dove-like desire . . . the smoke goes upwards . . . to God or something you replace God with . . . usually yourself.

—Bono[1]

The title of this book—*Gods and Guitars: Seeking the Sacred in Post-1960s Popular Music*—is misleading. For one thing, "popular music" is a label that defies easy definition.[2] And second, the songs considered represent but a small sample falling within that catchall category. My selection is eclectic, even random, owing as much to my age—born in the summer of love—and personal tastes as anything else. Inevitably, my choices will strike some as scandalous. The omission of certain artists from discussion will be as problematic to one group of readers as the inclusion of certain artists will be for another. This is unavoidable but still constructive if it encourages readers to reevaluate their favorite musicians in similar terms. Ultimately, my particular choices of artists, songs, and albums do not matter a great deal for the overall argument. One would reach similar conclusions if bringing the same questions to an entirely different list, I suspect. As I read song lyrics of the last forty or so years with attention to religious themes, I observe particular habits of writing and tendencies of thought that appear in a far wider range of songs than the narrow, selective list with which I work. These broad tendencies and habits concern me here.

Popular music studies can address a number of subjects: music and instrumentation (sounds), artist biography, fan culture, historical development within genres and the recording industry, and so on. Here, I reduce albums and songs to lyrics, to words on the page, giving only passing attention to such things as musical accompaniment, the dynamics of live performances, and connections between music and the sociological makeup of its audiences. Of course, every music fan knows that a good song is something to experience, not something to read about, and though I realize my approach has its limitations, I persist because many song lyrics are interesting *as texts*, and they reward close reading. This book is primarily literary in its approach, reading songs as writings resembling poetry, even if they are not poems in a formal sense.

The particular subject on which I focus as I read these lyrics is also unusual because as a rule we do not tend to emphasize religious content in entertainment media, though a burgeoning bibliography on religion in popular culture is in the offing. I distinguish religious media from media with religious content, and focus on the latter. I use the term "popular music" or "mainstream music" deliberately, to distinguish the songs discussed here from those intended for niche markets, such as the religious audiences of traditional gospel music, or contemporary Christian music. One way of defining popular music is to emphasize audience size, as opposed to such things as genre or technology. The authors of one textbook on the subject "use the term 'popular music' broadly, to indicate music that is mass-reproduced and disseminated via the mass media; that has at various times been listened to by large numbers of [people]."[3] For the most part, the music I consider has no connection to the activities of organized religion. Indeed, religion and popular music are occasionally hostile to one another, as evident in churches boycotting, protesting, or vilifying particular musicians, or musicians ridiculing religion. In light of this occasional dissociation and hostility, it is remarkable just how much sacred subject matter we hear on the radio.

I focus for the most part on music of the post-1960s, though this demarcation is not rigid. When we think about popular music, particularly rock and roll, there is an inevitable association of this particular art form with aggression, resistance, protest, and rebelliousness. Such iconic events as the 1969 Woodstock and Altamont music festivals, for instance, embody the youthful idealism and defiance of the establishment characteristic of that particular historical moment as the sixties came to a close. Musicians and their audiences symbolically gave notice of their decision to part company with the status quo, claiming in effect that their politics, fashion sense, sexuality, artistic tastes, and spirituality could move in any direction they wished, regardless of societal expectations. For many, this included movement away from traditional ways of thinking about religion, and from the traditional contexts for exhibiting religious devotion (like synagogues and churches). This did not mean, necessarily, that interest in religion itself declined, and consideration of the music of the post-1960s bears this out. Religious thinking is ubiquitous in the songs and albums of recent decades, and for many, mainstream music, at times even the cult of celebrity,[4] would offer a kind of spirituality and forum for reflection on metaphysical matters.

I focus on post-Woodstock, post-Altamont music because it represents a generation shaped in part by this antiestablishment attitude. My aim is to capture something of the spirit of the post-1960s, a period conveniently bookmarked by my two favorite albums, George Harrison's *All Things Must Pass* (1970) and Bob Dylan's *Modern Times* (2006). These musicians and these particular albums embody much of what interests me here. Both artists were iconic figures active during the volatile 1960s, a period of upheaval in opinions about society, politics, and religion in the Western world. Both also continued writing and performing into the decades following those heady days. These particular albums also bring into focus the central questions addressed in what follows. If organized religion lost its firm grip and there was a general movement away from institutional faith—and I am speaking in sweeping generalities here—then why is it that religious terminology and imagery remain such pervasive features of Western popular music in the post-1960s period? Why is it that the quintessential symbols of this antiestablishment *Zeitgeist*—mainstream pop musicians—so often turn to the sacred language of the Bible and the Church or other religious traditions? Harrison's religious convictions sound clearly through his solo music, in songs like "My Sweet Lord" (*All Things Must Pass*, 1970) and "The Rising Sun" (*Brainwashed*, 2002).[5] This is true of Dylan to a lesser extent (consider especially his gospel albums *Slow Train Coming* [1979], *Saved* [1980], and *Shot of Love* [1981]). However, what Dylan's massive musical output from the early sixties into the twenty-first century illustrates best is how religion provides writers with conceptual, metaphoric, and thematic resources for their artistic endeavors, regardless of religious orientation.[6]

In 1970, George Harrison released the first solo album by a former Beatle. His beautiful *All Things Must Pass* was critically acclaimed and was a clear expression of his Hindu spirituality. In 2006, the enduring Bob Dylan released *Modern Times*, which earned Grammy Awards for Best Solo Rock Vocal Performance ("Someday Baby"), and Best Folk/Americana Album. The album is rich with biblical allusions, as in its opening words ("Thunder on the mountain," in the song of the same name) that echo ancient Israel's Sinai experiences described in Exodus 19:16. We also find the narrator of "Spirit on the Water" banished from Paradise like Cain (cf. Gen 4:10-14) and sweating blood like Jesus (cf. Luke 22:44). Both Harrison's *All Things Must Pass* and Dylan's *Modern Times* demonstrate ways sacred language and subject matter appear outside traditional venues of religious discourse, in the medium of so-called secular, mainstream music. These album dates represent convenient, if randomly selected, points of reference framing approximately the following reflections. These artists, and these particular albums, also illustrate my central point. The decision of many to leave organized religion during the 1960s does not indicate a corresponding decrease in meaningful spirituality or engagement with religious questions and texts. Harrison and Dylan and a host of others present rich, insightful, often humorous, often critical, often ironic dialogues with religious subjects in their music. This book examines some of the ways in which, and some of the reasons why, they do so.

What kind of religion are we talking about here? Certainly, there are many mainstream musicians with a vibrant religious faith, and I discuss examples throughout. In many cases, however, the kind of religion introduced to popular songs is highly individual, often unconventional, and sometimes even eccentric. Songwriters often lack the precision and nuance that practitioners of religion and specialists in the academy might prefer. Whereas a great deal of discussion about religious questions—in religious studies departments, theological writings, houses of worship, creeds—strives toward a measure of consistency and clear definition, much of the music we hear is comfortable with ambiguity, paradox, and mystery.

This preference for a vague religiosity is evident, for instance, in Boston's "Higher Power," included with their collection *Greatest Hits* (1997). In this song, religion itself is not the primary topic addressed. It is not a theological statement. Instead, sacred terms contribute to the band's reflections on an entirely different issue. The singer acknowledges a transcendent being, even calling to this "Lord" for salvation, but he does not name that figure and refers instead to an ambiguous Higher Power. The song includes a reading (by actor Kimberly Jorgensen) of the "Serenity Prayer" written by Christian theologian Reinhold Niebuhr (1892–1971). The prayer's original form is as follows: "God, give us grace to accept with serenity the things that cannot be changed, courage to change the things that should be changed, and the wisdom to distinguish the one from the other."[7] Alcoholics Anonymous (AA) eventually adopted the prayer for its program,[8] in slightly modified form. The AA program encourages members to accept various premises, among them the need to "believe that a Power greater than ourselves could restore us to sanity" and the need to make "a decision to turn our will and our lives over to the care of God as we understood Him." Prayer is an element of this communion with the divine, and members are encouraged to practice "prayer and meditation" in an effort to "improve our conscious contact with God, as we understood Him."[9]

The use of the phrase "as we understood him" in the AA literature allows all members, regardless of their personal views about religion, to participate. Whereas Niebuhr would have in mind a more precise definition of "God" in the context of his prayer, this organization leaves specificity behind as a way of welcoming people with differing opinions and backgrounds. In the liner notes to Boston's *Greatest Hits*, the band expresses thanks to "the Narcotics Anonymous and Alcoholics Anonymous programs around the world for inspiring the song *HIGHER POWER*." By this statement, they show a degree of comfort with the undefined God or Power of the AA language ("as we understood Him"), even though more precise definitions of God are available to them in formal religious discourses. At the same time, they practice religion in a sense, constructing the song as a form of prayer addressed to this unknown Power.

Ambiguity regarding definitions of God and what constitutes genuine spiritual experience fits comfortably in the broadly diverse and tolerant milieu that is contemporary music. Boston and a host of other artists are clearly at ease incorporating spiritual language into their music, while avoiding narrow definitions of their terms. Perhaps a tighter use of terminology would exclude others, or stifle creativity. Furthermore, in this particular example Boston's motive for introducing religious language ("save me Lord," and so on) is ultimately nonreligious. Their liner notes include information about the potential harm stemming from drug use: "Less than 10% of all cocaine & heroin users are able to free themselves from addiction, even after prolonged treatment." They dedicate the song "Higher Power" to "those few individuals who have the heart to recognize the destructiveness of their addiction to themselves and those around them, and the fortitude to succeed against such a powerful force." They even include the detail "Boston is drug-free," using their celebrity status to bolster their campaign in support of addiction treatment and addiction prevention. What is clear is that the "religion" presented in the song "Higher Power" is a secondary concern. They use Christian discourse, adopting a theologian's writings (which they acknowledge), but this religious source does not absorb the songwriter's attention as a subject in itself. Rather, the song's sacred references serve another subject altogether (addiction prevention and treatment). Religion in popular songs is often connotative rather than denotative, hinting at forms of spirituality rather than offering clearly articulated viewpoints. What is more, we do well to remember that the integration of religious content into these artistic works is adaptation, and therefore "repetition without replication."[10] Artists do not mimic or regurgitate ideas found elsewhere. They recreate and rewrite. This implies new meanings as ideas move from one setting (sacred discourse) to another (artistic production), or, as Linda Hutcheon puts it, "when an adapted text migrates from its context of creation to the adaptation's context of reception."[11]

Robert Alter makes a similar point with specific reference to the Bible. He describes the canon as a "transhistorical textual community" that involves dialogue between received texts and readers who appeal to those writings for meaning and authority. However, even among communities of traditional believers it "has been imagined to endorse as a matter of divine revelation rationalism, sensualism, determinism, free will, and a good deal else." The concept of canon lacks fixity; there is no "singular, authoritative meaning, however much the established spokesmen for the canon at any given moment may claim that is the case." Alter goes on to observe that creative writers using the Bible are similarly flexible.

> Modern writers merely push to the next step this process of extending the range of meanings of the textual community in which they participate when they use the biblical canon [referring here to the specific writers he examines] to express vitalistic pantheism, or an individual fate of hapless victimhood, or a vision of cosmic pitilessness, or a notion of eternal recurrence.[12]

Songwriters, like the writers of fiction Alter examines, extend the range of meanings possible from creative reading of the canons.

As I listen to mainstream popular music of the post-1960s, I hear several recurring patterns in the lyrics that involve the use of sacred texts and religious discourse. Artists introduce sacred material (1) to articulate sincere religious convictions; (2) to reject, ridicule, and criticize religious beliefs and communities of faith; (3) to depict the sexual Other as a redeemer, and love and sexuality as a form of redemption; (4) to lay claim to moral high ground in advocating social justice causes; (5) to evoke a mythological other world, providing a form of escapism from real-world problems; and (6) to express perceived alienation, and voice resistance to and independence from authority. Not all references to religion are necessarily profound, of course, and we must be careful about reading too much into songs. Umberto Eco laments the tendency of modern readers to find symbolic meaning everywhere, to the point where "the symbolic diamond, which was meant to flash in the dark and dazzle us at sudden but ideally very rare moments, has become a neon strip that pervades the texture of every discourse. This is too much of a good thing."[13] It is easy to lose sight of the fact that texts can include "open unintentionality." If we proceed in reading everything as though it has a "second sense," then everything becomes "flat and dull," and the "lust for a second sense ruins our ability to see second or even one thousand senses where they actually exist, or have been placed."[14] And so it is that when Elton John sings about Jesus freaks "handing tickets out for God" ("Tiny Dancer," *Madman Across the Water*, 1971), or when Alice Cooper gets punched in the nose by a minister ("No More Mr. Nice Guy," *Billion Dollar Babies*, 1973), they are likely not making deep theological statements. What follows addresses songwriters who habitually return to religious subject matter and dialogue with it thoughtfully. As I listen to their songs and read their lyrics, I ask two guiding questions: *how* do they engage this material, and *why*?

INTRODUCTION

SPIRITUALITY IN POST-1960s LYRICS

At one point in Jack Kerouac's *On the Road*, the irrepressible Dean Moriarty meets Rollo Greb,[1] an individual who inspires Moriarty and somehow embodies the very qualities he seeks. Greb does not bow to authority and has "more books than I've ever seen in all my life," according to the narrator Sal Paradise, "two libraries, two rooms loaded from floor to ceiling around all four walls."[2] Greb is a scholar and music lover, with a thirst for experience and knowledge that is apparently insatiable:

> He didn't give a damn about anything. [. . .] He could hardly get a word out, he was so excited with life. Dean stood before him with head bowed, repeating over and over again, "Yes . . . Yes . . . Yes." He took me [Sal] into a corner. "That Rollo Greb is the greatest, most wonderful of all. That's what I was trying to tell you—that's what I want to be. I want to be like him. He's never hung-up, he goes every direction, he lets it all out, he knows time, he has nothing to do but rock back and forth. Man, he's the end! You see, if you go like him all the time you'll finally get it." "Get what?" "IT! IT! I'll tell you—now no time, we have no time now." Dean rushed back to watch Rollo Greb some more.[3]

1

Dean is searching for the indefinable "IT," and in Rollo Greb he sees an artist and sympathetic soul able to point him toward that goal. Greb lacks boundaries, moves in all directions, and seeks that same elusive dream, experience, or truth—call it what you will— that Dean and his friends are after. Dean's inability to articulate this longing makes the need for such spiritual preceptors[4] necessary. At a later point, Dean tries his best to capture in words what he means by that indescribable *it* but his vocabulary fails him again. When Sal asks for a definition of *it*, Dean admits his limitations—"'now you're asking me impon-de-rables—ahem!'"—and he turns to the efforts of musicians as an illustration to aid his response:

> ". . . somewhere in the middle of the chorus he [a jazz musician] *gets it*—everybody looks up and knows; they listen; he picks it up and carries. Time stops. He's filling empty space with the substance of our lives, confessions of his bellybottom strain, remembrance of ideas, rehashes of old blowing. He has to blow across bridges and come back and do it with such infinite feeling soul-exploratory for the tune of the moment that everybody knows it's not the tune that counts but IT—" Dean could go no further; he was sweating telling about it.[5]

Dean's longing for that vague authentic experience appears throughout the novel. On another occasion, he and Sal go to hear the great jazz pianist George Shearing, whose music so moves Dean that he has what is nothing less than an epiphany:

> Dean was sweating; the sweat poured down his collar. "There he is! That's him! Old God! Old God Shearing! Yes! Yes! Yes!" . . . When he was gone Dean pointed to the empty piano seat. "God's empty chair," he said. . . . God was gone; it was the silence of his departure. It was a rainy night. It was the myth of the rainy night. Dean was popeyed with awe.[6]

When he sees George Shearing again months later, the experience is the same: "'Sal, God has arrived.'" Dean is similarly enchanted with jazz musician Slim Gaillard when out on another road trip, shouting "'God! Yes!'" and "clasping his hands in prayer" during a performance. When Dean approaches Slim, "he approached his God; he thought Slim was God; he shuffled and bowed in front of him."[7]

Such fleeting encounters with the "divine" locate Dean among the poets and mystics. These experiences do not move Sal Paradise in quite the same way, but no matter. Dean's experiences are inimitable, contingent on his own state of mind and personal situation. The music scholar Rollo Greb, and the musicians George Shearing and Slim Gaillard communicate something to Dean Moriarty that may or may not be recognizable to anyone else. Whether he is right or wrong to credit these artists with genius and profundity and insight is beside the point—he thinks they possess them all. The search for *it* does not end with these players—while traveling south to Mexico City, Dean announces, "'Man, this will finally take us to IT!'"[8]—but music remains one of the important inspirations for Dean in his search for meaning.

Many music fans look to their favorite artists in the same way Dean Moriarty looks to Rollo Greb, George Shearing, and Slim Gaillard. They believe these musicians are people on the right path, moving toward enlightenment, who will help them find that indefinable *it* they so desperately seek. Call it what you want—an authentic existence, God, contentment, fulfillment, knowledge, truth, freedom. Our journeys are all different. Fans look to popular songwriters and musicians as independent thinkers who resist conformity and containment and compliance in much the same way Rollo Greb does when he shouts to his confining aunt, "'Oh, shut up, you old bag!'"[9] She represents an older generation, and an older way of looking at things, the establishment, and authority. To her nephew, she is someone standing in the way of liberation and free expression. Music fans of all ages and across all genres, find in their favorite band or performer their own mystical jazz master, their own Mr. Tambourine Man, whose inspired musical touch allows a glimpse of *it*, as though artists were conduits bringing that elusive insight and experience fans seek within reach.

Most musicians themselves probably find our high expectations a little unusual. There is a tendency among Bob Dylan's fans, for instance, to look to him as something of a mystic. Sam Shepard, in his poetic account of Dylan's Rolling Thunder Revue tour of the mid-1970s, refers to audience members at concerts as "College types going to see the prophet."[10] To Dylan, this kind of exaggerated assessment of him and his work is absurd. He too is searching for something—his own *it*—I suspect. When Ed Bradley of the CBS program *60 Minutes* asked him about his fans' high expectations during a 2004 interview, Dylan admitted to being puzzled:

> You feel like an impostor when someone thinks you're something and you're not. . . . you're just not that person everybody thinks you are, though they call you that all the time. "You're the prophet. You're the savior." I never wanted to be a prophet or savior. Elvis maybe. I could easily see myself becoming him. But prophet? No. . . . My stuff were songs, you know? They weren't sermons. If you examine the songs, I don't believe you're gonna find anything in there that says that I'm a spokesman for anybody or anything really.[11]

While Dylan seems genuinely mystified about his audiences, he acknowledges moments of youthful idealism in his autobiography *Chronicles: Volume One* (First Chronicles!) that resemble their high expectations: "I could transcend . . . limitations. . . . had a heightened sense of awareness, was set in my ways, impractical and a visionary to boot."[12] Fans suspect as much from their favorite performers. One of the reasons we search out these musicians in the first place, and hang on their every word, is a hunch; we suspect they see things we do not see, that they possess this heightened sense of awareness Dylan describes. They are on to something, and we want to follow.

I imagine Dylan (and others with him) would identify with Kerouac's Dean Moriarty, not George Shearing. Dylan looks to musicians, and literature, and any other sources of insight he can find to help him in his own quest; in his autobiography, he constantly mentions literary and musical influences. His search for that hidden, unattainable something is plain to see in his work. "Songs," he writes in *Chronicles*, "were my preceptor and guide into some altered consciousness of reality, some different republic, some liberated republic."[13] Songs provide something analogous to religious experience, something apart from the everyday, but ultimately the object of this mystical longing is hard to reach and hard to explain, a truth that is "obscure, too profound and too pure."[14] For Dylan-as-seeker, moments of illumination are fleeting and elusive. Sometimes he turns and someone—or *it*—is there; other times he is alone.[15]

Popular songwriters contribute to music fans' spirituality, vaguely defined in what follows as their search for and experience of *it*. Religious language abounds in contemporary songwriting, something that is remarkable because so many artists introduce sacred terms and images while simultaneously asserting their independence and freedom from all sources of authority. So much popular music habitually defies anyone or anything imposing conformity or confinement, whether real or imagined; it expresses a longing for spaces devoid of restraint. As the old Cole Porter song puts it, "I want to ride to the ridge where the west commences / And gaze at the moon till I lose my senses / . . . I can't stand fences / Don't fence me in."[16]

Whereas artists constantly resist boundaries, authorities, restraints, conventions, and "fences," religions, by definition, create them. Religions supply answers to questions, thus limiting speculative and innovative thought. Religions impose a way of looking at the world and the people and things in it, and they regulate behavior. Why then do songwriters repeatedly turn to them for inspiration? And how do they employ the vocabulary of the sacred canons and the traditions associated with them?

A NOVELIST AND A LITERARY CRITIC

In reflecting on these questions, two unlikely sources yield inspiration. The first is a novel in which the narrator speculates about the mysterious appeal of popular music.

> Why do we care about singers? Wherein lies the power of songs? . . . Maybe we are just creatures in search of exaltation. We don't have much of it. Our lives are not what we deserve; they are, let us agree, in many painful ways deficient. Song turns them into something else. Song shows us a world that is worthy of our yearning, it shows us our selves as they might be, if we were worthy of the world.[17]

A work of fiction is an unusual point of reference for an examination of popular music, but Salman Rushdie's 1999 novel *The Ground Beneath Her Feet* is one of the most insightful studies of the inexplicable lure of rock and roll available. By depicting his protagonist musicians as players in a modernized retelling of the Orpheus myth, Rushdie articulates through story what so many of us know by instinct but struggle to express. There is something transcendent, mystical, and even primal, about music at its best. Just as nature and poetry carried the Romantics toward what they called the Sublime, so also music transports audiences toward something beyond the everyday, toward *it*. Music transforms our day-to-day experiences into something else, something worthy of our yearning.

Songs provide a vehicle to articulate deep desire: the longing to have what is beyond our reach; to know what is beyond our ken; to express the inexpressible. To achieve this, songwriters regularly employ language and imagery originating within the canons and traditions of organized religion, and they often do so without commitment to a formal creed. Music provides color and texture to our sometimes mundane lives. Music fans know firsthand the power of music to transform the way they see the world. My interest here is to explore how the concepts and vocabulary of religious discourse contribute to this transformative art.

The second unlikely source guiding my reflections is a work of literary criticism. Harold Bloom's ideas about literary influence offer a compelling way of thinking about the relationship of popular music to religion. "The poet," Bloom writes,

> is condemned to learn his profoundest yearnings through an awareness of *other selves*. The poem is *within* him, yet he experiences the shame and splendor of *being found by* poems—great poems—*outside* him. To lose freedom in this center is never to forgive, and to learn the dread of threatened autonomy forever.[18]

Harold Bloom describes the poet (I will adapt his theory to include the songwriter; although they are not exactly synonymous, I will use the terms interchangeably) as an artist horrified to discover her most intimate and profound expressions are late. Someone before her has already said what she feels and writes. There is always an earlier poet, a precursor, who has penned it all before. The poet is always at risk, for this reason, of merely repeating the work of a powerful predecessor. If this is the case, how can an artist truly be an original, authentic genius? The only way to establish originality is confrontation with the earlier poetry. Writers must subvert and rewrite that earlier work in such a way that they diminish the one and assert the genius of the other. Religious discourse is, I submit, one of the precursors contemporary songwriters confront. They speak the language of religion but constantly confront it through creative rewriting.

Songwriters, Rushdie tells us, have the ability to create worlds in their music worthy of our "yearning." There is an ideal world we long for, something apart from and bigger than our experiences in the real world, full as it is with painful deficiencies. Similarly, the poets are also aware that there is something more to be experienced, that to which their "profoundest yearnings" point, to use Bloom's phrase. However, our abilities to imagine and speak about things apart from the everyday routines of life are limited. All we know is what we see and experience, and to describe anything beyond this requires a conceptual framework that includes more than the day-to-day realities available to us through the senses. Religion provides this conceptual other world.

Notice that both Rushdie and Bloom use the term "yearning." These writers help pinpoint two impulses at work in the artistry of contemporary popular music. One is the attempt by the poet-songwriter to articulate a vision of an ideal, other world. The world we live in is clearly broken in their view, but when the poet-song-writer attempts to articulate this vision of another world, she finds herself dependent on language inescapably shaped by religion. Second, the poet discovers that expressing her profoundest yearn-ings brings her face to face with what Bloom calls *other selves* or poetic precursors. In the case of the popular songwriters discussed here, these other selves include religious discourse. There are, Bloom argues, a variety of ways poets resist and escape the influ-ence of the great poetry that makes them anxious.[19] I will explore ways in which the poet-musicians of the post-1960s respond to this anxiety of influence, simultaneously embracing and resisting reli-gion in their songwriting.[20]

A FASCINATION WITH RELIGION IN POPULAR MUSIC

Like Rushdie's narrator in *The Ground Beneath Her Feet*, performer and producer Daniel Lanois experiences a deeply intimate connec-tion with music, one well described as a kind of spirituality:

> The pedal steel guitar is my favorite instrument. I've been playing it since I was a kid. It takes me to a sacred place. It's my little church in a suitcase. That's what I like to call it, my church in a suitcase.[21]

Religious references are everywhere in popular music. This music *is* religious in some senses (Bono, Rushdie, Lanois), and it depends on the language and imagery of religion (in ways analogous to Bloom's theory of poetic influence). There are allusions and quo-tations, parodies and adaptations, criticisms and celebrations, all of them dialoguing with sacred themes, concepts, symbols, rituals, and texts. This is not to say this use of terms and images articu-lates a coherent system of belief in all instances—often it does not—but the pervasive influence of religion and its texts is hard to miss. The conversations between religion and popular music appear in sounds and lyrics, concerts and videos, album covers and interviews throughout the industry, and across the spectrum of musical genres subsumed under the broad catchall label popular music. And so we are not surprised when reggae artists Bob Marley and the Wailers sing about Rastafarianism in songs like "Rasta Man Chant" (*Burnin'*, 1973) or "Zion Train" (*Uprising*, 1980), or when country singer Keith Urban thanks God for freedom from the devil's chains.[22] Nor do we find it remarkable that Rob Zombie features a large "666" in some stage performances and videos (cf. Rev 13:18),[23] or that a camera zooms in on a crucifix Bono places on a microphone stand at the conclusion of a U2 concert.[24] The poet Lawrence Ferlinghetti parodies the biblical "Lord's Prayer" in a reading of his poem "Loud Prayer" during The Band's concert The Last Waltz,[25] and Madonna's video for the song "Like a Prayer" (*Like a Prayer*, 1989) features a burning cross, a church and choir, and the singer with stigmata. Biblical material is obvious in the title and cover art for Marilyn Manson's *Holy Wood (In the Valley of the Shadow of Death)* (2000), which features a picture of the singer hanging on a cross. The subtitle is a quotation of Psalm 23:4. The list goes on, but these examples make the point that religion is pervasive in the various arts associated with popular music, such as lyrics, stage performances, videos, and album cover art.

Some musicians in the mainstream music industry are very open about their religious convictions, singing at times with evangelical fervor. Others are vocal in their criticisms of organized religion. Perhaps most often we see religious material introduced to popular music for artistic reasons, as it offers a rich source of imagery and symbolism. The integration of religion and music is so ubiquitous that a religious studies scholar can argue, without irony, "that some of the most important and interesting texts in recent U.S. culture which have overlapping concerns with liberation theologies are by Madonna."[26] Another can approach his analysis of Metallica claiming, again without irony, that they are "an emphatically religious band."[27]

According to Salman Rushdie, songs show us a world worthy of yearning. Music, Daniel Lanois claims, can take us to another place, a sacred one. Attempting to put our finger on what this means requires a consideration of music as religion, and religion in music. These are slippery issues because every artist is unique and every music listener draws their own conclusions about what spirituality is, and whether music has anything in it worthy of the term. Before attempting to unravel these ambiguities, I address five questions touching on this line of inquiry.

IS THERE MEANING IN SONG LYRICS APART FROM MUSIC?

The first question stems from Daniel Lanois' remark about the musical sounds produced by his steel guitar, and my interest in focusing on the words that accompany instrumentation: Can we find meaning in song lyrics apart from music? There is an ongoing discussion about this subject; some analysts emphasize lyrical content in their treatment of songs, others the aural qualities, and others still the mutual dependence of one on the other. Robyn Sylvan, for instance, makes "a deliberate choice not to focus on the lyrics of the music in question, not only because it is my opinion that this kind of approach is superficial and has been overdone, but also because I believe the major religious impact of the music takes place primarily at a nondiscursive level."[28] Jeremy S. Begbie criticizes overemphasis on lyrics and neglect of music. Writing from an explicitly Christian theological viewpoint, he observes that "Christian assessments of popular music . . . have too often focused on scrutinizing lyrics alone—'content analysis' (a term that gives the game away)—as if the musical sounds were no more than a transparent varnish on the words, which alone carry content."[29] He does not deny the significant place of words in music of the Western world, and qualifies his focus on musical sounds with the following remarks: "This is not because I believe music without words is superior to texted music, still less because I believe music can or should be sealed off from everything outside it. Instead it is because I do not want to lose sight of the peculiar properties of musical sounds, the way we make and hear them, and what they might be contributing in different contexts."[30] I agree with these views to a degree, but I maintain that many song lyrics are vibrant texts that reward close reading.

Some clearly disagree with me on this point. Keith Negus ridicules my decision to analyze lyrics, claiming, "Songs are experienced in the very way that they unfold as music in time, connecting with our bodies in a manner far removed from the intellectual contemplation and reflection implied [in Gilmour's writing]."[31] However, Negus does not give me credit for distinguishing between listening to songs and reading them. They are two different exercises. Furthermore, Negus does not explain why Bob Dylan the songwriter publishes his lyrics in book format, mixed with poetry, if the lyrics cannot communicate meaningfully and sustain analysis apart from musical accompaniment. It seems reasonable that if Dylan or another songwriter chooses to publish lyrics in some form (books, Web sites, album liner notes), they intend for people to read them.

It is commonplace to read plays intended for performance, and the situation is analogous with song lyrics. There is pleasure in reading *Twelfth Night, or What You Will* but it is a different kind of pleasure than seeing this Shakespeare play performed. It is not a matter of one version of the story being better; they are just different. I enjoy reading song lyrics in a way different than I enjoy listening to a CD or hearing a song during a concert or watching a music video. Each encounter with artistic energy offers a distinctly meaningful experience.

Too often commentators oversimplify the issue about whether lyrics can stand alone as texts by approaching the question as an all-or-nothing option. This is misguided. Obviously, many song lyrics, perhaps most, do not aspire to be anything more than entertainment (light fare like a dance song, say, Abba's "Dancing Queen" [*Arrival*, 1975]). In such cases, I agree there is little meaning in the words apart from the music. Other songwriters, however, attempt much more. When Joni Mitchell adapts W. B. Yeats' poem "The Second Coming" in her song "Slouching towards Bethlehem" (*Night Ride Home*, 1991), she is clearly engaged with something more self-consciously literary than other entertainment songs. "Slouching towards Bethlehem" is a work of literary interpretation.

Another way writers betray literary intentions is by their inclusion of song lyrics with albums and/or, as mentioned, the publication of song lyrics with or without poems, in book form.[32] Clearly the words matter and can and do exist on their own, on the page. This textual presentation is particularly conspicuous when the arrangement of the lyrics appears to follow an intentional layout, inviting readers to think about the visual presentation of the words on the page. Eddie Vedder's mostly handwritten lyrics included with Pearl Jam's *Ten* (1991) is a good example. The words to each song are visually unique, often appearing in nonlinear arrangements in ways reminiscent of certain poets.[33] To illustrate, the opening, handwritten words to Pearl Jam's "Black" appear approximately as follows:

SHEEtS	UNtOUCHED
SPREAD	BODY
ALL	REVOLVED
tAStED	tAKEN

Furthermore, only selected words for the song appear in the liner notes (cf. also "Porch" on the same album), which leads one to speculate about the significance of these particular terms written on the page. Why include these terms? Why omit others? Vedder's attention to spatial/visual considerations complements the instrumentation on the CD but in some respects remains independent of the music.

We can say the same thing regarding the common practice of including pictures as part of album liner notes, especially when they appear in relation to lyrics. Doodles and scribbles appear alongside handwritten words in the liner notes for the Pearl Jam album just mentioned. Joni Mitchell includes several of her own paintings in the liner notes to *The Beginning of Survival* (2004). What do these pictures mean?[34] What is their relationship to lyrics on the page, and recordings of the words and music on the albums? Other media (album art, pictures, musical accompaniment, music videos, and so on) contribute to the overall experience of song lyrics, but this does not rule out the possibility that the words themselves can have an independent, meaningful function apart from them.

Artists like Mitchell and Vedder are self-conscious as writers, as much artists with their pens as with their voices and instruments. Musicians may fail in the attempt to write intriguing lines, to be sure, but we must not rule out literary pretensions because they put these texts to music. My own emphasis in these pages falls on the lyrical content, with only occasional reference to musical accompaniment. That the music has an important relationship to those lyrics is not in dispute. It is just that my focus in this context is the religious *language* of popular song lyrics.[35]

Of course, sounds and choice of instruments can signify religious content as well. As the narrator in Jim Steinman's "Bat Out of Hell" (*Bat Out of Hell*, 1977) lays dying in a pit after a motorcycle crash, we discover how words and sound complement one another as they work in tandem to communicate a particular idea. The injured rider hears someone "tolling a bell." There is an allusion here to familiar lines from John Donne's *Devotions Upon Emergent Occasions*, Meditation 17 (1624), in which the poet reflects on the significance of tolling church bells marking the passing, or near passing, of members of the community:

> Who bends not his ear to any bell which upon any occasion rings? But who can remove it from that bell which is passing a piece of himself out of this world? No man is an island, entire of itself; every man is a piece of the continent, a part of the main. If a clod be washed away by the sea, Europe is the less, as well as if a promontory were, as well as if a manor of thy friend's or of thine own were. Any man's death diminishes me, because I am involved in mankind; and therefore never send to know for whom the bell tolls; it tolls for thee.[36]

The song "Bat Out of Hell" moves along at a quick pace for most of its nine plus minutes, giving a sense of the rider speeding along on his bike. However, as the song fades, we hear a chorus singing softly and soothingly, which contrasts with the song's otherwise frenzied pace and the rider's violent end ("the last thing I see is my heart . . . Breaking out of my body"). Through sound, we suspect this is an angelic choir, ushering the rider out of one world and into the next. Their singing complements the words of the song, including the allusion to Donne's meditation on death.[37] The combination of lyrics (bells tolling) and sound (singing angels) makes it clear that the rider is now dead.

My decision to focus on words over sound is not a denial of the symbiotic connection between them (Steinman makes the complementary relationship plain to hear, in this example). My decision depends, rather, on the nature of the questions I am bringing to the songs, questions exploring the ways in which song lyrics—words—dialogue with religious discourse.

WHY ENGAGE IN SUCH A SUBJECTIVE EXERCISE AS LYRIC ANALYSIS?

The second question touching on the study of religion and popular music is always lurking in the background of any conversation about meaning and value in songs: If we allow that no two people hear songs in exactly the same way, why bother analyzing them at all? Such an exercise is hopelessly subjective. The environments in which audiences experience songs vary widely (live performances, studio albums on a stereo, covers by other artists, movie soundtracks in a theater, hack renditions in a karaoke bar), and we bring different expectations to music depending on the artist performing the work. It matters, for instance, if we hear "Knockin' On Heaven's Door" while watching the 1973 Sam Peckinpah film *Pat Garrett and Billy the Kid*. Here it serves as background music as Sheriff Colin Baker (Slim Pickens) is dying with his wife by his side after he is shot. We can also hear this song as part of Bob Dylan's soundtrack album of the same name (1973), or as covered by Guns N' Roses on their album *Use Your Illusion II* (1991). The same song takes on new meaning in each setting because it means different things depending on the artists performing them, the assumptions audiences bring to those artists and songs, and the contexts in which they hear them.

Consider Nine Inch Nails' version of "Hurt" (*The Downward Spiral*, 1994)[38] alongside Johnny Cash's cover of that song on *American IV: The Man Comes Around* (2002). Here we can imagine the dialogue between these artists and their respective audiences producing different listening experiences. Our awareness that this was one of Johnny Cash's final recordings (he died in 2003) inevitably contributes to our reception of the song and its critically acclaimed video (which won the 2003 Grammy for Best Short Form Music Video). For my part, when I hear Cash singing about the people he knows going away, and an "empire of dirt," and a thorny crown, I hear an older man reflecting on his own mortality and that of loved ones, the temporal nature of worldly possessions, and the burden of perceived inadequacies. When I hear Nine Inch Nails perform the same song, most of these elements are still present but the emotional intensity is not the same. To hear these *younger* performers sing the same words eases the sense of despair because their (relative) youth implies they may yet find relief from their burdens. Cash did not have the same luxury.

Simon Frith approaches the issue of meaning with an emphasis on songs as performance and articulations of preexisting realities. After pointing out that sociological studies repeatedly find that many music listeners do not understand or even notice lyrical content, he speculates:

> What this suggests, I think, is the difficulty we face if, in interpreting how songs "mean," we attempt to separate the words from their use as speech acts. I would put the arguments this way: song words are not about ideas ("content") but about their expression.[39]

To illustrate this idea of songs as speech acts, he refers to love songs (which do not cause people to fall in love but allow them to articulate the experience of romance) and protest songs (which do not provide political ideas and arguments so much as slogans). Song lyrics are not "words, but words in performance."[40] Frith also calls attention to what he calls "lyrical drift": when listeners replace the original sense of a song with a new sense. He cites the example of the Republican Party's use of Bruce Springsteen's "Born In the USA" during the 1984 presidential campaign; what was originally a protest song became a patriotic boast in this context.[41] Listeners find meaning in songs independently of authorial intention when they internalize that music, and when those songs help them process and articulate their own unique experiences.

> Once we grasp that the issue in lyrical analysis is not words, but words in performance, then various new analytical possibilities open up. Lyrics, that is, are a form of rhetoric or oratory; we have to treat them in terms of the persuasive relationship set up between singer and listener. From this perspective, a song doesn't exist to convey the meaning of the words; rather, the words exist to convey the meaning of the song. This is as true of the "story song" or the *chanson* as of the most meaningless house or rave track, just as political and love songs concern not political or romantic ideas, but modes of political and romantic expression. Pop songs, that is, work with and on *spoken* language.[42]

We might carry Frith's point over to audiences' reflections on spiritual themes. Songs may not provide us with a systematic body of information on which to base religious beliefs, but they might help us articulate preexisting convictions, doubts, questions, and suspicions.

Subjectivity also exists in song analysis because of the tendency to think of songs in biographical terms, as if they inevitably reveal a songwriter's views. In thinking about religious elements in popular songs in the post-1960s, I do not mean to imply at any point that "this is what Paul Simon means" in a certain song, or even worse, "this is what Paul Simon believes personally." We could never understand completely what Paul Simon means in any given song, and we will always be at some remove from an individual's personal beliefs no matter how transparent their art and conversation about songwriting may be. Artists often describe the inspirations behind songs in interviews or liner notes, but this does not exhaust a work of art's potential meaning. For this reason, the *reception* of a song or a poem or a painting or a novel is an integral part of the communication process. Audiences receive and respond to songs, bringing bundles of emotions as well as varying experiences, knowledge, and expectations with them. Meaning resides in the interplay of artist and audience; there is a relationship between the two, with the song—lyrically and musically—serving as the bridge between them. I am focusing largely on lyrics (cf. Frith's emphasis on speech act and performance), but the principle holds on this particular point. Audiences have certain preconceived ideas about religion and spirituality, and popular music provides them with a way of verbalizing those beliefs, however vague they may be. Their particular interpretation of a song may have no connection to the artist in question (that is, there may be no similarity between authorial intent and what an audience member hears), but this does not matter. Bob Dylan never wanted to be a prophet or savior, as per remarks made during his *60 Minutes* interview, and George Shearing did not think of himself as God (presumably), but this does not stand in the way of fans that catch a glimpse of *it* in their music. We react like Dean Moriarty in our pursuit of meaning.

DOES IT MATTER IF WE RECOGNIZE RELIGIOUS PRECURSORS?

This book examines religious precursors contributing to lyrics: Does it matter if we recognize these influences? We bring all kinds of life experiences, knowledge, presuppositions, and biases to everything we read or hear. As we encounter texts—all texts—our ability to make sense of them and form opinions about them involves dialogue with all this information in our possession. For instance, it makes a great difference in our experience and interpretation of Yusuf Islam's music whether or not we recognize the influences of the Koran and Sufi poets. Those not overly interested in religious subjects will still enjoy the music, relieved to know, as many of us are, that "Cat Stevens" is back. The songs—I am thinking of the albums *An Other Cup* (2006) and *Roadsinger* (2009) here—sound great. However, those choosing to interact with Yusuf Islam's theology and interpretation of sacred traditions can hear/read his new work on a whole other level. Furthermore, while the recognition of religious traditions behind songs determines the nature of audiences' dialogue with music to a degree, so does the absence or presence of sympathy for those traditions. A songwriter's opinions about religion will register with listeners differently depending on their prior convictions (do they believe in God or not? do they have firm convictions about spirituality or are they open to hearing new ideas?).

The assumptions and knowledge we bring to song lyrics shape our interpretations, and while it is risky to think in terms of *the* meaning of a song, most will agree that some interpretations are better than others. Not surprisingly, if we give weight to the consensus of other listeners or to songwriters' stated intentions about the meaning of songs, we occasionally discover that our first impressions of a song are off track. When a young Homer and Marge Simpson hear on the radio Debby Boone's 1977 version of the Joe Brooks' song "You Light Up My Life," Homer concludes, "That guy she was singing about must've been really happy." He assumes the song is about romantic love. He reaches this conclusion based on prior knowledge (pop songs are often about romance) and present circumstances (he was in love at that moment; cf. Frith's point above). Marge, however, offers a very different interpretation:

Marge: "Actually, I think she's singing about God."

Homer: "Oh, well he's always happy. No wait, he's always mad."

There are many examples of what are arguably incorrect readings of songs. For one, many Christians concluded U2's "I Still Haven't Found What I'm Looking For" (*Joshua Tree*, 1987) signaled a departure from their Christian profession (which it did not).[43] However, when we identify such errors of interpretation, this does not invalidate song meanings *as experienced* by individuals or audiences. An element of subjectivity is inevitable if we are to take into consideration the listener's unique perspective. If, with Homer Simpson, we hear "You Light Up My Life" as a romantic love song—and I suspect most listeners do—it will give expression to our feelings regardless of what Marge says.

Religions provide adherents with a way of thinking about and ordering their life experiences.[44] Those with a religious perspective have at least some answers for life's many complex questions, a moral framework to help them make choices in day-to-day living, and some sense of how they should relate to others. Religious perspectives provide consolation when facing crises, and in most cases, a sense of purpose for this life and the promise that another life exists after death. Those who do not embrace organized religion still have similar needs and ask many of the same questions: What are my obligations to others? How do I determine right from wrong? Where will I find comfort and purpose? How do I make sense of the events in my life? They need to find their answers elsewhere. To a degree, music addresses some of these concerns. Our experience of songs is highly subjective, and at times we interpret them in ways that meet our individual needs so that they provide comfort, direction, and answers regardless of authorial intent.

IF IT'S ENTERTAINMENT, WHY ANALYZE IT?

My fourth question relates to popular music audiences and particularly those interested in discussing, interpreting, and debating the meaning of songs. We can imagine two distinct groups here, admirers and academics (or, enthusiasts and eggheads). Why analyze pop songs, the one group asks the other, if in fact they are intended for entertainment? This is a good question, and a hard one to answer to everyone's satisfaction. I will approach it in a roundabout way.

Philosopher Gregory L. Reece's *Elvis Religion: The Cult of the King* speaks to the remarkable energy people invest in their favorite subjects and the passion with which they embrace their much-loved celebrities.[45] There is endless enthusiasm among music fans for expressing opinions, likes, and dislikes; for demonstrating their affections for particular artists or genres; for entering into discourse about *their* music. Reece's study of Elvis fan subculture is a delightful introduction—often funny, always illuminating—to a world in which the lines between the love of a singer/movie star/icon and outright religious devotion are often blurry. Or we could consider another example of extreme fan loyalty, appearing in the documentary *Global Metal* (2007), directed by Scot McFadyen and Sam Dunn. This film follows their earlier *Metal: A Headbanger's Journey* (2005) with a look at heavy metal music cultures outside Europe and North America. They document examples of metal fans in such unexpected places as India, China, Israel, and Iran, where the faithful maintain fierce loyalties to their music of choice despite enormous familial, social, and even state pressure to avoid such extreme (and Western) lifestyles and aesthetics. Music is deeply important to many, and we should be careful about underestimating its significance for the construction of one's identity and outlook on life.

Music fans are also protective of their favorite artists, in part because of their tendency to weave their identities into the music, subcultures, and art forms they treasure. Why is that? It likely has something to do with the sense of connection we have with musicians.[46] Music is ubiquitous and tends to be somewhere in the background of so much that we do. Consequently, it often reminds us of certain times, places, spaces, and people in our lives. This is profoundly intimate. Music provides a soundtrack to our lives, as the saying goes, and so there is a close tie between nostalgia and music, which is why many people buy the same albums many times over, every time a new format appears (LP, 8-track, cassette, CD, MP3). This also explains in part why bands continue performing long after their careers peak, and why we spend so much money attending reunion tours. It is profitable for the artists and provides a chance for audiences to "go back." An album, artist, or genre can take a person somewhere else (cf. the citation of Daniel Lanois above: "It takes me to a sacred place"). During the time spent thinking about and writing this book, I have taken in shows by Midnight Oil, Ted Nugent, KISS (the original lineup!), Supertramp, Van Halen (not the original lineup), AC/DC, Black Sabbath (with Dio), Aerosmith, Bob Dylan, Cheap Trick, Megadeth, Rob Zombie, Ozzy Osbourne, Def Leppard, and Billy Idol, among others—all of these artists evoke certain memories and associations with my youth. At some level, their music is part of my story.

Thus, when writing about popular music, one must tread softly. Most music lovers are not Elvis impersonators, Apple Scruffs, Rusties, Deadheads, Bobheads, or members of the KISS Army, but this does not change the fact that for music fans of all kinds, this subject is important, and they will not suffer fools gladly. At the same time, for those who bring academic pretensions to their writing about the entertainment industry, there are also certain expectations placed on them by their peers, who evaluate such things as the nature of the questions asked and the methodologies employed for analysis. On the one hand, the potential readership for popular music studies includes interested fans anxious to protect the all-important music from disconnected blowhards, and on the other, peers in the academy who tend to prefer formal analysis to free-spirited, casual reflection: enthusiasts and eggheads.

There is a tendency to separate these categories, as though impermeable borders keep the academy and the real world apart. In reality, such borders do not exist. All that differs between these amorphous groups is the nature of the discourses in which they participate. Academics may ask different kinds of questions and articulate their findings in less than enthusiastic language, but despite all of this, most of them are still music fans. They buy the same CDs, download the same songs, attend the same concerts, and play their music just as loud when driving.

What happens if we bring these discourses together? When the two worlds collide, there are both challenges and opportunities. One of the challenges is an oft-heard criticism directed toward academics who examine popular music. The complaint often runs something like this: songs are entertainment, intended for pleasure and escape; to analyze a song is to suck the life out of it, and to read too much into it is to miss the artist's point altogether. Or, as Pete Townshend puts it, "Typewriter tappers / You're all just crappers / You listen to love with your intellect." These people are so out of touch and oblivious, "they don't give a shit Keith Moon is dead" ("Jools and Jim," *Empty Glass*, 1980). Townshend specifically identifies his targets in this song as "journalists who sneer. Vampires. Parasites."[47] What is often true of journalists is also often true of academics. I tend to agree with such complaints in many instances, at least when the academics in question look down on the ways others experience music, or when academics do not acknowledge their own relation to the artists in question (that is, are they fans of this music? ambivalent? antagonistic?). At times, writers appear so disinterested in the subject matter that it is reasonable to ask whether the sociologist or literary critic, anthropologist or musicologist even likes the music they discuss. Sometimes it is hard to tell. To read a book about a favorite band or singer by someone who appears to lack enthusiasm for the subject is tedious at best, annoying at worst. Rock and roll is fun, and books about it should avoid being stuffy at all costs.

Furthermore, to return to our focus on religion in popular music, we must be careful not to treat popular songs as we would formal treatises on theological questions. In comments about George Harrison's "lack of self-defense in controversial religious matters," Dale C. Allison Jr. does not accuse the singer of naïveté but instead offers two plausible explanations. First, the medium of songs is not conducive to systematic, nuanced treatments of the subject. Music is not, Allison notes, "an all-purpose vehicle. It can communicate much, but it cannot communicate everything." Music is well suited to convey the writer's feelings but not necessarily "one's rational analysis." Second, Harrison, like many of the writers mentioned in the present book, "was not a formally trained academic or intellectual, not even a writer of nonacademic prose. He was a religious individual who experienced God first through the heart and only secondly through his mind."[48] To approach Harrison and other writers on a purely cerebral level would be to miss the way they think and write.

For all these reasons, I find myself in the same awkward position as others who comment on popular culture media. The fans of film, television, comic books, or music represent (usually) large, diverse communities of devotees sharing particular interests. The forms and forums available to fans for expressing their affections and articulating their views are endless: blogs, fanzines, conventions, graffiti. Oftentimes, there are few controls or rules of engagement when it comes to dialoguing with others about their favorite entertainment media.

The academic community, by contrast, imposes all kinds of limitations on its members. There are many gatekeepers to satisfy, among them peer-evaluators, tenure committees, academic presses, and book reviewers. This system imposes certain restraints on those writing within it, shaping the style and tone of books and articles. Those engaging in formal study of popular culture through the usual channels of academic inquiry, such as scholarly journals, academic conferences, or classroom lectures, are often in the interesting position of speaking to their academic peers and the passionate fan simultaneously. Those wanting to dialogue with the former must meet certain expectations that can appear stifling to the latter. There is less tolerance for gushing celebrations of treasured subjects, or for pouring disdain on others ("I love this song!" or "I hate that one!"). There are expectations of an authorial posture of neutrality, or at least gestures in writing toward objectivity. Academic research involves the introduction of appropriate methodologies to the area of inquiry, as well as a formal tone.

All is not lost. Writing about the entertainment we enjoy need not be overwhelmingly stifling, and the borderline between fan culture and scholarly activity is porous—academics are fans, and attentive fans know their music as well as anyone.[49] Again, the distinction between these communities involves the nature of the discourse and the kinds of questions addressed, not the quality of the engagement with the music. A more constructive model involves listening to all interested parties who hear something in the music, whether the songwriters and performers themselves, audience members, critics and reviewers, or the diverse discourses falling under the umbrella term "academia." Susan Fast, in her book *In the Houses of the Holy: Led Zeppelin and the Power of Rock Music*, successfully blends the insights of different audiences in the context of academic writing. As part of her research, she posted a questionnaire on Led Zeppelin fan Web sites that includes the following introduction:

> I'm a musician and huge fan writing a book on Led Zeppe-
> lin's music that will be published by Oxford University
> Press. I want the book to include the opinions of a wide
> range of people who listen to Zep, not just mine, so I'd
> appreciate your taking a moment to answer the questions
> below. . . .[50]

Fast chose to incorporate a fan survey after seeing Rob Walser do
the same in the preparation of his book *Running with the Devil:
Power, Gender, and Madness in Heavy Metal.*[51]

    Lyricist Robert Hunter, best known for his songwriting col-
laboration with The Grateful Dead's Jerry Garcia, has this to say
about the role of different reading/listening communities:

> When fans hear a song they like, they internalize it, dance
> to it, sing along. Tape it, collect it, trade it. When scholars
> hear a song they like, they annotate it. There is more than
> one way to love a song. There are as many ways as there are
> listeners.[52]

    I hang on to Hunter's insightful words throughout this book
and offer my own idiosyncratic way of approaching popular music
as just another way to love songs. I confess to being a fan first but
choose to bring questions to the music that some might find stifling and formal, though I hope to demonstrate that all audiences
benefit—by gaining greater appreciation, fuller understanding—
from looking at familiar things in new ways. This does not mean
every reading is accessible to all, to be sure. For instance, the tech-
nical analyses of musicologists are often lost on those without their
expertise, just as the social nuances at play in certain musical subcultures involve subtleties easily missed by neophytes or the unini-
tiated. Not everyone understands the inner workings of mosh pits
or raves, for instance (myself included).

    William Echard locates himself in this interesting but awkward
space inhabited by the scholar-fan (a term he borrows from Richard
Middleton) in the opening of his book *Neil Young and the Poetics
of Energy.*[53] Echard credits the ongoing dialogues of Rusties (Neil

Young fans) for influencing his work, and he explicitly contextual-
izes himself as an analyst as "both a fan of Neil Young and a critical
scholar." While in his book he offers a "contribution to scholarship,"
he also aims "to make at least a small part of that implicit theory
[used by academics] more explicit, but not to altogether abandon
the position of the practically engaged fan." There is a risk here: "it
is inevitable that parts of the work will be too academic for some
fans and other parts too casual for some academics."[54] This strikes
me as a worthwhile gamble and a constructive balance.

There is often a cautious restraint in academic treatments of
popular music. Part of this is an educational system that prizes
objectivity, leaving a deeply ingrained suspicion of subjective
response. Scholars in all fields are well aware that pure objectivity does not exist, but they feign critical distance just the same.
Scholars may also face some embarrassment working on subjects
usually viewed as lightweight—a life spent analyzing Shakespeare
will always have a measure of respectability in certain circles, while
the close reading of graphic novels will not. Occasionally, however,
those doing serious work on popular music let their guard down.

An interesting example of this appears in Paul Nonnekes' *Three
Moments of Love in Leonard Cohen and Bruce Cockburn*. Nonnekes
describes his original and creative study as a series of "reflections"
on ideal masculine subjects in the work of the poets/songwriters
Leonard Cohen and Bruce Cockburn, inspired by such theorists
as French psychoanalyst Jacques Lacan, German theorist Walter
Benjamin, and French psychoanalytic feminist Julia Kristeva. For
Nonnekes, however, this exercise is more than a densely theo-
retical treatment of Cohen and Cockburn. It is also very personal,
something he makes explicit in the closing words of the book. He
describes his upbringing in the Christian church as the son of a
minister, and subsequent intellectual and spiritual developments,
stating how Cohen and Cockburn contributed to this process:

> I wish to say that, having been raised in this Dutch Reformed
> tradition, and now *informed by the encounter with Cohen and
> Cockburn*, I have arrived at a post-ecclesiastical vision of

masculine desire. I believe in paradise, and am attracted to images of paradise coming from the past, from tradition, while at the same time I possess an inability, unwillingness, and determined commitment not to believe in the images presented from the past and by tradition, especially those held in an exclusive manner. This, it seems, has left me in a quandary, but it is a dialectical quandary, and one that I am quite satisfied with.[55]

I am interested here in the way Nonnekes integrates the artistic contributions of these songwriters into his personal belief system, and then admits that he does so. He casts his remarks in explicitly religious terms ("paradise") and defines his new understanding in contradistinction to organized religion ("post-ecclesiastical"). When Nonnekes dedicates the book to his minister-father, he accomplishes the same thing: "For my father / whose dream of paradise / despite appearances, / is not that different from mine." The author draws on sacred discourse but self-consciously moves away from it while simultaneously redefining its terms. I choose this particular example not only to illustrate how a sophisticated, academic reading of popular music song lyrics can be personal, but also to provide an illustration of ways in which reflection on the dichotomy of sacred and secular can inform popular music analysis. Nonnekes finds in Cohen and Cockburn singer-songwriters who can help him think through questions touching on religious matters. All three of these writers, Cohen and Cockburn, and their interpreter Nonnekes, move into the sacred realm for inspiration but ultimately leave it for a space of creativity and reinterpretation (cf. the diagram illustrating this process in track five).

WHY POPULAR SONG LYRICS SPECIFICALLY?

My final question concerning the study of popular music and religion emerges from previous comments about academic engagement with songs: Why popular music? Why invest so much time in popular song lyrics? Opinions vary on whether songs are worthy objects of serious study. Academic and artistic snobbery is inevitably at play in some circles. It is not surprising that many view analysis of popular media as little more than an indulgence by fans and a frivolous waste of mental energy, and this is no less true for those working in the diverse fields of religious studies. To neglect this body of artistic work, however, is to overlook an important example of religious experience in contemporary society.

> Right under our noses, a significant religious phenomenon is taking place, one which constitutes an important development in the Western religious and cultural landscape. Yet, because conventional wisdom has taught us to regard popular musics as trivial forms of secular entertainment, these religious dimensions remain hidden from view, marginalized and misunderstood.[56]

When asked about my own interest in popular music (as one whose primary focus is biblical studies), I often suspect a hint of criticism lurking behind the question. Why study Ozzy when you can study Isaiah? I typically respond in terms recalling Don E. Saliers' short book *Music and Theology*, where he argues that the distinction between the secular and the sacred is not particularly helpful nor easy to make.[57] There is a sacral potential in secular music, he suggests. Consequently,

> we need not work with dichotomies between "sacred" and "secular" music as such. Perhaps we need much more to attend to what can be called the "sacrality" or even the "sacramentality" of music wherever and whenever we are moved out of ourselves and our habitual, common-sense world.[58]

Saliers singles out folk music at this point in his argument as a kind of theology but his remarks suit other genres equally well. Folk musicians and others often express and explore deeply religious questions. In some cases, he continues, we may find "stronger prophetic texts" outside the church.[59]

Those who criticize the general premise that mainstream popular music offers something of merit with respect to literary and/or theological content are guilty of the kind of elitism Mark Allan

Powell refers to in his *Encyclopedia of Contemporary Christian Music*. Powell is a respected, well-published New Testament scholar who has invested considerable time and energy into this major analysis of the Christian music industry. In his preface, he mentions that some question the efforts and resources put into this project, and his response deserves repeating in this context.

> I *hate* that kind of elitism. I regard the persons [i.e., the song-writers and performers] in this book as amateur theologians whose perspectives and insights on life and faith are every bit as valid as those of any Harvard professor or Rhodes scholar. That, I hope they realize, is why I approach their work in a critical vein. . . . it does not bother me that these poets lack the proper nuances of reflection or expression taught within the guild. Jesus was a carpenter, and Peter, a fisherman. Only Paul was a scholar, and he is generally the most boring of the three.[60]

The analogy between Powell's project and my own is clearly not a perfect one. He is writing about Christian artists who express their faith, in most cases, within the Christian music industry. (There are a few exceptions: Powell has entries on performers active outside these circles, such as Bruce Cockburn, Collective Soul, Alice Cooper, Creed, Bob Dylan, Elvis Presley, and U2.) My book is shorter on detail and wider in scope. I am interested in the religious language used by mainstream contemporary songwriters, Christian or otherwise, and attempt to identify particular patterns in their use of this material. I mention Powell's book, particularly his remarks about his authorial perspective as a religious studies specialist looking at the work of "amateur theologians," because of the respect he shows these musicians. My book is more literary in emphasis than theological, but I hope I can emulate Powell's manner of writing in this engagement with the fascinating literature of popular song lyrics.

Another instructive model of popular song lyric analysis focusing on religion is Dale C. Allison Jr.'s *The Love There That's Sleeping: The Art and Spirituality of George Harrison*. Allison, another

New Testament scholar analyzing popular music, states his goal as an attempt to sort through and interpret Harrison's "mixed bag of fragmentary feelings, religious poetry, secular love songs, perceptions of the world, and anxieties about life." His book is, in short, "a book about George's religious sentiments as they surface in his songs."[61] Allison offers a sympathetic and respectful reading of Harrison's religious material, confessing at one point, "I for one, despite being a Christian rather than a Hindu, appreciate George's infatuation with his God."[62] Allison is a religious studies scholar, yet, like Powell, he approaches the amateur theologizing of a singer seriously and with respect.

Some of the artists I mention write about their personal beliefs, others express no particular convictions and merely draw on sacred subject matter for artistic purposes, and others still are openly hostile to aspects of religion, or at least pretend to be for dramatic effect. I am not writing to evaluate their personal views. Instead, I merely describe religious dimensions in their work and I do so because I take their (oftentimes amateur) religious reflections seriously. We can learn much about religion, and perhaps even the reception of religion by audiences, if we listen carefully to these artists. Unlike many who study religion—including typically out-of-touch academics like me—rap and rock, country and pop, folk, blues, and jazz musicians have a unique contact with, and I suspect understanding of, the large numbers of people who listen to their work. Most of the musicians and poets I examine in this book write songs and perform them for extremely large audiences. The ability to sell millions of albums requires some awareness of what makes your fans tick.[63] By listening to the songs, we might catch glimpses of the ways large segments of the population think about sacred subjects. We can turn this around too. Inevitably, celebrities influence those who revere them. Does U2 shape the way their fans see the world? Their politics? Their passion for social justice? Their understanding of religion? Absolutely.

What draws me to this subject is this potential for religious insight. Of course, we must not be naïve. A writer's choice to write or sing about a recognizable religion, or draw upon a sacred text or concept, does not mean he fully understands the tradition or that his dialogue is particularly insightful. Like the narrator in Styx's "Come Sail Away" (*The Grand Illusion*, 1977) who mistakes aliens for angels, confusion is often on display. Whereas distortion of source material may indicate deliberate irony or forms of critique, it can also indicate simple misunderstanding. Jennifer Rycenga observes an example of the latter in an article about the progressive rock band Yes, where she remarks, "it is embarrassing how little [Jon] Anderson knows about Hinduism," with specific reference to the band's 1973 album *Tales from Topographic Oceans*.[64] Another form misunderstanding takes is insensitivity. Madonna's decision to name a song "Isaac" on her album *Confessions on a Dance Floor* (2005) angered some rabbis, who assumed she was referring to the sixteenth-century Kabbalist sage Rabbi Yitzhak (Isaac) Luria. According to an Israeli newspaper, cited in *Rolling Stone* magazine, Rabbi Rafael Cohen of Safed, Israel said, "Jewish law forbids the use of the name of the holy rabbi for profit. [Madonna's] act is just simply unacceptable, and I can only sympathize for her because of the punishment that she is going to receive from the heavens."[65] Madonna denies the song has any connection to the mystic sage, but even if that were the case, one suspects she might have anticipated the objection, given her interest in Kabbalah, and avoided potential offense altogether.

MUSIC AND SPACE

What purpose do sacred language and imagery serve in mainstream music? One reason I will put forward is the longing—shared by singers and audiences alike—to glimpse something apart from the real world we inhabit. There is a mystical, quasi-religious atmosphere created in many songs and albums, an inexplicable spirituality, an almost hymnic quality. Consider Bob Dylan's "Visions of Johanna" (*Blonde on Blonde*, 1963), Cat Stevens' "Peace Train" (*Teaser and the Firecat*, 1971), or Michael Jackson's "Will You Be There" (*Dangerous*, 1991). Each song introduces provocative lyrics with sacred associations (e.g., "Madonna," "holy," "River Jordan," respectively), and the musical accompaniment is contemplative,

even prayer-like. These and other songs offer alternate spaces to listeners, an imagined place separate from the deficiencies (Rushdie's
term) of the real world we all know too well. Music can, to recall
Daniel Lanois' remark, take us to "a sacred place." Lanois' spatial
metaphor is useful for thinking about the ways in which religious
content in popular music communicates.

Spatial imagery is a familiar way of thinking about music.
David B. Knight's *Landscapes in Music: Space, Place, and Time in the
World's Great Music*, for example, provides a fascinating exploration of ways "composers have represented, structured, and sym-
bolized real, imagined, and mythical landscapes in their tonal
compositions."

> Just as poets and novelists describe, painters paint, and
> geographers analyze landscapes, so many composers of
> orchestral music represent landscapes (and waterscapes)
> that are real, imagined, or mythical and reveal an awareness
> of various physical and human processes and attachments
> to place.[66]

Though Knight focuses on classical, orchestral music, this line
of inquiry presents an intriguing option for reflection on lyrical
popular songs.

As an illustration of the point, I offer a few remarks about Neil
Young's 2005 album *Prairie Wind*, a work that includes numerous
spatial references, a mixture of real and imagined geographies.
Young's *Prairie Wind* responds to the traumas of 9/11 and its violent aftermath.[67] In this album, we find the artist coping with the
sorrows experienced in real space by turning to an imagined one, a
place offering solace and a venue for political commentary.

Neil Young has a childhood connection to the Canadian prairies, having moved to Winnipeg, Manitoba at the age of twelve.
Apparently, his relatively short time on the prairies left an impression because, according to William Echard, Young treats nonurban
spaces specifically, and the earth generally, as "a life-source." He
tends to write about "the countryside—not wilderness but agricultural land—as his own personal refuge."[68] Echard does not discuss

Prairie Wind specifically, but his comment remains pertinent for this album nonetheless. The emphasis on agricultural space is obvious in *Prairie Wind*, and reading this geography in Young's songwriting as a "refuge" is particularly fitting.

Young returns home to this geographical space in this album, a place he specifically refers to as his Canadian prairie home in an earlier song ("One of These Days," *Harvest Moon*, 1992). The prairies are a literal space that takes on symbolic value, a place where singer and audience can find solace and reorientation. The world described in Neil Young's *Prairie Wind* stands in sharp contrast to the chaotic, violent, urban landscapes of the post-9/11 world, with its warmongering and restless anxiety. It includes numerous prairie images, some general (e.g., farmers, wind, buffalos, trains on straight prairie railroads), others specific, recalling Young's days in Canada during the late 1950s and early 1960s. In the concert DVD *Neil Young: Heart of Gold*, which features songs from *Prairie Wind*, the artist prefaces "Four Strong Winds" by songwriter Ian Tyson with comments about Winnipeg, "where I grew up" and "Falcon Lake," a popular holiday destination just east of the Manitoba capital. For Young, the prairies come to represent a return to a time of simplicity, innocence, and safety known in his youth and desperately missed in the post-9/11 world. Indeed, that tragedy and the subsequent military responses to it are prominent in Young's most recent work. The heroic efforts of passengers on United Airlines Flight 93 to subdue hijackers are the inspiration behind "Let's Roll" (released on *Are You Passionate?* [2002]), and the later *Living with War* (May 2, 2006) and *Living with War—In the Beginning* (November 27, 2006) represent Young's more overt commentary on the United States' foreign policy since September 2001. Young's political views are relatively subtle in *Prairie Wind* compared to *Living With War*, sounding a more introspective note, one concerned to find personal peace in troubled times. Still, it remains a politically engaged collection of songs. The album is both a reaction to the attacks that occurred on American soil in 2001 and the invasion of Iraq in the years following.

Prairie Wind opens with "The Painter," a song about a female character functioning, by all appearances, as Young's muse. She is able to bring order out of chaos, an idea suggested by her ability to harmonize colors picked from the air: green to green, red to red, yellow to yellow, and so on. The songwriter needs her because he fears he may get lost while traveling during turbulent times. Where does she lead him? This muse-Painter takes the album's narrator back to the prairies, reintroducing color and contentment to an otherwise troubled life. Following the opening song's invocation, the world he rediscovers in *Prairie Wind* includes music (guitars and piano ["This Old Guitar"[69] and "Far From Home"]), family (mother, daddy, uncle, sisters), nostalgia (Elvis ["He Was The King"]), and simple faith (an old church ["No Wonder"]). Significantly, the singer embraces this return to his roots, even insisting they bury him on the prairies so he will always be close to home ("Far From Home"). This retreat to comforting prairie spaces is necessary because "that song from 9/11" keeps ringing in his head ("No Wonder").

Throughout *Prairie Wind*, the Canadian landscape of Young's songs alternates between real and imagined spaces. There are unambiguous geographical markers—proper names—that recall recognizable, mappable places: the Red River ("It's A Dream"); Cypress River (a town in Manitoba, Canada; "Prairie Wind"); the Trans-Canada Highway ("Far From Home"). However, the prairiescape of this album, with its recurring references to cliché signs of the North American plains—buffalo, wheat, wind, old churches—is mostly, and logically, an artistic creation, a re-imagining and re-presenting of distant memories. So completely reworked is the prairie space of this album that the singer openly acknowledges his revisionist tendencies. He is aware of a place on the prairie where evil and goodness mingle, but he deliberately ignores potential corruption of this space ("Prairie Wind"). Young is constructing, here and throughout *Prairie Wind*, what amounts to a virtually Edenic, prelapsarian world, one distinct from the corrupted urban world he wants to escape.

This implied accusation of moral lapse, and the tropes of a fall and loss of paradise, are familiar in popular music. For instance,

Neil Young, with David Crosby, Stephen Stills, and Graham Nash, turned Joni Mitchell's song "Woodstock," from her 1970 album *Ladies of the Canyon*, into an enormous hit. The song expresses a longing to return to "the garden." Kelton Cobb points out that "Rock and roll, before it splintered into a multitude of niches in the 1980s, was heavy with the theme of lost paradise," citing among other examples this line from Mitchell's song.[70] Cobbs' remarks demonstrate that statements about morality are somewhat commonplace in popular music generally, and found in Neil Young's work specifically. Furthermore, Young and some of his contemporaries operate with the spatiality of the Genesis garden/wilderness binary as a vehicle to articulate a kind of moral perspective. A morality is at issue when Neil Young invites us—those listening to *Prairie Wind*—to go to the prairies, though he admits most choose to ignore him ("Prairie Wind"). What he is calling for is a kind of return to garden innocence.

Despite the pastoral, peaceful mood of *Prairie Wind*, Young's songs incorporate an understated yet sharp polemic against the United States government's responses to the 9/11 disaster, specifically in his song "No Wonder." The songwriter seems unable to shake the memories of the 2001 attacks on the United States and the subsequent military reactions. He walks through a pasture, attempting to escape the pain he feels, but at the same time "America the Beautiful (That song from 9/11) / Keeps ringin in [his] head." Young does not actually sing the words "America the Beautiful" on either the *Prairie Wind* recording or the *Neil Young: Heart of Gold* DVD performance of the song, though they appear in the lyrics provided with the CD. If Young has in mind a specific performance of "America the Beautiful," it may be the stunning rendition by mezzo-soprano Denyce Grave during the prayer and remembrance service honoring victims of the 9/11 tragedy on September 14, 2001 at the Washington National Cathedral. This allusion clearly locates the song in a moment of grief and mourning. Young may also be referring here to the fundraiser concert "America: A Tribute To Heroes," in support of 9/11 victims' families (released as a CD and DVD in December 2001). During this event, Willie Nelson led a number of musicians and actors, including Neil Young, in a performance of "America the Beautiful."[71] This concert was also a moment of national mourning.

Young follows this line with another musical inspiration, this time one focusing on the violence following the 9/11 disaster. He hears Willie Nelson singing on the radio, which may refer to the country singer's performance of "America the Beautiful" just mentioned. It is also possible he knows of Nelson's antiwar song "Whatever Happened to Peace on Earth," written in protest against the United States' invasion of Iraq and first performed on January 3, 2004. The lyrics articulate a very clear perspective and political opinion regarding the Iraq invasion. He invokes the biblical commandment "Thou shall not kill" alongside the accusation that oil is the motivation behind the war. Truth, he sings, is "my weapon of mass protection," and that truth, again drawing on biblical writings, can set people free (cf. John 8:32).[72] Obviously, these lines allude to the questionable intelligence cited as justification for the war.[73]

The geography in Neil Young's *Prairie Wind* combines a real, physical, named space and an idealized, constructed one in which Young and his sympathetic listeners escape turmoil. This is not a complete retreat. The compassion of "When God Made Me" reminds listeners of their obligations to other human beings and articulates one possible alternative to the violence of both 9/11 and the military actions that followed, namely a world determined to show compassion to others. It is at this point that Young's album takes a theological turn because he reminds us that God made us to be caring and tolerant. The spatial movement described in *Prairie Wind* is also not a complete retreat because the artist continues to offer commentary on political processes, engaging in an ideological debate. However, the movement to a space of refuge provides the singer with a safe, restorative place from which to carry on this struggle. Young's album helps us understand why an artist like Daniel Lanois describes music in spatial terms ("It takes me to a sacred place").

Just as Neil Young creates a symbolic this-worldly space to retreat from sorrow and fear, so too other artists create otherworldly spaces to engage other challenges and questions. These alternative worlds often appear sacred in character. Religions provide a way of organizing our interaction with the world and all the people and experiences we face therein. When organized religion does not play a part in a person's life (and even when it does), art forms provide another venue for engaging our most intimate and pressing concerns. The remainder of the book examines some ways this happens.

RELIGION ON RECORD
POPULAR MUSIC'S ANXIETY
OF INFLUENCE

The . . . songs of Ormus Cama are rants in praise of the approach of chaos,
paradoxically composed by an artist working at the highest level of musical
sophistication. The songs are about the collapse of walls, boundaries, restraints.
They describe worlds in collision, two universes tearing into each other, striving
to become one, destroying each other in the effort. Dreams invade the day, while
waking's humdrums beat in our dreams.[1]

The narrator of Salman Rushdie's novel *The Ground Beneath Her Feet*
here grasps for the words to capture the profound and mysterious
power of rock music to represent and facilitate transformations.
When society is on the cusp of change, and of course society is
always on the cusp of change, the artist/musician has a role to play.
Artists can point to that which society should leave behind, while
presenting a vision of what the future could be. Contemporary
popular music tends to define itself over and against something,
whether earlier music, political positions, or society's values and
expectations. It is oppositional in one way or another. At the very
least, if new music is to endure, if it is to be relevant and interesting,
it must distinguish itself by taking style and lyrical content somewhere different. The most enduring songs do far more than that.

Rushdie's narrator speaks of collapses and the breaking of boundaries, of universes "tearing into each other." It is within those moments of confrontation that something artistically startling emerges. Many songs by the fictional Ormus Cama stem from "his horror at the profligacy with which the New World squanders its privileges," leading him to berate "his admirers for their wantonness, for the licentious debauchery of their ways."[2] His magical music is born out of contrariness, defiance, anger, and personal pain, but audiences hang on his every word: "Prophesying doom, he is the best beloved of the allegedly doomed. . . . the anathematized young of the Western world are enchanted."[3]

Though *The Ground Beneath Her Feet* is fiction, Salman Rushdie still manages to capture something of the spirit of rock-and-roll culture and its fascination with, and ability to point audiences toward, something beyond the mundane. He quite possibly models his character Ormus Cama on the late Jim Morrison (1943–1971) of The Doors, a connection suggested by the latter's "drug addiction, his Roman wilderness of pain, and his dogged attempt to break on through to the other side—to the underworld in which he tries to resurrect the spirit of his dead love, his Indian Eurydice [Vina Aspara]."[4] There are also shades of Queen's Freddy Mercury (1946–1991) in this character. Like Ormus Cama, Mercury (born Farrokh Bulsara) was a musician of East Indian descent (born in Stone Town, Zanzibar, Tanzania), who grew up in India and became a rock-and-roll god to Western audiences. To the extent that Cama is also a brilliant musical poet, transfixing audiences during a tumultuous period of cultural upheaval, he resembles Bob Dylan as well.

When thinking about rock and roll, the name Salman Rushdie is not the first to come to mind, and he himself would agree that the circles he inhabits as part of the literary intelligentsia, and those of the giants of the entertainment industry, meet only awkwardly. When describing an Anton Corbijn photograph of himself and U2's lead singer Bono, for which the photographer suggested the two exchange glasses, Rushdie observes, "There I am looking godlike in Bono's Fly shades, while he peers benignly over my uncool literary specs. There could be no more graphic expression of the difference between our worlds."[5] He remains, however, an insightful and passionate music fan. In one collection of essays, to illustrate, he includes a glowing review of a Rolling Stones concert, describing the band as "amazing. Their force, their drive, the sheer quality and freshness of Mick's singing and the band's playing. . . . The Rolling Stones may not be dangerous now, they may no longer be a threat to decent, civilized society, but they still know how to let it bleed. Yeah yeah yeah WOO."[6]

There are hints of Rushdie's appreciation for The Rolling Stones in his fiction. A devilish narrator lurks in the pages of his controversial novel *The Satanic Verses*. Making his presence known early on in the story, he asks the reader, "Who am I? Who else is there?" We catch a subtle echo of The Rolling Stones' "Sympathy for the Devil" in this line of questioning, specifically the repeated line in the song, "Pleased to meet you, can you guess my name?"[7] We find a further link between the satanic narrator of the novel and a pop music intertext when he offers a sly response to his own question: "Who am I? Let's put it this way: who has the best tunes?"[8] The expected answer is of course the devil. The satanic narrator's second phrase brings to mind lyrics by the late Larry Norman, made famous by Cliff Richard: "Why Should the Devil (Have All the Good Music)."[9]

Salman Rushdie, one of the world's best-known authors and arguably its most controversial, recognizes the lyrical quality of many pop songs. With reference to Frank Zappa and the Mothers of Invention, Elvis Presley, John Lennon, Randy Newman, Paul Simon, and Tom Waits, this Booker Prize-winning novelist admits, "In all this [songwriting] there is much for literary folk to study and admire. I don't subscribe to the lyrics-are-poetry school of rock aficionado over-claiming. But I know I'd have been ridiculously proud to have written anything as good as this."[10] Rushdie even entered the rockstar's domain on one occasion, famously joining U2 on stage at Wembley Stadium in 1992. This was the band's way of showing solidarity with Rushdie during his "exile" following the publication of *The Satanic Verses*, after the Ayatollah Khomeini issued his infamous *fatwa* calling for the author's death. U2 also put music to Rushdie's poem "The Ground Beneath Her Feet," found in the novel of the same name.[11] The song is part of the soundtrack for the movie *The Million Dollar Hotel* (2000).[12]

I include remarks about Salman Rushdie and *The Ground Beneath Her Feet* because this writer recognizes the fundamental importance of antagonism and the pressing of boundaries that is so central to much popular music. In trying to comprehend his unlikely friendship with the world's biggest band of the 1990s, Rushdie makes the following remarks by way of explanation:

> I've been crossing frontiers all my life—physical, social, intellectual, artistic borderlines—and I spotted, in Bono and Edge, whom I've so far come to know better than the others, an equal hunger for the new, for whatever nourishes. I think, too, that the band's involvement in religion—as inescapable a subject in Ireland as it is in India—gave us, when we first met, a subject, and an enemy (fanaticism) in common.[13]

Fanaticism leads to repression. Fanaticism ends dialogue and rejects alternative viewpoints. Fanaticism is dangerous, and therefore rightly called "an enemy." Fanaticism stifles creativity and exploration, and is therefore problematic for artists. For many artists, a sense of urgency to push back against rigid borders and boundaries, anything that hinders or limits expression, and a "hunger for the new, for whatever nourishes," informs and motivates the creative process. Salman Rushdie's vision of the task of writer and musician, as artists simultaneously defying established limits while searching for the new and the nourishing, captures well a recurring tendency in popular music's dialogue with religion.

It is a curious thing that rock and pop music of the post-1960s, which so often fashions itself as the embodiment of rebellion against authority, remains so thoroughly steeped in notions of the sacred. While many stepped away from organized religion during the last generation, a fascination with religious themes remains. Yet the recurring embrace of religious elements in popular songwriting is rarely straightforward. It usually involves the kind of struggle Rushdie describes in his protagonist's music: "The songs are about the collapse of walls, boundaries, restraints. They describe worlds in collision, two universes tearing into each other, striving to become one, destroying each other in the effort." Songwriters of the post-1960s indeed draw on the rich resources of religion for inspiration but, when they do, it is no mere passive borrowing. What occurs is a kind of poetic struggle where universes tear into one another.

HAROLD BLOOM AND THE ANXIETY OF INFLUENCE

Every artist is a cannibal, every poet is a thief;
All kill their inspiration and sing about the grief.

—U2, "The Fly," *Achtung Baby* (1991)[14]

Harold Bloom is, according to one recent treatment of his work, "the most famous living literary critic in the English-speaking world."[15] One of Bloom's most enduring contributions is in the area of influence theory. What is the relationship between a poet and his or her predecessors? According to Bloom, "strong poems are always omens of resurrection. The dead may or may not return, but their voice becomes alive, paradoxically never by mere imitation, but in the agonistic misprision performed upon powerful forerunners by only the most gifted of their successors."[16] We find in these words a summary of some of Bloom's central ideas about the nature of literary influence. Strong poems involve resurrection because they inevitably dialogue with earlier poems, thereby bringing the "voices" of those older works back to life. However, the influence of one poet/poem on another poet/poem is never a simple matter of borrowing or imitation. Instead, the relationship between poets and their precursors is agonistic (combative), involving misprision, or an act of sedition. This combative response exists because artists need to assert their individuality and unique creative genius.

Poets continually face "inescapable precursors,"[17] earlier influences that contribute to and potentially overwhelm their own work. Those who follow poetic greatness chronologically are therefore

anxious, fearful that their own work is nothing more than repetition and imitation of what another has already said. Introducing
Freudian imagery, Bloom observes strategies employed by chronologically late, influenced writers for overcoming, even killing, their
poetic ancestors. There are two key drives at work. One is the tendency to imitate the poetic parent; the other is the urge to overcome
the poetic parent in an Oedipal struggle, as the child poet asserts her
poetic originality. The poet overcomes through a process of rewriting and misreading the precursor, a process involving continued
indebtedness to, and liberation from, the poet's source. Or, as U2's
Bono puts it, poets are thieves who steal and kill their inspirations.

As a way of approaching the subject of religious content in
popular music, I propose an adaptation of Harold Bloom's theory.
This model offers a way of accounting for the dynamics at play
as song and sacred discourse meet. As poets (in a sense),[18] songwriters struggle with a kind of anxiety of influence. Religion is an
inescapable precursor for songwriters in the Western world, and
writers and audiences respond to this precursor in all kinds of
ways. Songwriters, like poets, are cannibals and thieves, borrowing from the resources available to them but often trying to stifle
and kill those inspirations in the process. They cannot escape religious influence completely, though they find ways of misreading
it. They write their own poems and stories using religion's terms as
part of the process of finding their own unique voice and demonstrating their distinctive poetic genius. (For a visual representation
of this process, see the diagram in chapter 5.) As Bloom puts it,
"Any strong literary work creatively misreads and therefore misin-
terprets a precursor text or texts."[19] I am clearly adapting Bloom's
theory by suggesting that religion broadly, and especially the Bible
and Christian discourse, functions as a massive "poetic" precursor
for English language songwriting in the Western world.

POPULAR MUSIC OF THE POST-1960S

The 1960s and early 1970s were times of remarkable change, with
liberalizing trends in politics, fashion, and sexual mores. Those
years were also a time of aggressive activism, demanding new and

consistent civil liberties for all citizens, including blacks, gays, and women. Religious alternatives presented themselves as never before, with the arrival of the International Society for Krishna Consciousness, the Moonies, and the Scientologists, among others. It was also a time of persistent fear. The Cold War loomed large, raising the specter of nuclear holocaust, a drama reaching its apogee during the Cuban Missile Crisis of 1962 when "a hard rain" very nearly fell. This was also an era marred by the violence and destruction of the Vietnam War. This unpopular conflict proved to be a foreign policy disaster, creating a rift between the American government and many of its citizens, and an atmosphere of mistrust.

In 1965, Bob Dylan offered a now-familiar turn of phrase that captured the mood of the day, particularly the willingness to challenge authorities, whether individuals in positions of power or institutions. Even presidents, he sang, must stand naked sometimes.[20] Everyone is vulnerable to scrutiny, according to the song. Just as Dorothy found a rather pathetic and weak manipulator of machines behind the curtain in Oz, so too the promises, ideals, and plans of the most exalted and revered people and offices of the land prove to be a chimera when examined closely. The implications are twofold: officeholders should beware because power is contingent, limited, and fleeting; and everyone else would do well to be cautious about trusting others to guide them. The only one you can trust, Dylan added in a later song, is yourself.[21]

Dylan takes aim at a variety of targets in "It's Alright, Ma (I'm Only Bleeding)," a song that continues to speak with great force in live performances decades after its first release.[22] Dylan draws attention poetically to the dangers of stasis because the only alternative to constant rebirth is death. Those who are not actively growing, adjusting, changing, and adapting to new situations and times inevitably fall prey to fools' disillusioned words, advertisers' cons, those urging conformity to party platforms, promoters of false morals, false gods, and pettiness. And yes, religious leaders and institutions are among the fools who speak empty words, a category of the disingenuous or disillusioned that includes doomsday preachers and the purveyors of glow-in-the-dark statues of Christ.

This song illustrates the compulsion to push back against boundaries described by Salman Rushdie in *The Ground Beneath Her Feet*, something prevalent in popular music of the 1960s and later. Dylan is certainly not alone among the songwriters of his generation in using music to reevaluate long-held assumptions and to question authority figures, including those representing religious institutions.[23] Many were challenging religious boundaries. Don Lattin examines emerging trends in American religious life during the 1960s, which he defines as stretching from January 20, 1961, the date of John F. Kennedy's inaugural address, to November 18, 1978 and the mass suicide of members of the Peoples Temple. These dates cover a period that witnessed "the idealism, religious activism, and social commitment that defined the best of the Sixties" at the beginning, to a tragedy that saw "the spiritual and political dreams of the Sixties [collapse] in a collective nightmare."[24] Spirituality was in transition, witnessing such phenomena as reform in Roman Catholicism, the arrival of Eastern spiritualities to North America, the appeal of rock and roll as "another vehicle for spiritual transcendence," as well as the emergence of such religious leaders as the Reverend Sun Myung Moon and Jim Jones.[25]

While it is customary to associate the American religious experience of the 1960s with movement toward exotic spiritualities, the growing interest in such organizations and trends as the Hare Krishna, transcendental meditation, and experimentation with psychedelics does not, in fact, represent "Nixon-era religion" very well. Mark Oppenheimer offers a helpful correction to our thinking on this point by calling attention to countercultural trends *within* the more established institutions of American religious life. Most Americans were not hippies or cult members, active proponents of gay rights or feminism, or engaged in drug use or social protest, and even though generally membership numbers in mainstream religious organizations declined in the post-War era, these institutions remained an important part of the social and religious fabric.[26]

Oppenheimer concentrates on the experience of more traditional religious communities during this period, and his apologetic for this emphasis is convincing. Cults and sects, he notes, are often "brief flashes" that may not survive long-term. They do not provide an opportunity to study the interplay of religion and culture. However, "Looking at Nixon-era religion not through cults and sects, but rather through the counterculture's manifestations in mainline denominations, should point the way toward a new kind of church history," Oppenheimer argues. Such a history should work to understand "how the counterculture functioned not on the fringes of society—on communes and around gurus—but in the traditional denominations that must interact with America, or die."[27] There was a new freedom within organized religion of the period, an openness to move away from the conservative patterns of worship that were—in the opinion of many—out of step with modern society.

RELIGION IN UNEXPECTED PLACES

Some pushed for reform within traditional Christian and Jewish communities, and others looked outside those institutions for religious options, but what about those who did not participate in organized religion at all during the 1960s and later? If the 1960s witnessed a growing distance between individuals and institutional religion, where did the "religious impulse" find expression for nonadherents? I take the term "religious impulse" from Robin Sylvan, who traces ways musical subcultures provide an orientation and sense of community traditionally provided by religion.

> Observers of culture and scholars of religion have said many things about the slow decline of religion and the death of God in Western civilization. Yet for millions of people . . . religion and God are not dead, but very much alive and well and dancing to the beat of popular music; *the religious impulse* has simply migrated to another sector of the culture . . . a genuine religious impulse went underground and became entangled in the hodge-podge hybrid now called popular music.[28]

Robert Detweiler and David Jasper make a similar point, though with reference to literature:

Much has been written and said about the seculariza-
tion of the European mind since the Enlightenment, and
the demise of religious perspectives under the pressure
of the great ideologies of progress in the nineteenth century . . . what we are suggesting here is *a persistence of the
religious spirit* and its insights which still must be taken seriously, its incorporation into our culture still acknowledged
by all those who either fear it, continue to subscribe to its
power, or celebrate its apparent demise. The energy and
difficulty of the interdisciplinary debate that lies at the heart
of our concerns may yet be central, even crucial, for us and
for those who will follow us.[29]

Whereas Detweiler and Jasper observe this "persistence of the religious spirit" in creative writing, and Sylvan observes an enduring
"religious impulse" manifest in musical subcultures, my own focus
combines these approaches and shifts the emphases. I am interested
in popular music, with Sylvan, though I approach popular songs as
texts, bringing primarily literary questions to them. In doing so, I
consider a different body of writings than Detweiler and Jasper,
and place less emphasis on the community/audience dynamics of
popular music than Sylvan. Despite different foci, Detweiler, Jasper, and Sylvan agree that an enduring hunger for spiritual meaning manifests itself in human artistic endeavors.

My guiding questions are simple ones. First, how did and
how do the massive changes in attitudes toward religion in recent
decades find expression in popular music, and second, if there was
in fact, in very broad terms, a shift away from traditional religiosity
in Western society, why does religious discourse continue to play
such a prominent role in so-called secular music? Clearly popular
culture provides some sense of the sacred for audiences. Sylvan
refers to "a growing body of scholars who recognize that, as traditional institutional religion has become increasingly irrelevant
to many people, the sector of popular culture has become the new
arena for their religious expression." With reference to musical subcultures, he adds that they serve "as the functional equivalent of

religion for the people involved."[30] Bruce David Forbes and Jeffrey H. Mahan introduce examples of critics who look at forms of popular culture *as* religion, noting that for these analysts, "the emphasis is not on traditional forms of religion, but on the way that significant cultural activity takes on the social form and purpose of religion."[31] So what does it mean to suggest that popular culture media, and music specifically, functions as an alternative religious experience?

As noted, it is surprising that music embodying the longing for separation from symbols of authority, and giving expression to a sense of alienation, still habitually embraces the language of established religions and their texts. There are many reasons songwriters introduce overt religious references and experiment with vague spiritualities in their music. For one thing, the introduction of religious imagery is often ironic in its intention. The gods inhabiting popular songs are often quite unlike the deities of traditional religious beliefs, doing and saying things in songs that are quite unexpected. Too, religious imagery often appears in songs simply because of its massive influence on the English language, something particularly true of Christianity. It is hard to avoid terms that have at least some association with the Bible or the church's traditions.

However, there are many instances of song lyrics born out of thoughtful reflection on religious subject matter and recalling actual moments in the spiritual lives of artists. Some mainstream writers acknowledge openly their religious beliefs, as we see, for instance, in Sinéad O'Connor's *Theology*, where she expresses her longing to make something beautiful with a stolen Bible "for U" ("Something Beautiful").[32] O'Connor capitalizes "U" because she directs this prayer to the God who forgave her soul, something she learns from the stolen Bible. O'Connor, who is an ordained priest,[33] explains to one interviewer that she really did steal a Bible on one occasion and made the promise referred to in the song.[34] Other albums exploring dimensions of songwriters' religious views include Alice Cooper's *The Last Temptation*, George Harrison's *Brainwashed*, and Yusuf Islam's *An Other Cup*, each of which I examine later.

Other writers are less certain about matters of faith but still describe their search for truth or encounters with the divine. An interesting illustration of the latter appears in Burton Cummings' eponymous 1976 album that opens with the song "I'm Scared." The events he narrates in the song actually occurred, according to claims made in an interview.[35] As a piano player he was concerned about his hands getting too cold on a winter day in New York City, so to escape the elements he entered the Cathedral of St. Thomas. The song captures a moment in time, an experience that left the impression that there is something more, just out of reach. While sitting in the church there was a vague presence, "something in the air" as he puts it in the song, though he could not identify who or what it was. At other times, songwriters are more active in their quest for meaning. The narrator in Pete Townshend's "The Seeker" is looking under chairs and tables for answers to life's many questions.[36]

While some share openly their personal search for religious meaning or encounters with the divine, others are equally vocal about their rejection of religion. Examples are legion.[37] Ironically, songs that reject religion still depend on a theological vocabulary to articulate their opinions, in much the same way atheists define themselves in relation to something they deny exists (that is, a-*theos*, no god). In fact, we can think about a lot of the music of recent decades as engaged in a form of competition with establishment religion. Stephen H. Webb asks two interesting questions growing out of the antagonistic dialogue some popular music has with Christianity in particular. The first is whether Christianity can survive the age of rock and roll, "the quintessence of popular culture," especially because Christian identity insists on standing apart from values embedded in popular culture. The second question reverses the order of the first:

> One could also ask: Can rock and roll survive the death of Christianity? Some scholars think we live in a post-Christian culture. . . . If this is true, and if rock has risen to prominence as a substitute religion by organizing a counter-Christian process of social formation, what will happen to rock when

it has nothing to work against? In other words, if the power of rock and roll depends on its competitive and ambivalent relationship to Christianity, in a purely secular culture, rock just might sound boring.[38]

This is a very interesting question. Contemporary songs, and the subcultures that identify with this music, define themselves over and against a sacred Other. Just as poets define themselves in a competitive relationship to earlier examples of poetic genius, so too songwriters who employ sacred themes cannot escape religious precursors and inevitably rewrite them in their own artistic work. They need that religious precursor to define themselves. Webb's question remains. Does rock music need religion/Christianity? At the very least, we might suggest that as long as Christian discourse figures so prominently in the psyche of the culture, there will be a desire to dialogue with it. As long as organized religion is a part of our world, there will be an appetite to provide commentary on its activities.

Reference to religion in the music of recent decades is widespread. However, is there a dominant quality to this engagement with sacred discourse? I suggest that resistance defines the relationship between religion and popular music, in two senses of the term. The first is resistance as a response to the anxiety of influence, a confrontation with the inevitable religious precursor as part of the creative writing process. Songwriters creatively rewrite religion. The second form of resistance relates to the struggle with authority characteristic of the counterculture movement that commenced in the 1960s. Mark Oppenheimer warns us against simplistic attempts to account for this period of history, reminding us that a "coherent 1960s never existed" because it is "a complex phenomenon, not easily reduced to political or social trends."[39] Still, Oppenheimer adds, "*Something* happened" during this time, "whatever the exact dates."[40] When listening to the music of the 1960s and 1970s, one *something* we observe is a growing suspicion and distrust of traditional sources of authority. Brian May of Queen clearly has this generation in mind when he refers to those growing up with the

threat of nuclear war ("the mushroom cloud"), and those angry
with the politicians who allowed this arms-race crisis to happen
in the first place (Queen, "Hammer to Fall," *The Works*, 1984). The
lyricist taps into the widespread tendency of this generation to
ask, in effect, whom can we trust? Will the government hear our
concerns? If not, we will scream louder and louder until it does. A
similar suspicion of authority, and anger at apparently indifferent
powerbrokers, and the willingness to protest and demand reform,
entered the religious sphere as well.

CRITIQUING RELIGION: POPULAR MUSIC ON THE OFFENSIVE

As we retreat from religion, our ancient opiate, there are
bound to be withdrawal symptoms. . . . The habit of worship is not easily broken.

—Salman Rushdie[41]

Popular music typically assumes an antagonistic attitude toward
society. As Robin Sylvan puts it, "The oppositional stance of white
youth culture is one of the main reasons why teenagers began to
turn to the rhythm and blues music of the African American community in the first place. It was a means of rebelling against the stifling conformity of mainstream 1950s culture."[42] This oppositional
stance of musicians and their audiences extends to religion as well,
and this contrarian position takes many forms. I will briefly mention four, which sometimes overlap with one another.

To begin with, some use art as a way of expressing their outright rejection of religion, their unbelief in a transcendent deity or
any kind of postmortem existence. We often find songs verbalizing
doubts about the existence of God framed as a type of existential
despair. Country singer Robbie Fulks observes that the world may
be full of wonders, but in the end the human experience is "mea-
ger" because God does not exist.[43] The band Bad Religion is also
explicit about its atheism; their name itself originates "from their
mutual distaste for organized religion."[44]

A second form this contrarian attitude takes is questioning the notion of a benevolent God based on pain and injustice in the world. The singer of Nine Inch Nails' "Heresy," for instance, identifies religiously motivated violence in the world as a reason for his skepticism: "[He] demands devotion atrocities done in his name / Your God is dead and no one cares / . . . Will you die for this?" Not infrequently, arguments questioning the existence or goodness of God based on the observation of personal or collective pain employ an angry tone. This is true of Gary Numan's "A Prayer for the Unborn." Here the singer accuses "you" of not listening to a cry for help. Later in the song, after the death of an unnamed "she," the singer addresses the object of his prayer again: "If you are my father / Then love lies abandoned and bleeding." His views on religion can be quite unambiguous at times: "I won't pray here / Or bow my head / I won't praise your name / I won't kneel down."[45]

More times than not, songs questioning the premises of religious faith articulate agnosticism or confusion about eternal truths. In such cases, the singer is not necessarily hostile to the idea of a transcendent being, just unable to find answers, as in The Who's "The Seeker": "I won't get to get what I'm after / Til the day I die" (*Meaty Beaty Big and Bouncy*, 1971). On other occasions, we hear laments over a lost faith or memories of some (usually vague) experience of the divine, as in Billy Joel's "River of Dreams" (*River of Dreams*, 1993): "I've been searching for something / Taken out of my soul / Something I'd never lose / Something somebody stole." There is nostalgia in such songs, perhaps recalling a time of simplicity, when one could find answers more easily. At the same time, there may be an implied criticism here. Those who search for meaning without success may be calling attention to the insufficiency of divine revelation and/or the inability of God's people to communicate religious truth convincingly and clearly.

A third form of opposition to religion involves criticism of faith communities from the outside. By this, I have in mind songwriters who describe problems within institutional Christianity (usually) or at least individuals within them, but who do so merely as spectators. There is no sense of connection between the singer and the group described and no attempts to engage in dialogue with them. For instance, "Devil in a Midnight Mass" by the Toronto-based band Billy Talent appears on their second album, *Billy Talent II* (2006). The song deals with sexual abuse in the Roman Catholic Church. It clearly evokes the ecclesial setting of the abuse, and identifies the priestly perpetrator as one who kills "the boy inside the man." Musically, the song effectively captures the male victim's anger. According to singer Ben Kowalewicz, the song is based on

> a story I read about a priest in Boston who had been arrested for child abuse and the church kept moving him from parish to parish. The Supreme Court tried and convicted him of molesting 150 kids over a 30 year span and while he was serving his sentence another inmate broke into his cell and murdered him. I stumble upon these stories, they don't necessarily have to be directly personal but it's things like this that move me. I'm a big advocate for children's rights and this song looks at sexual abuse. It's not against the church or anything, it's more about that individual betrayal between adult and child. I don't have the answers but hopefully if I sing about a certain issue it will get people talking about it.[46]

Kowalewicz clearly addresses the topic from a distance (the song is not "directly personal"). He criticizes the church's practice of "moving [this priest] from parish to parish" but does not enter into any kind of dialogue with it, such as calling for reform or invoking biblical or ecclesial teaching in the promotion of "children's rights." For this reason, Billy Talent's song is different from those fitting in the next category.

A fourth oppositional stance involves those who criticize religion from within, not only artists sympathetic to the faith tradition in question (for example, Christian artists criticizing Christianity) but songwriters who use the terms of a faith tradition as part of their critique of attitudes and practices. Bono's rant during the live version of "Bullet the Blue Sky" on *Rattle and Hum* (1988) is a well-known example, in which he refers to "a preacher of the old time gospel hour stealing money from the sick and the old." His response to the immoral behavior of greedy televangelists involves simultaneous identification with religion and rejection of certain activities by other religionists. The God he puts his faith in does not need their money.[47]

A very clever illustration of criticism from the inside appears in one of Dylan's lesser-known masterpieces. The narrator of the song "Dignity" hears the tongues of men and angels but adds the detail that there "wasn't any difference to me."[48] He is looking everywhere for dignity but cannot find it. Interestingly, the lines play off a biblical passage: "If I speak in the tongues of mortals and of angels, but do not have love, I am a noisy gong or a clanging cymbal" (1 Cor 13:1). According to Paul, loveless Christianity is little more than empty noise. Dylan finds no difference between the speech of angels and men, meaning he cannot distinguish between them. All he hears is noise. This lack of clarity in the sounds implies, according to Paul, an absence of love among people of faith. In this example, Dylan is an insider in the sense that he uses the biblical text as a basis to criticize those who read the Bible. This insider category would also include avid believers who criticize their fellow religionists for whatever reason, again, using insider terminology.

Contemporary songwriting critically analyzes religion in diverse ways. Moving from one end of the spectrum to the other, we have those who reject religion completely, others who find religion incomprehensible or inaccessible, and finally those who observe and question aspects of religious beliefs and praxis as either outsiders or insiders, the latter using its terms and values as a basis for commentary. One constant through these kinds of songs, whether articulating atheism, agnosticism, nostalgia, or mere indifference, is the use of terms and phrases from religion itself. Obviously one cannot deny the existence of God without mentioning that God (hence the term "atheism," which presupposes the term "theism"). One cannot criticize religion without entering into dialogue with religion. Here then, we have a well-represented category of religious content in contemporary songwriting. There are many examples of writers taking some kind of critical stance against religion, representing the range of opinion just described. The examples that follow focus on the last category, criticisms of religion from within.

CRITICISMS OF RELIGION FROM WITHIN

I do not mean to say that all songwriters who challenge religion or religious practices using its terms are believers, only that they choose to criticize religion from the perspective of an insider, and/ or they choose to use core teachings as a basis for criticism.

Kanye West's "Can't Tell Me Nothing"

Consider, for instance, Kanye West's 2007 album *Graduation*, where we find such an appeal to core values in the process of questioning Christian beliefs.[49] In "Can't Tell Me Nothing," the rapper relates a dream in which he discovers he can buy his way into heaven but, before he does so, recklessly spends his money on jewelry. The songwriter clearly draws on several biblical images here, including passages that contrast material, earthly wealth with true heavenly treasure.

> Do not store up for yourselves treasures on earth, where moth and rust consume and where thieves break in and steal; but store up for yourselves treasures in heaven, where neither moth nor rust consumes and where thieves do not break in and steal. For where your treasure is, there your heart will be also. (Matt 6:19-21; cf. 6:24; Luke 12:33-34)

When the narrator delays buying his way into heaven, telling God he will return later, he buys a necklace, gets himself arrested, and spirals into increasingly stupid behavior. The sentiment behind these lines, and specifically the phrase "To whom much is given, much is tested" alludes to Luke 12:48: "From everyone to whom much has been given, much will be required; and from the one to whom much has been entrusted, even more will be demanded." Wealth is clearly one of the things the singer has in abundance. On first glance, we might assume the implication is that wealth and possessions distract the unwary from important spiritual considerations.

However, West is not moralizing here. There is a tension developed in "Can't Tell Me Nothing" between the expectations others place on the singer, and his personal reality. (The video seems to emphasize this distinction, featuring the artist in two different locations. In one he is largely alone in a desert and appears distraught, in the other he is confident and boisterous in an urban setting.) On the one hand, some maintain that money should change him (so that he makes better choices, presumably) and cause him to forget his origins. On the other hand, this is not an easy thing to do. He did not grow up as part of the wealthy and privileged Cosby family, he points out. This sense of distance between the singer and others also emerges out of persistent, troubling questions. Though he is aware that Jesus sacrificed himself for others, this alone does not provide all the answers he wants (e.g., the reasons for wars). Here he articulates a classic theological conundrum, namely, how do we account for the origins of evil if in fact God is good? The singer cannot accept easy answers. The tensions between the rapper and others come to a head as he asserts his individuality: "This is my life homey." While it might be troubling to some, he asserts his individuality through ostentatious displays of wealth (parking "sideways" and letting "the champagne splash").

Despite the bravado, there is some reserve in the closing lines of the song. Life can be dressed in one of two ways. On one extreme, the "devil wear Prada" and on the other, Adam and Eve "wear nada." The singer does not choose either extreme, claiming he is "in between." The song is not about extreme wealth (champagne and big cars) in the end, but the critical tendencies of those who examine his life: "Ya homies looking like 'Why God?' / When they reminisce over you, my god." West challenges those who reduce complex social realities and even theological subjects to simple answers and tidy categorizations, just as he questions those who make quick judgments about the way he lives his life. His middle position, "between" nada and Prada, appears to contrast those fixated on this world ("Prada," possessions, fashion) and those fixated on the next world ("heaven"). West rejects both extremes. My main point here is that this performer enters this conversation about identity, expectations, and even theodicy using religious, particularly biblical language. He speaks therefore as an insider.

Arcade Fire's Parodic Bible

My second illustration of challenge from within also uses the Bible in what amounts to a sophisticated criticism of aspects of the contemporary Christian church.[50] In 2007 Arcade Fire's album *Neon Bible* was one of the darlings of the entertainment world,[51] praised by critics and commercially successful. The album includes a harsh critique of contemporary North American church life, though this critique does not extend to Christianity itself. What is interesting about Arcade Fire's approach to religious subject matter is the way they construct their commentary on church and society. *Neon Bible* is a clever parody of Christianity, one that recalls Mikhail Bakhtin's descriptions of medieval carnivals; according to Bakhtin, carnivals introduce "a second world and a second life outside officialdom."[52] The band does this very thing, ridiculing the official ecclesial authority by usurping its rightful place, in effect, through an unofficial, popular culture medium. They not only recorded their album in the sacred space of a church (literally), they even call the finished product a "bible." These comments on Arcade Fire's use of parody in *Neon Bible* also draw on Linda Hutcheon's definitions of the term.

According to Kelton Cobb, the jeremiad is widely used as a narrative framework in popular culture.[53] It offers a variation on the lost paradise script that calls for a return to Edenic innocence. The jeremiad has a biblical origin, of course. In the Hebrew Scriptures, the prophets like Jeremiah warn the people of covenant violations and call them to repentance. Literary critics apply the term "jeremiad" "to any work which, with a magniloquence like that of the Old Testament prophet (although it may be in secular rather than religious terms), accounts for the misfortunes of an era as a just penalty for its social and moral wrongdoings, but usually holds open the possibility for reforms that will bring a happier future."[54] Cobb observes writers and artists in popular culture constantly returning to the flexible form of the jeremiad to express their conviction "that we have corrupted our obligations toward a providential order that surrounds us." There are numerous variations of this theme because artists differ in their views regarding "what it is that constitutes corruption, and what it is within us that persists in causing it." What they share in common though is the use of paradise myths to explore "the shortcomings of human life" as they address the question "what went wrong?"[55]

In *Neon Bible*, Arcade Fire presents two kinds of religiosity in dialogue, one we might call a genuine, biblically informed spirituality, and the other an expression of religion tainted by commercialism and self-interest. The band assumes the role of prophet in the jeremiad tradition, calling the audience to be wary of the latter. Why do they do this? Because "a golden calf" still gives its light ("Neon Bible") and the "lions and the lambs ain't sleeping yet" ("The Well and the Lighthouse"). Cobb continues:

> The covenant/jeremiad script is a good one for juxtaposing an ideal order to our boundless imaginations for deviancy. Through it, a stubborn moral faith that persists in the culture continues to have a voice, promoting repentance and invoking a more exalted and inclusive idea of justice than the one that prevails. It offers a proven device for inventorying both a society's sins and the contents of its conscience.[56]

Indeed, Arcade Fire's *Neon Bible* juxtaposes an ideal order with forms of deviancy, and occasionally we hear hints of a stubborn moral faith. Some characters in the songs cannot escape a persistent, nagging conscience. Value systems clash in the *Neon Bible* world as greed meets scruple.

In addition to being a jeremiad, *Neon Bible* is also a parody. As such, it has some qualities of the "carnivalesque," Bakhtin's term for the transgressive energies of medieval carnivals during which unofficial culture would mock official culture, temporarily[57] resisting political oppression and totalitarian order—political, ecclesial,[58] or social—through laughter, parody, and grotesque realism. Bakhtin's image highlights liberation from fixed values and imposed modes of behavior. Those normally subjected and silenced have occasion to speak, and freedom to treat the sacred as profane, to mock and ridicule authority figures, and to cast off social expectations.

The term carnivalesque does not suit this particular text in every respect; there is no attention to bodily functions and grotesque imagery in Arcade Fire's lyrics, for instance. For this reason, I also have in mind Linda Hutcheon's definition of parody as I approach this album. For Hutcheon, parody in literary history is neither "that ridiculing imitation mentioned in the standard dictionaries" nor "a mode of discontinuity which rejects earlier kinds of textual reference to other works." Rather, she sees parody as "operating as a method of inscribing continuity while permitting critical distance. It can, indeed, function as a conservative force in both retaining and mocking other aesthetic forms; but it is also capable of transformative power in creating new syntheses."[59] The "collective weight of parodic *practice*," she argues elsewhere, "suggests a redefinition of parody as repetition with critical distance that allows ironic signalling of difference at the very heart of similarity."[60] Irony and parody are "double-voicings, for they play one meaning off against another."[61]

Arcade Fire's second album offers a parody of Christian symbols. They not only identify this album as a kind of bible,[62] but they connect their music to sacred imagery in other ways as well. For instance, the liner notes number the songs and the verses within them, using larger and smaller fonts in a format recalling chapter and verse divisions in modern Bibles. The liner notes further evoke a mood suitable for something called a bible by including pictures of organ pipes, stained glass windows and churches, and people in water with crosses on their wetsuits, suggesting baptism. According to the notes, the band recorded and mixed the album "at 'the church' in Quebéc," and "St. James Anglican Church in Bedford, Québec, [and] the Église St. Jean Baptiste in Montréal." When they say they recorded and mixed the album at the church, the band means this literally. They lived and worked in a nineteenth-century church near Montréal for the year it took to complete the album.[63] Not only does this decision to bypass a more traditional, modern, technologically sophisticated recording studio contribute to the album's fresh, original sound, the preference for a "sacred space" over a "secular" one has metaphoric value. This expression of unofficial culture assumes the place of official, authoritative religious activity as it constructs its own bible.[64]

The band introduces sacred elements to the album in still other ways. They acknowledge the contributions of "Gospel Singers" and direct thanks to "the Ven. Dr. Brian A. Evans, Archdeacon of Bedford" and the Église St. Jean Baptiste in Montréal "for allowing us to use their organ." The album's cover has a picture of an open, glowing (neon) book (presumably a bible). These visual clues indicate to the band's audience—before they hear a note—that Arcade Fire is presenting a kind of sacred text. This bible draws on various symbols—the sacred sounds of church organs, a chapter-and-verse style of lyric presentation, explicit references to the Bible and ecclesial practices—and in doing so parodies and comments on contemporary Christianity. The words *neon bible*[65] simultaneously suggest a modern, urban landscape complete with commercialism (neon), and such things as religious authority and moral directives (bible). The song lyrics do the same.

Arcade Fire's *Neon Bible* is replete with the unexpected twists and inversions implied by the term carnivalesque. Furthermore, the album is rich in biblical imagery, and this is no surprise given the principle songwriter's background. Win Butler grew up in the suburbs of Houston, along with his brother and fellow band member Will Butler, before moving to Québec, and he describes his father's side of the family as "really nonreligious" and his mother's side as "really religious." He refers to his maternal grandparents as "martini-drinking Mormons" and says he attended Mormon Sunday school as a child. He also listened to his maternal grandfather, "who would cheerfully undermine the church's dogma."[66] Elsewhere, Butler mentions that he studied "scriptural interpretation." With reference to the band's first album *Funeral* (2004), a Montréal-based magazine reports, "The album's inception can be traced back to 1999, when Houston, Texas-born singer Win Butler moved to Montreal to study scriptural interpretation at McGill [University]."[67]

Butler recalls another way religion loomed large during his days in suburban Texas, and his remarks are instructive when considering the *Neon Bible* songs. He mentions the many megachurches in the area and claims he had contact with them: "I've been exposed to that quite a bit—the commercial church." These institutions embody for him a kind of religion "fused with the culture, [which] becomes more commercial." This stands contrary to what religion should be in his opinion: "I'm always suspicious when religion isn't countercultural."[68] Implied in these remarks is Butler's view that religion has two faces. On the one hand, there is a kind of genuine spirituality (countercultural), and though he does not elaborate the point in this context, he does refer to the Bible as "still relevant." On the other hand, he criticizes religion when it aligns itself too closely with culture and commercialism (megachurches). This second form of religion betrays the influence of contemporary society, presumably its uglier qualities.

This dual perspective contributes to the ambivalence toward religion evident in the *Neon Bible* songs. There is such a thing as authentic, genuine spirituality, but it has a materialistic, commercially driven doppelganger that mimics distasteful features of the modern world, and herein lies the band's social critique. They use biblical and ecclesial imagery as part of a critique of certain religious institutions, those "fused with the culture" and manifesting the greed and selfishness of the contemporary world. Within the lyrics of Butler's songs and his comments about them, we find references to both kinds of religion. There is a bible that is poison ("Neon Bible"), and *the* Bible that is "relevant." A church can also have a doppelganger. On the one hand, it can kill: "working for the Church while my family dies" ("Intervention"). On the other, "the church" depicted in the album's liner notes indicates a site of creativity, the sacred space in which the band creates its prophetic music, its jeremiad. An overview of selected lyrics in *Neon Bible* illustrates the band's vision of these contrasting manifestations of religion.

The song "(Antichrist Television Blues)" involves three distinct speeches. The first speech (vv. 1–2, 9) is a soliloquy presenting the narrator's rationale for not wanting to work downtown, ostensibly because planes are crashing into buildings two by two. This obvious allusion to 9/11 articulates a perfectly understandable fear, and a credible reason for wanting to avoid the rigors of a regular job in an urban setting. Presumably, most listeners would be sympathetic to his despair at first, but when we jump ahead to the third speech (vv. 7, 10–14), addressed to his daughter, we become a little suspicious of his motives. He tells the thirteen-year-old girl that he worked for minimum wage when he was her age, and he will not allow her to do the same when a better opportunity exists. He is coaxing this little "bird" to get on the stage and sing. She may be tired and afraid, but he insists she perform and convince the men watching[69] that she is "old for [her] age." Initially there is gentleness in his terms of endearment, but his words—and the musical accompaniment—become increasingly frantic as the song proceeds, as if the girl is reluctant to perform as he wishes. This culminates when his tone changes toward the end of the song and he tells her he is through being cute and nice. He will force her to sing.[70] His words almost suggest violent coercion.

It is in the second speech, directed to God (vv. 3–6, 8), that we piece together the narrative in more detail. This self-identified Christian narrator attempts to justify his actions, explaining to God that people must work hard and receive compensation for their labors. He also tells God that his daughter is quite mature for her age—as if he does not already know—perhaps anticipating the same objection that the men watching the girl, and the girl herself, appear to recognize.

This father is clearly looking for permission to allow his "bird in a cage" to perform for pay. In an effort to provide a persuasive case, he appeals to a biblical precedent. He asks God whether he intends to seat his daughters (plural in verse 4 of the song) at his right hand, clearly alluding to the Gospel story where a parent puts the same request to Jesus:

> Then the mother of the sons of Zebedee [James and John]
> came to [Jesus] with her sons, and kneeling before him, she
> asked a favor of him. And he said to her, "What do you
> want?" She said to him, "Declare that these two sons of
> mine will sit, one at your right hand and one at your left, in
> your kingdom." (Matt 20:20-21; cf. Mark 10:35-40, though in
> Mark's version the mother does not appear)

The parent in the song obviously knows this story but appears to
overlook the fact that Jesus does not grant the mother's request
(20:22-23), making his appeal to this particular biblical passage
rather odd, even foolish. Butler is certainly aware of this, and by
having his narrator make such a request, it is clear that the father's
actions do not enjoy divine commendation (or the songwriter's
approval).

This father has other biblically based arguments in support
of his case. He claims to have God's best interest in mind, wanting a child on the TV screen so the whole world will discover his
true word. He refers to his daughters as "lanterns" and God as the
"light." These lines allude to Jesus' metaphors of a city on a hill and
a hidden lamp:

> You are the light of the world. A city built on a hill cannot
> be hid. No one after lighting a lamp puts it under the bushel
> basket, but on the lampstand, and it gives light to all in the
> house. In the same way, let your light shine before others, so
> that they may see your good works and give glory to your
> Father in heaven. (Matt 5:14-16)

According to some reports,[71] the band occasionally refers to
"(Antichrist Television Blues)" by the title "Joe Simpson," after
the father of pop star Jessica Simpson, who would therefore be the
bird in the cage mentioned in the song. Regardless of the referent
intended, the song clearly describes a parent willing to exploit his
children for personal gain. This father may tell his girl to perform
and demonstrate to the men watching that money has nothing to
do with it, but his words ring hollow. He is the one with an aversion

to the idea of his daughter working for minimum wage, as he once did, and he is the one who becomes wealthy thanks to her talent. This is evident in the fact that he holds the purse strings tightly; if the girl does not sing, he threatens he will not buy her any gifts. He has an opportunity to escape the workaday world by living off the profits earned by his celebrity child.

There is a polyphonic quality to this song's lyrics. On the one hand, the father is a person of Christian faith and biblically literate, evident in his choice of terms and phrases (possible allusions to Prov 26:23-24; Isa 29:13; Matt 5:5, 15:8, 20:21). At the same time, this father recognizes that his actions are morally suspect. If this were not the case, he would not need to explain himself to God in the first place (vv. 3-6, 8). This recognition of moral shortcoming is most evident in the song's closing words, which follow immediately on his announcement to the girl that he will no longer be cute and nice. Returning to prayer, he cries as the song closes, "O tell me, Lord, am I the Antichrist?!" This conflicted father is aware of two kinds of sacred discourse. One is the commercially driven religious agenda that attempts to justify the exploitation of a child using biblical tropes (sitting at Jesus' right hand; a city on a hill). The other is the father's religiously informed conscience, traces of what Kelton Cobb calls "a stubborn moral faith" (see above). Despite his own rhetoric, he is aware that what he is doing is wrong. His desperate last question is the largely stifled voice of conscience, perhaps something implied by the use of parentheses in the song's title (i.e., it is a muted confession, partly hidden away). The father in this song holds in tension two separate discourses. He is dialogical, debating with himself, driven both by genuine religious ideals, and more selfishly motivated religiosity that hopes to profit from immoral actions. In his final question, he again draws on biblical discourse (antichrist: 1 John 2:18) but this time with a different tone, one of fear (the music is frenzied as he speaks the words) and perhaps confession.[72]

The narrator of "Keep the Car Running" is anxious about a vague sense of impending doom not unlike hints of the same in "Windowsill."[73] This song describes the contents of a recurring dream situated in a city that involves unidentified men coming to take the sleeper away. He has told them his name, but just the same he does not want them to find him. The recurring call to keep the car running signals his intention of fleeing before (or when) they arrive. The narrator does not tell us explicitly who these men are, or why they frighten him. He also lives with a deep-seated fear that he has known his whole life, right from infancy. This fear is distinct from the men themselves, and he adds the detail that those men do not know "when It's coming."

The capitalization of "It's" (as it appears in the liner notes five times) suggests he is referring to a specific crisis, perhaps the biblical judgment. The reference to the biblical passage about the lion lying with the lamb elsewhere on the album—an image frequently linked to the millennium/kingdom of God in some Christian circles—lends support to this reading (see "The Well and the Lighthouse" and Isa 11:6, 65:25). This still does not explain the identity of the men he is running from, who are at least aware of the singer's fear, even if they do not know where and when the expected crisis will occur. It seems plausible they could be religious teachers who preach fear to their congregations, even if their messages lack clarity and detail (i.e., the when and where of divine judgment). Though it is risky to link a songwriter's biography to poetic lyrics, it is striking that Win Butler is so open about his connections to organized religion during his childhood. The fact that the singer wants to run from them suggests his desire to leave behind the fearmongering that traumatizes him.[74] He cannot escape the fear itself, it would appear, because he continues to have disturbing dreams, but he can avoid those who promulgate that fear.

If this reading is correct, it supports the suggestion put forward earlier that *Neon Bible* distinguishes actual, genuine religious content from institutions and other manifestations of that religion that are suspect in the songwriter's view. The narrator of "Keep the Car Running" wants to distance himself from those who represent the kind of piety that thinks it appropriate to frighten children in the name of God.[75] This song resembles "(Antichrist Television

Blues)" in that it comments on what is arguably a form of child abuse—broadly defined—by religious authority figures.

We find a further narrative about the frightening power of institutional religion in the song "Intervention." It tells the story of a "soldier" whose efforts on behalf of the church produce destructive consequences. While working for that institution, he reports, his family is dying. This story appears to involve the plight of those inside the church who are simultaneously its victims. Indeed, some of these people sing hallelujah but are frightened as they do so.

The song opens with a king taking back his throne and the sowing of "useless seed." Here we have an allusion to the parable of the sower (Matt 13:1-9, 18-23; Mark 4:1-9, 13-20; Luke 8:4-8, 11-15), in which a dutiful farmer scatters seed. According to Jesus' parable, some of the seeds do not produce crops because of the nature of the soil, competing plants (thorns), or birds. The seeds themselves are fine. The king in the song "Intervention," by contrast, sows "useless seed." There is a carnivalesque quality to this image. The seed in Arcade Fire's version of the parable is itself ineffective, and the king of the song, who parallels the diligent, well-meaning farmer of Jesus' parable, is abusive. We see a further inversion of values in the soldier's story; the church does not care for the hard-working individual but is instead responsible for his demise.

The soldier in the song is a vulnerable member of a religious community. The image of a soldier is a common one in Christian discourse,[76] but even though he is fighting for the church, he is afraid and his life is falling apart. A church that once provided genuine care for its members and carried out the honest, biblically mandated work of spreading the gospel and its love (that is, spreading good seed, as in Jesus' parable) now exploits and abuses its members.

Finally, I turn to the album's title track. According to the song "Neon Bible," distinguishing pain and hope is no easy thing because they resemble one another. Like other songs on the album, this one describes moral ambiguity in a world where a "golden calf" offers the only light, skewing better judgment in the process. The narrator uses the first person in his dialogue with an unnamed individual who holds a position of moral authority, saying to him, "What I know is what *you* know is right" (emphasis added). By the song's end, however, the narrator recognizes that the lessons learned from this source are suspect and the value system offered to him is corrupt: "It was wrong but *you* said it was right" (emphasis added). Again, a carnivalesque reversal is at play, now with reference to ethics—right is wrong, wrong is right. This mixed-up logic is the poison of the age, and the light provided by the golden calf is more blinding than illuminating. The biblical image of the golden calf raises again the notion of religious authority figures—Aaron the priest plays a part in that story (Exod 32:1-6). The implication from the song is that the "*you*" providing bad advice is also a religious authority figure. After recognizing the dangers of distorted values, the narrator retreats from this confusing light, announcing he will only read at night from now on, as if to say darkness provides a better source of illumination than the alternatives available to him.

Here again, *Neon Bible* addresses commercialism (it is a *golden* calf after all) and a self-interest that acts to the detriment of others. Despite reference to "the world," there is a specifically urban setting evoked because the poison of the age, and the golden calf, light up "the city." This is consistent with the use of the word neon in the song's title, typically associated with downtown signage and commercial spaces, and Butler's reference to suburban megachurches in the interview cited above.

Neon Bible is an illustration of unofficial culture resisting official—in this case ecclesial—culture, questioning its coercion and abuses by presenting a parody of the church and its biblical basis of authority. Returning to Linda Hutcheon's definition of parody for a moment, I note her emphasis on the potential of parody as a constructive force.

> Parody is endowed with the power to renew. It need not do so, but it can. We must never forget the hybrid nature of parody's connection with the "world," the mixture of conservative and revolutionary impulses in both aesthetic and social terms. What has traditionally been called parody

privileges the normative impulse, but today's art abounds as well in examples of parody's power to revitalize.[77]

{Arcade Fire's carnivalesque lyrics subvert and ridicule authoritarian, commercially driven Christianity. The band, in this carnivalesque reversal of roles, takes the place of the Church through their symbolic act of choosing to record in that venue} They cannot escape ecclesiastical fearmongering and commercially tainted religiosity, so they confront and undermine its claim to authority. Arcade Fire's album functions as an alternative bible, replacing *the* Bible in effect, and through parody the band censures the questionable ethics and practices of churches in consumer culture. This repetition of religious images involves, according to Hutcheon's definition of parody, a critical distance that permits "ironic signalling of difference at the very heart of similarity."

POPULAR MUSIC'S CONFRONTATIONS WITH RELIGION: FINAL THOUGHTS

Rock songs, Rushdie tells us, "are about the collapse of walls, boundaries, restraints." When free-spirited, opposition-prone music meets religion, something artistically original emerges. It is combative, rewriting a religious precursor in ways recalling Bloom's description of poetic anxiety. By bringing sacred content out of the officially sanctioned venues of religious discourse (houses of worship, canonical texts, and so on) artists reevaluate religiosity without restraint, without walls or boundaries that limit creative thought. The conclusions they reach vary, from outright rejection of the sacred, through expressions of agnosticism, to genuine faith. Others are indifferent about religion altogether, finding only linguistic and symbolic resources in its various discourses to aid in the songwriting process, even when the subjects addressed have nothing to do with metaphysical concerns. Finally, these dialogues with spiritual concepts often involve a clear sense of perspective, as artists engage the sacred discourses as either insiders or outsiders.

The progressive rock trio Rush describes a modern-day Tom Sawyer, whose "mind is not for rent / to any god or government"

(Rush, "Tom Sawyer," *Moving Pictures*, 1981). Mark Twain's character is a freethinking individual not subject to anyone or anything. This Tom Sawyer attitude captures well the creative approach to religion exemplified in the contemporary music mentioned in this chapter. This push away from restraints and authority coincides with an insistent return to religious subject matter. This constant circling into and out of the religious sphere (see the diagram in track 5) collapses walls, boundaries, and restraints, causing collisions of universes as dreams invade the day and waking's humdrums beat in our dreams.

CHURCH IN A GUITAR CASE
COMFORT AND COMPASSION IN POPULAR MUSIC

"Our lives are not what we deserve," Salman Rushdie writes in a passage cited earlier. They are, "let us agree, in many painful ways deficient."[1] This is one reason why faith in God figures prominently in the lives of so many. Life is a struggle, to put it mildly, and faith offers a way of dealing with the slings and arrows that flesh is heir to. One with a religious outlook maintains there is purpose and meaning in all of life's experiences, and looks to a higher power for consolation.

Rushdie maintains that music offers something to those whose lives are painfully deficient. Just as religious discourse offers reassurance to people of faith, so too songs, in their own way, respond directly to calamity. In this chapter, I will consider ways in which popular music narrates personal and corporate tragedy, how songs express the fears and anxieties of individuals facing loss and communities struggling with injustice. In both instances, songwriters draw on religious language and imagery in their efforts to turn life into something else, and show us a world worthy of our yearning.

Why do popular songs, which are by definition forms of entertainment, dwell so often on troubling, often tragic subject matter? There are probably many reasons for this constant return to dark themes.[2] Singers have always responded to calamity, from the

Hebrew laments of ancient Israel to the present. What is interesting about the post-1960s era, though not unique to that period, is the parallel emergence of a growing secularism. The use of a religious vocabulary to articulate grief, and to express hope and longing for deliverance and relief, remains, but there is less sense of connection to formal religious communities. We continue to hear this precursor (established religion) as songwriters struggle to articulate their unique poetic vision under its long shadow, but many integrate this material into songs dealing with mundane subjects. This is a familiar pattern. For this reason, before turning to examples of popular music's response to grief and injustice, we will consider the use of religion in songs about nonreligious topics.

USING RELIGIOUS LANGUAGE
FOR NONRELIGIOUS PURPOSES

John Lennon released the intriguing "God" in 1970 on the album *John Lennon/Plastic Ono Band*. No doubt many at the time could identify with this lyrical rejection of religious and political symbols. For Lennon, God is merely a concept "by which we measure our pain." This statement implies that religion is an individual and social construct, a narrative allowing people to contextualize their lives within something much bigger. Religion is the ultimate Otherness, a reality apart from our world but one still bringing meaning to it. Politics can do this as well. Ideologies allow individuals to be a part of a larger community, one comprised of those sharing a vision of how to make the world a better place. Lennon, however, is highly suspicious of religious and political worldviews, troubled by the violence carried out in the name of ideology. In an ideal world, there would be "nothing to kill or die for," he sings elsewhere.[3] Lennon's song "God" does not voice suspicion of organized religion and politics only. He also lashes out at the idolization of celebrities. As audience members, we love our heroes, perhaps needing to believe that a select few can rise above the ordinary to achieve great things—even if we ourselves cannot. The songwriter questions this idea, challenging our naïveté in the process. Lennon's scorn about the value of celebrity is rather original when compared to the self-aggrandizement of many pop-music icons.

"God" is remarkably poignant, honest, and sad. In this poem, Lennon frankly admits that he is not able to believe in various things, naming a selection of religious symbols, texts, leaders, celebrities, and politicians to illustrate his point. Perhaps the song's most interesting idea is the thrice-repeated reference to the end of a dream. On one level, it most certainly refers to the breakup of The Beatles, though whether the call to his "dear friends" to press on refers to his bandmates, their fans, or both is unclear. However, given the long list of things the songwriter does not believe in— the Bible, Jesus, Kennedy, Elvis, and more—there is certainly more at stake here. His disillusionment stands opposed to the idealism that grand narratives like religion and politics offer. Lennon even acknowledges his complicity in nurturing one particular fantasy, admitting he was a "Dreamweaver," presumably signaling his immense influence as part of the Fab Four (further indicated by the words "Yesterday" and "I was the Walrus" which allude to two of their songs). Lennon has escaped all this, however. He is now "reborn," a term parodying words spoken by the very same Jesus rejected earlier in the song (cf. John 3:3). This rebirth is an intellectual awakening. He can only believe in himself now, not the iconic songwriter who *was* the Walrus (that is, a celebrity, a Beatle), just John Lennon the man.

Lennon's "God" illustrates a nonreligious use of religious language. He released this song in 1970, a post-1960s anthem signaling a break from traditional spirituality and authority structures. It is an assertion of individuality and love. All he believes in, the songwriter claims after his catena of rejected objects of faith, is "Yoko and me," a phrase illustrating how love and sexuality come to replace the salvific experience central to many religious traditions (cf. chap. 3). We also find in this song the continued appeal of religious discourse among writers outside traditional venues of religious contemplation. The song's title and provocative lyrics make use of a sacred vocabulary even though it is a statement, ultimately, about his nonreligious worldview.[4]

As is obvious from its title, religious language figures prominently in U2's "God Part II" (*Rattle and Hum*, 1988) as well, a tip of
the hat to Lennon that borrows the general structure of "God" (i.e.,
the singer lists things he does not believe in) and alludes to another
of his well-known songs (with the words "instant karma"). Here,
however, the language is not so cynical, and ironically, it reverses
some of the claims made in the Lennon precursor. Whereas Lennon
asserts his unbelief in religion in toto, the U2 lyrics suggest the need
for discernment when thinking about the spiritual realm. The singer
does not believe the devil's lies, but this is not a rejection of the spiritual realm outright.[5] The internal logic of this song suggests there
is such a thing as "truth" apart from the individual, and requires
that spiritual realities do exist, even if we should avoid some.

There are other points for comparison. Both "God" and "God
Part II" place limits on the potential of rock and roll; Lennon does
not believe in Elvis or The Beatles, and U2 does not believe music
can change the world. Instead, these songs urge listeners to think
for themselves, to be wary of those people and things that deceive
or give false hope. For Lennon, these include government, celebrity, and religion. For U2, the devil, violence, and drugs are among
the villains. Despite their theological differences, both Lennon and
U2 use these songs to address subjects that are not about religion,
for the most part, employing a sacred image ("God"/"God Part II")
to give commentary on a string of dissociated topics (cf. Boston's
"Higher Power," discussed in the preface).

Religious language does not require a spiritual object to be
meaningful. In other words, a person does not need to be a believer
to find beauty and welcome sentiment in sacred writings (witness
the number of weddings and funerals in which the Bible plays a
significant part, even when those involved are not particularly
religious). For this reason, theological language often contributes
to commentaries about nontheological subjects in popular songs.
As these examples show, even though writers differ in their views
about religion (and Lennon and Bono clearly disagree on theological matters), they continue to use its language in support of their

particular agendas, and they do so in similar ways. Other examples of nonreligious uses of religion are not hard to find.

THREE-MINUTE TRAGEDIES: CATHARSIS, RELIGION, AND POPULAR SONG

I turn now to reflections on the use of music in response to personal and collective trauma. Many songwriters reveal a persistent curiosity about spiritual themes in their work, even some who celebrate their freedom from societal expectations and organized communities of worship. David Chidester looks at the interesting test case rock and roll presents in relation to the study of religion. There is a striking ambivalence at work in this particular genre of music. For many in the religious establishment, "rock and roll appears as the antithesis of religion: not merely an offensive art form but a blasphemous, sacrilegious, and antireligious force in society."[6] At the same time, however, rock music "has sometimes embraced explicitly religious themes, serving as a vehicle for a range of religious interests, from heavy metal Satanism to contemporary Christian evangelism."[7] Though this apparent contradiction—a simultaneous escaping from and embracing of religion—defies simplistic explanation, we find one clue to this constant return to religious symbolism in lyrical narratives about human tragedy.

There are all kinds of songs dealing with painful experiences, and religion often figures prominently in these lyrical stories. Again, the artist's personal connection to the faith tradition providing a source of language and imagery is of secondary importance. The language of sacred discourse contributes to commentaries on nonreligious issues (like Lennon's "God" and U2's "God Part II"), regardless of whether or not the writer has any personal investment in the tradition.

Like "God" and "God Part II," the title of Paul Simon's "Wartime Prayers" (*Surprise*, 2006)[8] obviously includes a religious term. And like those other songs, its principal subject is nonreligious. Through references to and descriptions of prayer, the song responds to a tragedy and makes a political statement. In this song, Simon distinguishes prayers spoken during peacetime with those made during wartime. The former are private, silent cries for love. The latter emerge out of deep wounds, and are cries to drive away despair. When peacetime prayers end, and when wartime prayers are necessary, we also hear a third form of speech, according to the singer. Standing in contrast to the prayers of the desperate is a troubling public discourse. At such times, those anxious to hear the words of God are dependent on "lunatics and liars." The singer contrasts himself with a group described as holy, masterminds, and genius marketers, who are, one suspects, synonymous with the lunatics and liars. We might have other reasons to be wary of people referred to as genius marketers: "In popular cultural terms, good talkers are mistrusted as well as admired: people who have a 'way with words'—the seducer, the salesman, the demagogue, the preacher—are people with power, and the power to use words is a power to deceive and manipulate."[9] The lunatics and liars command an audience, but we suspect their rhetoric and warmongering are dangerous and misguided, given the destructive consequences of war.

The way Simon represents authentic prayer is noteworthy. The introduction of a mother holding her babies close in the last verse, uttering a wartime prayer, paints a picture of a family whose father is fighting in a distant land, or who perhaps died in the conflict. Maybe the "liars and lunatics" are responsible for that conflict. The prayerful mother's sincerity and desperation, and the narrator's humility (he admits he is no mastermind) seem far removed from the marketing geniuses and holy people mentioned elsewhere in the song. The singer lacks pretension; he does not claim to be holy, or a genius. He only hopes to find some wisdom and put away envy and rage. The mother caring for her children offers her wartime prayer to "drive away despair." The narrator mentions families torn apart; hers is clearly one of them.

Do the lunatics and holy people who contrast with these sincere supplicants represent the public face of foreign policy? Though the song does not mention the Iraq crisis explicitly, it is hard not to think of that conflict, justified as it was—in the opinion of some—on questionable intelligence (arguments claiming Iraq possessed weapons of mass destruction). Even weak evidence can sound convincing in the hands of genius marketers. In a National Public Radio interview, Simon mentions he "started writing [this song] before the invasion of Iraq," when he had some sense of what was coming. With reference to the album *Surprise* as a whole, he refers to the challenge of writing in the post-9/11 period, "in a world that was permanently altered."[10] Authentic prayer provides a means of coping with pain, disaster, and uncertainty.

Active and Passive Responses to Tragedy

Paul Simon sings about real-world crises in this song (politics, war, broken families), but to do so he introduces the language of religious ritual (prayer). This is a familiar pattern. When people experience trauma they often draw on their imagination to cope with and explain their experiences. Songwriters represent and respond to grief and violence in at least two ways. Many songs voice *active* responses to injustice and sorrow. This is most obvious in songs articulating political opinions or advocating on behalf of those in need. For instance, the 1985 famine-relief composition "We Are the World," written by Michael Jackson and Lionel Richie and performed by the supergroup USA for Africa, is a clear call for action. The song identifies a need and then appeals to listeners to respond: "there are people dying and it's time to lend a hand." Religious imagery contributes an important line of argument to this plea for generosity: "As God has shown us by turning stones to bread / So we all must lend a helping hand." The introduction of a religious reference contributes to the emotive force of the song's plea for compassion, even though there is some confusion in this allusion to Jesus feeding the hungry.[11]

While active response songs deal with actual situations for which real solutions are in reach, others involve fantasies of healing, comfort, and justice for dilemmas lacking any options for actual compensation (such as, the death of a loved one). Here, artists imagine responses to trauma that offer forms of escapism, narratives that provide solace and a strategy for coping with a crisis, even though no tangible correction to the problem exists. Religious terminology often plays a key role in such attempts to compensate for loss. We may call these *passive* responses to grief, and most of the examples in what follows fall under this heading. Both forms of creative response to trauma, passive and active, provide audiences with an opportunity to experience emotional catharsis.

Music and Catharsis

The philosopher Aristotle (384–322 BCE) observed theatergoers watching frightening and sad subject matter who were not distressed in the long term by what they saw. Quite to the contrary, they walked away from the theater having experienced a kind of relief, what he called "the pleasure of pity and fear." For the ancient Greeks, tragedies describe a protagonist's downfall, someone who is guilty of *hamartia*, an error in judgment, or *hubris*, excessive pride. This does not sound like something audiences should stand up and cheer about, but Aristotle maintains that watching tragedies on the stage, or reading about them in poetry, is a healthy exercise. When writing about this in his *Poetics*, he observes that

> tragedy is . . . an imitation of a noble and complete action, having the proper magnitude; it employs language that has been artistically enhanced by each of the kinds of linguistic adornment, applied separately in the various parts of the play; it is presented in dramatic, not narrative form, and achieves, through the representation of pitiable and fearful incidents, the catharsis of such pitiable and fearful incidents. (Aristotle, *Poetics*, 6)

Readers of Aristotle debate the meaning of this somewhat obscure phrase about a catharsis of incidents or emotions. The Greek word *katharsis* can mean "clarification," "purification," and "purgation," and the context in this passage seems to suggest that what is clarified, purified, or purged can be either the "incidents" in the play, or the emotions of "pity and terror" the play evokes.

If catharsis means "clarification" then the function of tragedy is largely pedagogical. We benefit from watching or hearing about tragedies because they can teach us. When the hero in the story falls, we take warning and learn to avoid his mistakes. However, if catharsis means "purification," the experience of viewing or hearing a tragic story helps us—audience members—deal with our emotions. After encountering true examples of tragedy in poetry and drama, we are less likely to misdirect our pity and fear to inappropriate objects. Reading Aristotle's catharsis in this second sense, as "purgation" or cleansing of the emotions, suggests a washing away of pity and fear. Watching a tragic play, or reading a heart-rending story, relieves us of painful and unwanted emotions. This is one reason why those sad songs say so much. This interpretation is consistent with Aristotle's use of the term "catharsis" in another context, here with reference to music:

> Any affection which strongly moves the souls of several persons will move the souls of all, and will only differ from person to person with a difference of degree. Pity, fear, and inspiration are such affections. The feeling of being possessed by some sort of inspiration is one to which a number of persons are particularly liable. These persons, as we can observe for ourselves, are affected by religious melodies; and when they come under the influence of melodies which fill the soul with religious excitement they are calmed and restored as if they had undergone a medical treatment and [*katharsis*] purging. The same sort of effect will also be produced [i.e., by appropriate music] on those who are specially subject to feelings of fear and pity, or to feelings of any kind; indeed it will also be produced on the rest of us, in proportion as each is liable to some degree of feeling; and the result will be that all alike will experience some sort of [*katharsis*] purging, and some release of emotion accompanied by pleasure. We may add that melodies which are specially designed to purge the emotions are likewise also a source of innocent delight to us all. (Aristotle, *Politics*, 1342a.4-5)

Here the clustering of music, religious experience, and catharsis is intriguing, and though I stop short of calling contemporary, mainstream music "religious melodies," I suggest the results are

similar for some listeners. Music and poetry offer therapeutic bene-
fits for audiences. Furthermore, since Aristotle was commenting on
Greek theater when he spoke of tragedy—the works of dramatists
like Aeschylus (ca. 525–456), Sophocles (ca. 496–406), and Euripides
(ca. 485–406)—there is a religious dimension to all this. The theater
played an important role in Greek civic life. It was also a religious
affair. The theater originated as part of Dionysian festivals, and
popular dramas regularly revolved around religious themes, such
as the need for fidelity to the gods.

So why is it that audiences, both ancient and modern, enjoy
hearing, reading, or watching tragic stories? Typically, tragic figures
are neither all good nor all bad. They embody both qualities, which
allow us to identify with them. Oedipus was not an evil man, nor
were Othello, King Lear, Sméagol/Gollum, or Anakin Skywalker/
Darth Vader entirely devoid of goodness. Stories about the downfall of "normal" characters frighten us because we recognize the
possibility that we might repeat their mistakes, or experience their
pain. This ability to identify with storytelling makes emotional
engagement possible, and this is where Aristotle's theory of catharsis comes in. He suggests that we can experience sentiments like
pity and fear because of this identification, but we can do so from
a distance. The actors on the stage make mistakes and suffer the
consequences while we, as spectators, participate emotionally in
the tragedy from the safety of our theater seats. We learn valuable
lessons and find some relief from the anxieties and fears we carry
with us.

Personal Trauma

It may seem unusual that a musician would deal with personal
tragedy through the medium of what is ultimately entertainment,
yet it occurs frequently. The fact that audiences listen to this music,
born as it is out of sorrow, implies that the inclusion of dark themes
does not distract us from the enjoyment of the music.

Two concerns often addressed in popular songs are mortality
and the ravages of aging. Consider, for instance, Ron Sexsmith's
Time Being (2006). The opening song on this album explores

emotions and concerns presented by the unrelenting ticking of the clock. "Hands of Time" fits in with a long line of poetic writings that address the perennial anxieties stemming from the passing of youth, and the specter of death; time may look friendly, but it will eventually leave us "high and dry," Sexsmith sings. This discomfort with the passing of time also appears in John Mayer's "Stop This Train" (*Continuum*, 2006), where he admits his fear of getting older. Similarly, Pete Townshend laments the loss of youth in "The Sea Refuses No River" (*All The Best Cowboys Have Chinese Eyes*, 1982): "We tried not to age / But time had its rage." This subject is not unique to songwriters, of course. John Milton's (1608–1674) "On Time" is one example of a response to the passing years in the English poetic tradition, one courageously confronting the inevitable losses we face with the passing years:

> Fly, envious Time, till thou run out thy race,
> . . .
> And glut thyself with what thy womb devours,
> Which is no more than what is false and vain,
> And merely mortal dross;
> So little is our loss,
> So little is thy gain.[12]

Time takes much from us, but ultimately "mortal dross" costs us nothing. Milton steels himself against the passing of time by looking to the divine recompense that awaits us:

> . . . long Eternity shall greet our bliss
> . . .
> When once our heav'nly-guided soul shall climb,
> . . . we shall for ever sit,
> Triumphing over Death, and Chance, and thee O Time.

This turn to religion as a source of comfort is one solution to an anxiety-ridden existence that involves fear of the unknown future.

Another solution common in popular music is resignation toward the inevitable. Put on a brave face when confronting your own mortality, the death of friends and loved ones, and loss of

youth, and celebrate the present moment. Ron Sexsmith chooses
this option. He dedicates the album *Time Being* to the memory of
two "good friends," and presumably they are in mind as he sings
about the pain of losing a loved one in "Hands of Time." The singer
finds comfort in the present moment, accepting that we are, inevitably, in the hands of time. As Milton tells us, time will glut itself
on all that is mortal. Sexsmith acknowledges this fact yet chooses
to celebrate that which is near at hand. If the present time is all we
have, he sings, "Honey, I won't change a thing." This creates a striking ambivalence regarding the inevitable parting of the ways lovers must make: "As drunk on life as death is sober / When we say
goodbye." Separation and death will come, but we will be happy,
living to the fullest. Religious language, while not prominent, is
present in this song. The opening line is a prayer, with the singer
calling out simultaneously to the Lord and "the hands of time."
However, the particular solace the singer finds is in a loved one, the
one who moves her "snow white hand" in his.

Sexsmith's song "Some Dusty Things" on the same album
casts the notion of passing time in a positive light, though even here,
a sense of finality and distance between the past and the present is
haunting as he observes how precious their time on earth "was."
The use of past tense is conspicuous. Consider also the album's
final song, in which the singer returns to reflections on one of his
lost friends. The song "And Now the Day Is Done" again plays off
the image of passing time, but here he is no longer thinking of his
own grief but of the sorrow felt by a friend. The singer will never
know about the load that friend had to bear when he "walked that
lonesome road." All the narrator can hope for now is that he found
comfort either toward the end of his life, or in death.

Artistic representations of human tragedy provide us with a
way of visiting scary but important places, for visiting emotions
that we might otherwise be inclined to neglect. None of us enjoy
dwelling, for instance, on our personal mortality or potential for
evil, or society's neglect of the poor, oppression of the most vulnerable, or the destruction of the environment. However, rather
than putting our heads in the sand, we can sit in the comfort of

our theater seats, with Aristotle, and take an emotional, cognitive journey somewhere between escapism and experience, relieving our anxieties but facing our fears. We do this by reading literature, watching a play or movie, or listening to our iPods. The experience is educational, emotionally liberating, and cleansing.

Religion and Tragedy

The tendency to employ metaphysical, otherworldly, and religious terminology when confronting the tragic resembles the ancient Greek dramas mentioned above. These complementary subjects—religion and tragedy—allow listeners to consider painful subjects and experience a form of escape simultaneously. Unadorned prose rarely provides satisfactory articulation of catastrophic events, and this explains in part the constant introduction of metaphysical categories in stories about mundane but tragic events. Writers do this in different ways, and for different reasons. Commenting on Led Zeppelin's song lyrics, Susan Fast points out that "the mythologies constructed by Led Zeppelin are meant to evoke the extradaily, especially the past or the magical, in a much more general way [than most progressive rock bands do], and this was a conscious decision on the part of the band."[13] So while Led Zeppelin makes use of various literary sources,[14] the band is not interested in over-intellectualizing their music. In support of this claim, Fast cites Jimmy Page, who contends, "some so-called progressive groups have gone too far with their personalized intellectualization of beat music. I don't want our music complicated by that kind of ego trip—our music is essentially emotional like the old rock stars of the past. . . . We're not going out to make any kind of moral or political statement." Fast finds in these words a distinctive quality of Led Zeppelin's lyrics. Page's statement indicates a deliberate move away from "the kind of intellectualization that occupied many progressive rock bands [and] toward greater physicality and undefined (or at least under-defined and therefore more interpretively open) spirituality."[15]

There are other reasons for introducing scenarios outside normal daily experiences. Bob Dylan's "Seven Curses" illustrates a further function of metaphysical language when narrating the tragic.[16]

This song tells the story of Reilly, who faces hanging after stealing a horse. His daughter brings gold and silver to the judge in
order to buy back her father's freedom. This judge, however, is not
interested in money and tells the girl, "The price, my dear, is you
instead." This demand for sexual favors horrifies her father, but
she insists on doing everything in her power to save him and yields
to the judge's demands. Once "the price was paid," however, the
judge does nothing to save Reilly from the gallows.

There is no satisfying solution available to the victims in this
story—the father is dead, the judge robs the girl of her honor, and
he escapes justice. Is there any possibility of relief for the story's
victims or for the audience listening to the narrative? Yes. The
songwriter introduces metaphysical language to help one cope
emotionally with the crimes committed. It is not representative of
any particular religion—compare Fast's reference to "undefined
(or at least underdefined and therefore more interpretively open)
spirituality"—but it is religious in some sense. While not a sacred
story, it does appeal to sacred categories as a response to catas-
trophe and is thus able to accomplish an emotional catharsis for
the audience. The singer curses the evil judge, imagining an eternal state of torment where he is beyond the healing touch of doc-
tors, where no one sees or hears him, where no one hides or buries
him, and most significantly, where "seven deaths shall never kill
him." There may not be justice for the vulnerable in this life, but
the imagination permits fantasies of appropriate consequences for
those guilty of horrendous crimes. And these consequences are not
subject to the mundane limits of time and space.

Contemporary pop music constantly turns to dark themes,
whether the myriad painful experiences endured by individuals or
larger social justice issues. Most religions provide ways of coping
with grief and fear, offering conceptual frameworks for explaining
trauma. Catastrophic events may be the work of a devil or demon,
meaning people are victims, or permitted by a benevolent god who
chastises people of faith to instruct them, as a parent disciplines
a child. Some cope with sorrow knowing that a better life awaits
them in some postmortem existence. Not all people have a religious

frame of reference, but they still need to deal with the more difficult aspects of the human experience. This need to confront, analyze, and make sense of trauma is universal.

Following Aristotle's lead, the following observations are possible: we enjoy watching and reading sad stories; we experience a catharsis of unwanted emotion when artists make us feel gloomy or frightened; and finally, artists regularly turn to transcendental or religious discourse as a vehicle for responding to human tragedy. Aristotle includes music in his analysis of the arts, recognizing its potential for "purging our emotions and lightening and delighting our souls." His insights translate nicely into the modern context. If we listen carefully, we can find tragedy, catharsis, and religion clustered regularly in contemporary songwriting. Song lyrics obviously do not provide systematic representations of a religious worldview, but these three-minute tragedies have the potential to introduce spirituality in unexpected places.

Confronting a Troubled Past: An Example

We find such a use of sacred and metaphysical language in a fantasy of healing and comfort on Meat Loaf's 1993 album *Bat Out of Hell II: Back Into Hell*. The lengthy (10:15) "Objects in the Rearview Mirror May Appear Closer Than They Are,"[17] written by lyricist Jim Steinman, describes three incidents in the life of a young male who is haunted by the persistent memories of his childhood and youth. Time references suggest progression in the story. As the song opens with episode one, the sun is bright. By episode two, the sun has set, and in episode three, there are stars in the night sky. This shifting in narrative time coincides with indications that the protagonist is aging as the stories unfold. The various scenes describe the main character growing up, moving out of the house, and discovering love, all of which suggest a gradual loss of childhood innocence. Each brief narrative also involves tragedy.

The first story is about the death of a childhood friend. The singer remembers his tears at the time of the accident but also imagines that his friend is behind him in the present moment. The narrator is unable to escape his past. The haunting presence of earlier events and people, a hyperactive memory, is even more obvious in the second and third episodes. The second story recounts the violence experienced at the hands of his abusive father, who hits him repeatedly. Though he lived with threats and fear as a child, he remains a victim as he recalls the abuse in the present, now that the singer is an adult. Those "terrors are still intact." He still hears his father's voice and feels him grabbing and pulling him back. The final episode introduces relief and a kind of redemption, though here too there is sorrow. He describes a beautiful woman who brings "salvation." She also haunts him, like an "angel rising up from the tomb!" This final story provides healing after the traumas endured earlier in life, using her body to dress his wounds, because sexuality and love provide solace and salvation.

This woman is particularly interesting in light of the music video for the song. Referral to music videos complicates lyric analysis, of course, because videos introduce further authors and interpreters to the mix. Songwriters (like Jim Steinman) compose songs that musicians (like Meat Loaf and the various instrumentalists) and producers interpret in their performances and recording efforts. Music videos add still further layers of commentary, ones that are particularly influential for music fans; indeed, some may only know a song through its video. Simon Frith comments on the relationship of sound and image (as in ballet, opera, or film scores), pointing out that the relationship between different art forms is not uniform. In opera, for instance, the composer plays the biggest part in conveying narrative meaning, more so than a librettist or director. In film, however, the director and screenwriter communicate narrative meaning primarily, not the musical composer. "There is," he concludes, "a different relationship between sound and image, between the use of sound to bring out the meaning of what's seen (film), and of image to bring out the meaning of what's heard (opera)."[18] Frith argues that music videos resemble operas in this respect more than film.[19] We might add the caveats that music videos can suggest *possibilities* of song meanings, and that music videos are not determinative in any sense because of distribution.

Many people still hear songs apart from videos (through CDs, MP3s, concert performances).

In the case of "Objects in the Rearview Mirror May Appear Closer Than They Are," the music video offers compelling images to complement the music and lyrics available from the CD, suggesting possible meanings to take from the song. The woman is a particularly interesting character. She resembles an angel rising from the grave, suggesting she is dead at the time the narrator tells the story. This simile also contributes to a quasi-divine quality in this woman. She plays a dominant role in the video. While flirting in the back seat of a car, she is sitting significantly higher than the boy is, requiring him to look up to her face. Since she is "an angel," there is something approximately divine about her.

More intriguing still is the hint of a maternal quality in this woman. As noted, the song lyrics suggest maturation. In the video, however, the angelic beauty who offers him salvation is clearly older than the young actor. The erotic level of meaning is obvious enough as the couple are together in the back seat of a car, a cliché signaling adolescent sexuality and an image familiar to Steinman and Meat Loaf fans—the well-known "Paradise by the Dashboard Light" is an obvious example (*Bat out of Hell*, 1977). Nevertheless, there seems to be more going on here. There is a brief moment in the video where she is present in the childhood home during the story of the abusive father, even though the song lyrics do not mention the woman during this scene. This angelic woman combines, it appears, shades of erotic, maternal, and quasi-religious symbolism. The Oedipal overtones are hard to miss and particularly striking given the absence of any maternal figure in the familial second episode. The boy's mother is mentioned nowhere in the song's lyrics.

Our primary concern in this section is the introduction of religious language as a response to trauma. This song illustrates the point, dealing as it does with death, abuse, and lost love all at the same time. There are at least three ways religious concepts contribute to Steinman's narrative. First, we see the integration of the theological ideas of resurrection and reunion with the dead in a song that explores how great pleasures and terrors linger in the memory with remarkable intensity. This idea of reunion with the departed, we will see in the next section, is a familiar trope in popular songs discussing death. In this particular example, these reunions are both happy and frightening, as the narrator meets again a long-lost childhood friend and an absent lover, as well as his violent, abusive father. Second, this song acknowledges that some of the traumas people encounter are so damaging that individuals are unable to rescue themselves. Salvation and rescue must come from the outside, an external Other able to bring healing. This too is a religious notion, at least as Steinman presents it with his angel of mercy. Finally and more generally, religious terms and ideas—salvation, angel, resurrection—contribute to the emotive force and intensity of the song. Steinman and his interpreter Meat Loaf are not making theological statements in these songs, but they are integrating religion into their storytelling.

Music and Mortality: Reuniting with the Dead

It seems incongruous that entertainment music introduces mourning as its subject matter as often as it does. As noted, Ron Sexsmith's *Time Being* is an example. His lyrics deal with mortality, and he dedicates the album "to the memory of [two] good friends." Other examples include KISS's "Detroit Rock City" (*Destroyer*, 1976), inspired by the death of a fan; "I'll Be Missing You" by Puff Daddy & The Family (*No Way Out*, 1997), a tribute to Notorious B.I.G. (murdered in 1997); and Elton John's "Candle in the Wind" (*Goodbye Yellow Brick Road*, 1973), mourning the death of Marilyn Monroe. U2 dedicates their album *The Joshua Tree* (1987) "To The Memory of Greg Carroll 1960–1986." Carroll was a Maori from New Zealand, hired by the band in 1984. He eventually settled in Dublin, where he died in a motorcycle accident involving a drunk driver. Bono and Larry Mullen Jr. accompanied the body back to New Zealand and attended his funeral, after which Bono wrote the song "One Tree Hill" (*The Joshua Tree*) in response to the experience.[20]

When lyricists deal with personal grief through the very public medium of a published song, audiences can share in the pathos of one mourning the loss of a loved one. Here too religious themes provide songwriters with a suitable vocabulary. Sacred imagery provides an appropriate reverence for memorializing the dead. It can be emotive and, more importantly, holds out the promise of reunion. The hope of reunion with the departed is a recurring theme in pop songs, a clear illustration of a *passive* response to trauma.

Robbie Robertson, former guitarist and songwriter for The Band, opens his eponymous first solo album with the rather touching "Fallen Angel,"[21] a song dedicated to former bandmate Richard Manuel, who committed suicide in 1986. There were other tributes to Manuel following his death, including The Band's "Too Soon Gone," written by Jules Shear and Stan Szelest and released on the 1993 album *Jericho*. Eric Clapton (with Stephen Bishop) wrote "Holy Mother" in Manuel's honor (released on the album *August*, 1986). The lyrics of this song are in the first person singular, suggesting a plea either that the Holy Mother bring comfort for the one grieving Manuel's death, or that the call for help is from Manuel himself, asking her to take away the pain. The narrator feels like the end has come and confesses he would rather be in her arms tonight.

Robbie Robertson's tribute is particularly interesting. His song assembles a cluster of religious, often biblical terms and phrases and concepts: writing in the sand (cf. John 8:6, 8); crossing into a land of shadows (cf. Ps 23:4); kneeling; the angel Gabriel blowing a horn; a chosen one; and so on. The most significant use of biblical language appears in the title phrase; the idea of a fallen angel has biblical roots (cf. Rev 12:9).

What is striking about Robertson's play with this language is the complete reversal of the usual sense of the words. Manuel is not a villain of course, and the word "fallen" carries the sense of departure and death, not evil and disobedience. In fact, the name of the fallen angel in the song is Gabriel, a powerful and good angel, not an evil one. "I lost a friend," Robertson writes, "Come down Gabriel and blow your horn." The instrumental link—the horn—is consistent with phrases in the Bible that present God's angels as musicians (such as 1 Thess 4:16), and naturally it is an appropriate image in a tribute from one bandmate to another.

As noted, the promise of reunion with the departed dead is a recurring theme in pop songs involving grief, and Robertson's "Fallen Angel" is no exception. Various lines addressed to this angel imply his continued existence and nearness. The songwriter is searching for the angel (Manuel) and seeing him in his dreams, even inviting him to come. At times, there is uncertainty about his friend's proximity—"If you're out there"—but at other times, there is confidence they will meet again.

Similarly, Eric Clapton introduces this idea of seeing a loved one again in the heavy-hearted "Tears in Heaven" (cowritten with Will Jennings; *Unplugged*, 1992). The song is Clapton's response to the death of his four-year-old son Conor in 1991.[22] As the title indicates, this beautiful elegy appeals to religious imagery, imagining what might happen when father and son reunite in heaven. Speaking in the first person, the songwriter addresses his child, asking if they will experience again the intimacies shared in life, asking if the boy will remember his name and hold his hand. Like Robertson's "Fallen Angel," the song involves a mix of certainty and doubt, at times using hypothetical language ("If I saw you . . ."), at others confidently asserting that beyond that "door," there is peace. This quasi-reunion theology takes many forms. A very different kind of reunion appears, for instance, in "Living Years" by Mike and the Mechanics, where the songwriter mourns the death of a parent but finds comfort in his baby's cry, hearing in it his father's "whisper" (Mike and the Mechanics, "Living Years," *Living Years*, 1990).

Songs on David Gray's 2002 album *A New Day At Midnight* (2002) incorporate reflections on the subject of life and death as well, including the longing for reunion with a parted loved one, especially, the closing track "The Other Side."[23] The death of the songwriter's father is an inspiration here. The whole album is grounded in Gray's personal experiences, to the point that he remarks "with *A New Day At Midnight* I'd taken the personal as far as I cared to go."[24] In a *Rolling Stone* interview, he speaks of the personal nature of this album. When asked about the ways the death of his father influenced the songs, Gray admits, "That's what the core of this record deals with."[25] Gray's songs resemble Clapton's "Tears in Heaven,"

Mike and the Mechanics' "Living Years," and Robertson's "Fallen Angel" in that the lyrics are responses to a specific death, a particular personal tragedy, and they fantasize about a reunion between the living and the dead.

The brief tragedies narrated in popular music provide important emotional connections for audiences. There is a link between uncomfortable or frightening storylines and our own deep-seated anxieties. On occasion, songs allow us to confront our demons and personal tragedies, and then help us deal with them. At times, pop musicians create narratives allowing *passive* responses to grief that offer fantasies of healing and comfort (such as reunion stories). These provide a way of dealing with traumas for which there are no satisfactory remedies or solutions. Other songs present *active* responses to injustice and sorrow, mobilizing audiences to take action in support of justice (calls for social justice, political and humanitarian action, as in "We Are The World"). We turn now to other examples of this second category.

THE SACRED RHETORIC OF SOCIAL JUSTICE: ROCKING FOR THE POOR AND OPPRESSED

"Human song that arises from a paradoxical world of beauty, injustice, and human suffering is," Don E. Saliers writes, "intrinsically theological." It follows, he continues, that "Singing has always been at the heart of social and political movements."[26] At this point, we turn from songs of introspection, examining personal loss and grief, to songs integrating religious elements in commentaries about oppression and injustice. The list of musicians engaging in activism or supporting causes is long and varied. This involvement does not always link directly to their music (that is, they do not always write songs directly about these causes), though their celebrity status helps raise the profile of the issue at hand. I mentioned Boston's efforts in support of drug prevention and rehabilitation. Bryan Adams raises money for breast cancer research through the publication of his photography.[27] Bob Geldof's writing on Africa helps raise awareness of the ravages of poverty in that continent.[28] Paul McCartney, Rob Zombie, and members of the band Boston are longtime vegetarians who support animal welfare initiatives. The list goes on.

The benefit concert is a forum musicians often use to promote their causes. Bookending the period approximately covered in this book are two significant examples of the integration of popular music and social justice movements—George Harrison's "Concert for Bangladesh" (1971) and Sir Bob Geldof's "Live 8" (2005).[29] Harrison organized his event in support of those suffering the consequences of a devastating cyclone and political unrest in Eastern Pakistan (what would eventually become the independent country of Bangladesh). As Tom Petty put it during his speech at George Harrison's 2004 induction to the Rock and Roll Hall of Fame (as a solo artist), "Years before Live Aid, George invented the idea of rock and roll giving back to the people."[30] In addition to fundraising and media exposure for the plight of East Bengalis, the "Concert for Bangladesh" set a precedent for the enormous potential of celebrity-driven social justice movements.

It is easy to be cynical when wealthy musicians take the stage in support of a cause. Publicity sells records, and no doubt there are musicians whose reasons for activism are open to question. The sheer number of cause-related events might lead some to question the motives behind them. Since Harrison's Bangladesh concert, there have been many such concerts of note. Bob Dylan organized "The Night of the Hurricane" at Madison Square Garden in support of the wrongly convicted boxer Rubin "Hurricane" Carter (December 8, 1975). The series of "Farm Aid" benefit concerts began September 22, 1985, organized by Willie Nelson, Neil Young, and John Mellencamp. Actor George Clooney organized the concert telecast "America: A Tribute to Heroes" in support of 9/11 victims and their families (September 21, 2001). Tom Cochrane organized "Canada for Asia," a televised fundraising benefit in support of relief efforts following the tsunami disaster of December 26, 2004 (January 13, 2005). There will always be cynics, but no one can deny that genuine compassion motivates many of these celebrity initiatives. In his study of Harrison's Hindu spirituality, Allison observes the "combination of otherworldliness and authentic social concern" in the Bangladesh project.[31] Harrison wrote the song "Bangla Desh" for the concert, the lyrics to which Allison describes as "simple and straightforward, [revealing] a sincere humanitarianism."[32] Harrison himself states his motives at the outset of the song, describing how a friend needed help, "before his country dies."[33] The friend in question is musician Ravi Shankar. According to Harrison, Shankar encouraged him to raise some money to support the poor in Bangladesh.[34]

A similar sincerity is evident in the ongoing work of Sir Bob Geldof on behalf of Africa's poor. He has been tireless in his efforts for more than twenty years, most notably in the organization of Live Aid and Live 8, and more recently through his bestselling book *Geldof in Africa*, cited above. Geldof has his critics, but few question his passion for humanitarian efforts on behalf of Africa's poor.

U2, Human Rights, and Political Activist Aung San Suu Kyi

U2 is closely associated with social justice initiatives as well. I focus here on one example of their support for a cause that illustrates how musicians can integrate religious discourse into their politically engaged songs. In the notes to their albums *How to Dismantle an Atomic Bomb* (2004) and *No Line on the Horizon* (2009), the band calls to their fans to "Support Aung San Suu Kyi. Help us free Burma. For Freedom! For Burma! Take Action!" Aung San Suu Kyi is the figurehead of the pro-democracy movement in Myanmar (formerly known as Burma). The military dictatorship in Myanmar placed the activist, author, founder of the National League for Democracy party, and 1991 Nobel Peace Prize Laureate under house arrest in 1989, with only brief reprieves since then.

One of the most remarkable features of Aung San Suu Kyi's story is her steadfast refusal to leave her country, even though the government once made this option available to her on the condition she would not return. When asked about her decision to remain under house arrest rather than flee the country, she offered the following explanation:

> I never forget that my colleagues who are in prison suffer not only physically, but mentally for their families who have

no security outside—in the larger prison of Burma under authoritarian rule. Prisoners know their families have no security at all. The authorities could take action against their families at any time. Because their sacrifices are so much bigger than mine I cannot think of mine as a sacrifice. I think of it as a choice. Obviously, it is not a choice that I made happily, but one that I made without any reservations or hesitation. But I would much rather not have missed all those years of my children's lives.[35]

Referring to this dilemma in the song "Walk On" (on *All That You Can't Leave Behind*, 2000), which U2 dedicates to Suu Kyi, Bono describes the activist as a "bird in an open cage" who is able to leave but will only do so when truly free.[36] In addition to hinting at the offer of a conditional release, Bono likely alludes here to Suu Kyi's published work. She writes about the plight of imprisoned pro-democracy supporters in Myanmar, describing their children as those who "have known what it is like to be young birds fluttering helplessly outside the cages that shut their parents away from them."[37]

U2's album *All That You Can't Leave Behind* includes a subtle reference to the prophet Jeremiah on the album cover—the alphanumeric symbol "J33→3"—that seems to indicate that this biblical prophet is significant for the ideas presented through the songs.[38] Furthermore, references to Aung San Suu Kyi in the album's liner notes indicate that her story is also relevant. The band's interest in Aung San Suu Kyi is further evident by the use of her image in performances at this period of their career. For instance, during three songs on the *Elevation 2001 / U2 Live From Boston* DVD ("Gone," "Wake Up Dead Man," and "Walk On"), Bono wears a button on his guitar strap with a picture of the political prisoner, and he also dedicates "Walk On" to her as he begins to sing this song. There is also a photograph in the liner notes to U2's *The Best of 1990-2000 & B-Sides* (2002) showing Bono wearing a T-shirt with her name and picture on it.

I suspect Bono finds in Jeremiah's story an ancient parallel to Aung San Suu Kyi's heroic efforts on behalf of her people. The symbol J33→3 is shorthand for Jeremiah 33:3, which offers the encouraging words, "Call to me and I will answer you, and will tell you great and hidden things that you have not known." Jeremiah was active during a period of political turmoil that reached its apogee with the fall of Jerusalem in 586 B.C.E. He announced Judah's demise, and because of this unpopular proclamation, the government of the day placed him in prison. Jeremiah was simultaneously strong and fragile, much like the latter-day prophet Suu Kyi. His courage is evident in his willingness to make unpopular announcements about the downfall of the nation and his criticisms of its leadership. His frailty is evident in his repeated struggles with timidity (1:6) and fear when facing violence (11:18-12:4). Jeremiah frequently returns to descriptions of his internal anguish (4:19; 9:1; 10:19-20; 23:9).

Both Jeremiah and Aung San Suu Kyi announced political change to the consternation of the government of the day. King Zedekiah of Judah placed Jeremiah in prison for claiming Nebuchadnezzar of Babylonian would conquer Jerusalem and take Judah's king into captivity (32:3-5; the prophet's words proved to be true [39:4-7]). Aung San Suu Kyi also directs her message at the ruling establishment. The ruling military regime in Burma commenced in March of 1962 following a coup under the leadership of General Ne Win, "a xenophobic, eccentric and ruthless dictator."[39] Myanmar's government responded to Aung San Suu Kyi's call for reform in the same way Zedekiah did to Jeremiah's message. Both prophets ended up in prison.

Here popular songwriting employs the language and stories of the Bible for nonreligious purposes. *All That You Can't Leave Behind*, and "Walk On" in particular, addresses a political question, not a religious one, and uses the Hebrew prophet's story as a way of telling the story of the modern political prophet, Aung San Suu Kyi. Jeremiah models the same courage and frailty evident in Suu Kyi's ongoing struggle. Religious discourse now serves an explicitly political purpose.

Those Sad Songs Say So Much

Popular music can be a positive force, whether by providing individuals with a way of exploring their personal sorrows and anxieties (catharsis), or by raising awareness and funds for social justice causes. We have also seen that while music voices skepticism and suspicion about institutional religion (as in Lennon's "God"), it also functions as a substitute for much that those communities of faith offer (such as a way of confronting fear and crisis). [Robin Sylvan argues that musical subcultures provide fans with "as all-encompassing an orientation to the world as any traditional religion," adding that "musical subculture provides almost everything for its adherents that a traditional religion would."[40] Attention to lyrics provides further insights into the reasons why music so often and so easily meets the needs of audiences. It is true that belief in something greater than oneself (the power of celebrity), the communal worship of that celebrity (fan culture), and the shaping of codes of behavior (such as fan subculture as an influence on dress, speech, values, politics, and so forth) all have loose parallels with dimensions of religious life. It is also true that there is a vocabulary in popular songs that draws on the language of traditional religion, and often hints at a vaguely defined transcendent Other. Song texts draw on a pool of discourse that for centuries and millennia served as the means of expressing human longings, questions, and fears—indeed, they still do. When songwriters incorporate elements of these discourses, they tap into habits of thinking deeply ingrained in our cultures and languages. The songs themselves do not offer a systematic way of thinking about spirituality; the songwriters and audiences may, or may not, know much about religion in any formal sense; but the imagery and terms used in this music have ancient roots. Popular music may provide but a pale reflection of the human quest for meaning and truth, but it is a reflection nonetheless.

OUTRAGEOUS RELIGION
SEX, DEFIANCE, AND OBSESSION
WITH THE SACRED

In the world of popular music, religion appears in the most unexpected places. I consider in this chapter songs that articulate individuality and freedom from restraint, often rejecting received wisdom and values in the process. Here again we find examples of the wider oppositional tendencies so typical in popular songwriting.[1] I include here lyrics that mix religious ideas and concepts with reflections on gender and sexuality. Strange as it sounds to twenty-first century sensibilities, there remains in society an almost Victorian tendency to view overt, uninhibited sexuality with trepidation. Because sex remains in some ways a forbidden pleasure in respectable society, the parading of sexual liberty in the various popular music arts—through lyrics, dance, videos, fashion, and so on—involves an act of resistance. Some who hear this music and watch these subcultures as outsiders (for example, religious conservatives) tend to find such a blatant decline in morality, as they see it, frightening.

I also examine here songs that introduce elements of horror and a fascination with the macabre. We often find this in hard rock or heavy metal music, though it is not unique to these genres. These songs differ from those examined in chapter 3 because rather than exploring ways of coping with frightening subjects, these songs embrace them, celebrating the sinister, menacing, and gloomy. Heavy metal in particular tends to introduce a lot of dark religious imagery, especially content with apocalyptic overtones, and there is often a shift in the valuation placed on binaries as well, with emphases falling on darkness over light, the devil over God, and so on.

These two categories—sex and horror—may not appear to have much in common, but I bring them together because both involve, first, a longing for liberation from convention, and second, the desire for an Other, whether an object of sexual desire or an experience outside the realm of the familiar and respectable. Songs acting out rituals of seduction, and the aggressive sounds and outlandish performances of hard rock music, express a yearning for a world free from conventions and restraint, and in both categories, religious language provides songwriters with a rich vocabulary and source of imagery.

PARADISE BY THE DASHBOARD LIGHT: SEX AND RELIGION IN POPULAR MUSIC

In a song discussed in chapter 2, John Lennon says he "just" believes in himself, Yoko Ono, and the love they share.[2] The "just" implies he does not believe in anything else, including God, despite the song's title. In pop song narratives, sexuality often replaces religion and religious experience. In this particular example, love becomes an object of faith in the context of a song that explicitly rejects belief in anything else considered sacred. The love shared between John and Yoko is a substitute for God and religion, among other things. Elsewhere, Lennon celebrates this romance using religious imagery in other ways. In "Dear Yoko" (*Double Fantasy*, 1980), he claims a divine blessing lies behind their profound union because the goddess smiles on their love. And again, in The Beatles' single "The Ballad of John and Yoko" (1969), Lennon tells the story of their marriage and honeymoon using an evocative reference to crucifixion. The hyperbolic language hints at a comparison between the singer's plight (media intrusion when lovers want to be alone) and Jesus' sufferings, suggested further by the use of "Christ" for emphasis in the phrase "Christ . . . They're gonna crucify me." There is nothing new here. Describing romantic love in exaggerated terms, including the use of sacred terminology, is commonplace in poetry and popular music, as is the tendency to link sexuality with spirituality. It works both ways too; mystics in different religious traditions introduce erotic language to express their communion with the divine.

When popular songs establish links between sexuality and sacred terms, the sense is obviously quite different than it is in the context of religious worship. The use of religious language in secular songs usually serves hyperbolic ends, celebrating both sexuality and the object of affection (usually feminine) with language traditionally directed to God as an act of obeisance. Quite often, these adaptations of religious language appear in redemption narratives, with sex standing as an equivalent for heaven or paradise. Heaven is lying in another's arms (Bryan Adams, "Heaven," *Reckless*, 1984; Lionel Richie, "The Closest Thing to Heaven," *Time*, 1998). It is also common to celebrate the healing touch of lovers by identifying them as saviors. Examples of this terminology abound: Jann Arden's "Saved" (*Happy?*, 1997), The Rolling Stones' "Heaven" (*Tattoo You*, 1981: "You're my saving grace"), Burton Cummings' "You Saved My Soul" (*Sweet Sweet*, 1981), Queen's "Save Me" (*The Game*, 1980), k.d. lang's "Save Me" (*Ingénue*, 1994), and The Cult's "Sweet Salvation" (*Ceremony*, 1991), to name but a few. Occasionally the reverse is true, with romantic/erotic language providing a way of articulating spiritual love. The song "Something," on The Beatles' 1969 album *Abbey Road* is one of George Harrison's best known compositions. On the surface, it suggests the songwriter's love for a woman, and indeed his first wife Patti (Boyd) Harrison once said it was about her. However, some devotees of the Hare Krishna movement claim George admitted the song was really about Krishna. George added, "I couldn't say 'he,' [in the song] could I? I had to say 'she' or they'd think I'm a poof."[3]

In most instances, however, religious language provides the vocabulary to speak about romantic love and sexuality. U2's 1991 album *Achtung Baby* provides a colorful illustration of this blurring of sexuality and sacred terms.[4] The song "Who's Gonna Ride Your

Wild Horses" includes various phrases from sacred discourse when describing a loved one, such as hallelujah and heaven. When this woman opens doors, others cannot close them, language alluding to Jesus' words in John's Apocalypse:

> These are the words of the holy one . . . who has the key of David, who opens and no one will shut, who shuts and no one opens: "I know your works. Look, I have set before you an open door, which no one is able to shut." (Rev 3:7-8)

We also learn that the woman addressed in the song left the singer's heart empty, allowing any spirits that come along to haunt him. Here too we appear to have an allusion to a biblical passage, this time Jesus' teachings in the Gospel of Matthew:

> When the unclean spirit has gone out of a person, it wanders through waterless regions looking for a resting place, but it finds none. Then it says, "I will return to my house from which I came." When it comes, it finds it empty, swept, and put in order. Then it goes and brings along seven other spirits more evil than itself, and they enter and live there; and the last state of that person is worse than the first. (12:43-45)

The singer is heartbroken, and the subtle reference to this passage, which includes the words "the last state of that person is worse than the first," captures well the lament of a jilted lover.

This song also uses the archaic second person "thee" with reference to the female object of his affection, a term recalling the language of the King James Bible and one typically associated with the divine (cf. the use of archaisms in recitals of the Lord's Prayer, as in "hallowed be Thy name, Thy kingdom come"). The woman in question is elevated in status to a godlike figure. The singer not only casts the woman of his desire in these quasidivine terms, he also repeatedly asks the titular question. What are these wild horses all about? The next song on the album, "So Cruel," explains.

"So Cruel" also includes the use of sacred terms in the singer's description of a woman: God's dove (an allusion to the biblical flood narrative; see Gen 8:8-12), angel, and so on. The singer returns to the wild horse metaphor of the previous song, though here he explicitly identifies them as "the horses of love and lust." The Edge, guitar player for U2, once described an album as "not just . . . a few songs you might have hanging around. For us in particular it's a collection that adds up to something more than just a few songs. It needs to have an overall logic that connects and complements and maybe not *resolves*, but has a beginning, middle, and end."[5] It seems reasonable, given this approach to preparing albums, to look for recurring themes from song to song. Assuming that one song provides a reliable measure for deciphering the language of another, we have in the "Who's Gonna Ride Your Wild Horses"–"So Cruel" sequence a clear use of religious terminology to relate the experience of romantic, sexual love. Both songs are about sex—"love and lust"—and the mutual seduction of the singer and the woman addressed.

Popular songs regularly depict sexuality as the equivalent of salvation and heaven. They also depend on the hyperbolic language of religious discourse to represent the sexual Other, as the U2 songs indicate. The hackneyed use of the term "angel" in love songs further illustrates this habitual use of sacred imagery in songs about romance and sex. Examples abound: Jimi Hendrix, "Angel," *The Cry of Love* (1971); Madonna, "Angel," *Like A Virgin* (1984); The Jeff Healey Band, "Angel Eyes," *See The Light* (1988; written by John Hiatt and Fred Koller); Eurythmics, "Angel," *We Too Are One* (1989); Aerosmith, "Angel," *Big Ones* (1994); Dave Matthews Band, "Angel," *Everyday* (2001); Sebastian Bach, "Angel Down," *Angel Down* (2007).[6]

Why do artists write this way? For one thing, it is the language of seduction. Nothing surprising there. By elevating the status of a woman or man to that of a god/dess or angel, and by claiming that sexuality brings a kind of salvation, the flatterer ingratiates him or herself to the one desired. David Usher's 2005 album *If God Had Curves* presumably puts femininity and sexuality in place of God. The narrator of Aerosmith's "Angel" explicitly asks the woman addressed to "save me tonight," using language associated with religious redemption, but the objective is clearly sexual: "What can I do, I'm sleeping in this bed alone."

We see a very different use of biblical language in songs exploring gender inequities and the marginal status of women (and in
these songs, too, sexuality remains a concurrent issue). One pattern
that emerges is the introduction of female characters from biblical stories. This device allows the songwriter to present a female's
perspective with the help of well-known precursors. These ancient
stories about such characters as Eve, Jezebel, and Mary Magdalene
provide a template to explore gender dynamics in the modern
world. Listeners immediately recognize such names, and the stories about them are emotively charged.

Alicia Keys and the Song of Solomon

Sinéad O'Connor's "Dark I Am Yet Lovely" (*Theology*, 2007) illustrates this use of biblical narratives involving women, in this case
drawing on the poetic romance called the Song of Solomon, though
the unnamed woman in the story is not as well known as those
named above (cf. Song 1:5-6).[7] Whereas O'Connor puts the biblical
passage to music, retelling the ancient story without extensive commentary, Alicia Key's poem "Lilly of the Valley"[8] uses the Song of
Solomon as a vehicle to tell a modern story, one about a vulnerable
and exploited individual. She takes the title phrase for her poem
from Song of Solomon 2:1: "I am a rose of Sharon, a lily of the val-
leys. As a lily among brambles, so is my love among maidens." The
poet warns Lilly (as she spells it) not to dance for a villain, an "evil
one" who is presumably a male. Whoever this person is, the term
clearly introduces devilish overtones with all the destructiveness
the image implies. In Scripture, the evil one is controlling (1 John
5:19), dangerous (Eph 6:16), and a source of violence (1 John 3:12).
Despite her use of the singular (evil *one*), the dangerous figure in the
poem is a collective term because the poet tells Lilly not to "let *them*"
destroy her (emphasis added). Keys offers a short commentary on
this poem and clarifies the identity of these destructive individuals.
Lilly is a stripper, one forced to sell herself if she is to "make it." The
evil one is her (presumably male) audience. Her performances for
them have a high cost. When Lilly dances for this audience, they
leave her feeling worthless. According to Keys' notes, women like

Lilly have "pain in their eyes." The Song of Solomon provides Keys with a way of presenting this woman's inner beauty. The lily of the valley in the biblical poem is truly beautiful and genuinely loved, and the male lover in that ancient poem recognizes that beauty (4:1). He loves her sincerely, unlike the voyeurs watching the Lilly in Keys' story.

Many of Alicia Keys' songs and poems explore matters of gender and include assertions about the dignity and independence of women in a hypersexed society that objectifies them. She resists the distorted priorities of this superficial world, for example, in "Cosmopolitan Woman," penned in response to a visit to AIDS-ridden Africa. The emphasis on surface beauty in the magazine indicated by the title is shallow and of no consequence, when compared to the plight of those at the AIDS clinic she visits. In contrast with those who fixate on a woman's physical appearance and sexuality, she regularly returns to glimpses of a female's inner beauty, her soul, a "glow" coming from the inside.[9]

Alicia Keys does not limit her treatment of the sexual exploitation and devaluation of women to formal poetry. She returns to the subject in various songs as well. In "A Woman's Worth" (*Songs in A Minor*, 2001),[10] she criticizes men who do not recognize a female's value. Women in her songs are not always powerless. At times, they assert their independence from men, or control over them, as in "Slow Down" (*The Diary of Alicia Keys*, 2003).[11] The songwriter also highlights certain imperfections in male characters. In the poem "Still Water," men are shallow, dirty, and mean, and have "polluted" souls.[12] At the same time, the songwriter admits that a man can have immense power to bring either happiness or pain to a woman (as in the poem "Is It Insane?").[13]

When the narrators of popular songs represent the male perspective, allusions to sacred imagery generally tend to be part of the process of seduction. To win over the object of desire, the singer often flatters the woman, describing her as an "angel" or looking to her for salvation of some kind or another. By contrast, when the narrator represents a female's perspective, allusions to sacred imagery often highlight marginal status, as in Alicia Keys' use of the Song of Solomon in a story about a vulnerable woman ("Lilly of the Valley").

Joni Mitchell and Mary Magdalene

Joni Mitchell introduces the name Magdalene in two songs with similar intent, both of them exploring the plight of helpless females. In "The Magdalene Laundries" (*Turbulent Indigo*, 1994), the first-person speaker identifies herself as an unmarried girl, a Jezebel in the opinion of others who assure her she will not reach heaven. Instead, they send her in shame to work with the sisters. Mary Magdalene and Jezebel are female characters in the Bible traditionally associated with sexual immorality. It is worth noting, however, that the biblical stories about them do not offer unambiguous evidence in support of this conclusion.[14] This fact makes the use of their names in Mitchell's "The Magdalene Laundries" particularly poignant. The listener is sympathetic to the girl whose story is told in the song. We have no reason to suspect she is an evil person, regardless of what others say about her. As Mitchell tells the story, the girl goes to the laundries because men leer at her, but what does this mean? Since we hear nothing about her directly (was she a flirt? promiscuous?), the only thing we know with any certainty is that these men are lecherous. The girl alone, however, carries the weight of punishment for their misdeeds, a situation resembling the Gospel narrative about the woman caught in adultery, where only the female faces judgment (John 7:53–8:11). Just as later Christian interpreters vilified characters like Jezebel and Mary Magdalene, so too those around the girl in the song demonize her, accusing her of sexual sin without justification. They are completely devoid of compassion.

Mitchell's song describes the plight of pregnant, unmarried, unwanted females, referred to as prostitutes, temptresses, and fallen women. All of them are sent to work at the Magdalene laundries. During the nineteenth and twentieth centuries, asylums often run by Roman Catholic orders took in prostitutes, unwed mothers, and other girls/women of questionable character, keeping them in convents and assigning them to hard labor.[15] The song gives one of these unfortunate girls a voice, one who cannot understand why they call a place so devoid of compassion Our Lady of Charity.

Mitchell's critique of the Christian Magdalene laundries is particularly clever and pointed because she turns Christian teaching itself back on the cruel taskmasters of the asylum. If these heartless nuns actually saw their "groom," meaning Jesus, they would not throw their accusatory stones. Here again Mitchell alludes to the story of the woman caught in adultery (John 7:53–8:11). In that story, vigilantes bring a fallen woman to Jesus and are ready to impose the death penalty for her crime. Jesus' famous answer— "Let anyone among you who is without sin be the first to throw a stone at her" (John 8:7)—results in the male accusers leaving the scene one by one. Mitchell's allusion to this passage is appropriate because interpreters often link Mary Magdalene to this Gospel story (even though the evangelist does not give the woman's name). Mitchell thereby makes explicit the connection between this Mary Magdalene story and the experience of those in the Magdalene laundries. It follows that these girls deserve the same compassion that Mary Magdalene receives in the Gospel of John. Jesus does not condemn the woman caught in adultery: "'Woman . . . Has no one condemned you? . . . Neither do I condemn you'" (John 8:10-11).

John's story makes it clear that the female brought before Jesus is no worse than her male accusers who want her punished, implied because they leave after Jesus' challenge to them. Jesus treats the woman in the Gospel story with dignity and ultimately saves her life from the crowd of vigilantes. The reference to the stone-throwing asylum nuns invites comparison with the accusatory religious authority figures in the Gospel story. The sisters, like the mob in the Gospel, are in no position to throw stones. They are no better than the inmates forced to be in the laundries.

Mary Magdalene appears in another Joni Mitchell composition as well, the song "Passion Play (The Story of Jesus and Zachius [sic] . . . The Little Tax Collector)" (Night Ride Home, 1991). This song brings together in compressed form elements of the Gospel narratives about Mary Magdalene, Zacchaeus, and the crucifixion of Christ. Mitchell contrasts one who is kind and redeeming, who heals and searches the heart, with others who enslave and force the vulnerable to "do the dirty work," though the songwriter does not explain exactly what this means. Jesus is a liberator in the song, reaching out to the trembling Magdalene and healing the heart of the first-person narrator Zacchaeus.

The song describes the desperate situations of the marginalized and vulnerable Magdalene, Zacchaeus, and a group of unidentified slaves. The songwriter introduces Magdalene as the song opens, trembling like items blowing in the wind on a clothesline, an image recalling again the Magdalene laundries discussed earlier. To this vulnerable woman, a man (Jesus) is both kind and redeeming. Zacchaeus is also in need (cf. Luke 19:1-10). He is a person of status (a tax collector) but also a sinner with a broken heart. Jesus, described as the "magical physician," comes to his aid.

It is difficult to determine who is responsible for the sadness known to Magdalene, Zacchaeus, and the other slaves mentioned in the song, but the recurring terms Exxon and radiation hint at the impersonal, greedy, and destructive corporate world. The scene of Jesus' crucifixion may support this conclusion. It is a marketplace, a wicked location devoid of the divine presence where we hear the pounding of deadly nails as the crucifixion takes place. The song leaves us wondering if the slaves will still gain their freedom after the crucifixion, or if others will continue forcing them to do the "dirty work" now that their protector is gone.

This song makes explicit use of biblical material. In addition to the characters, there is a direct quotation from the King James Version of the Lord's Prayer: "Thy kingdom come / Thy will be done." It may be relevant that the Lord's Prayer includes supplication for the sustenance of those economically vulnerable: "give us this day our daily bread" (Matt 6:11; Luke 11:3). In this intriguing song, Mitchell succinctly relates some of the variegated visions of liberation found in the New Testament Gospels. In "Passion Play (The Story of Jesus and Zachius . . . The Little Tax Collector)" we hear about desperate souls who find a magic physician's healing touch. However, this message is easy to miss in those places of business that kill saviors and stifle the efforts of liberators.

OUTRAGEOUS RELIGION: OBSESSION WITH THE SACRED

> This pretentious, ponderous collection of religious rock psalms is enough to prompt the question, "What day did the Lord create Spinal Tap, and couldn't he have rested on that day too?"
>
> —Marty DiBergi (Rob Reiner), reading a review of the album
> *The Gospel According to Spinal Tap*[16]

When I was about 15, a friend played Iron Maiden's "The Number of the Beast" for me, which begins with a Vincent Price imitator reading an adaptation of Revelation 12:12 and 13:18 in the Revised Standard Version:

> Woe to you, Oh Earth and Sea, for the Devil sends the beast with wrath, because he knows the time is short . . . Let him who hath understanding reckon the number of the beast for it is a human number, its number is Six hundred and sixty six.
>
> Revelations [*sic*] Ch. XIII v.18[17]

My friend then pulled out the family Bible and showed me the passage with the number "666." Neither of us knew anything about the verse other than its vague connection to the mysterious name Satan, and for this reason the song, and the Bible verse, were even more enticing. What we were listening to in "The Number of the Beast" and reading in the book of Revelation hinted at something forbidden and dangerous, even rebellious, as esoteric and arcane subjects often do. This might explain in part the appeal of heavy metal acts like Iron Maiden—they often flirt with themes that are just on the edge of what is familiar and safe, respectable and permissible. This was probably the first time I consciously considered religious subject matter in relation to songs. The combination of a powerful style of music, the slightly eerie reading of this strange, mysterious biblical passage, and a general awareness that many viewed Iron Maiden and their kind with a measure of disdain (and

a bit of fear) was intoxicating. In some strange way, the music provided a conduit to something beyond the everyday and mundane;
an Otherness with tremendous appeal. To my mind, heavy metal/
hard rock music is attractive in the same way as gothic novels and
horror movies. What do these media have in common?

It is a curious thing that horror characterizes so much entertainment. We usually apply the term to books and movies in contemporary culture, grouping fear and dread with the pleasures of
reading and attending the cinema.[18] The fascination with terror is
certainly not unique to contemporary society. Throughout history
and across cultures we find artists appealing to the monstrous for
a variety of reasons. Though it goes beyond the purview of this
book to explore the function of horror in any detail, a few general
remarks help introduce the subject matter of this chapter. This is
pertinent to the larger argument of the book because horror-influenced music liberally introduces religious elements (like the biblical number of the beast). A glance at a few album covers alone
makes this obvious:

AC/DC's *Highway to Hell* (1979) shows Angus Young with
devil horns and tail

Black Sabbath's *Heaven and Hell* (1980) shows angels
smoking

Ozzy Osbourne's *Blizzard of Ozz* (1980) shows the singer
holding a cross

Dio's *Holy Diver* (1983) shows a priest cast into the sea by a
devil in what appears to be a parody of Revelation 20:10

Metallica's *Master of Puppets* (1986) shows rows of crosses
in a cemetery

Marilyn Manson's "Personal Jesus" (2004; single) shows a
chi rho, an ancient symbol for Christ

Slayer's *Christ Illusion* (2006) shows a pierced hand, recalling the crucifixion

So what function does horror serve, particularly when manifested in music? And what does religious imagery contribute to this music?

Our Fascination with Horror

The practice of demonizing enemies is ancient. According to Mircea Eliade, one of the functions of religion is to define sacred space,[19] which is one way of recognizing what is monstrous and potentially dangerous:

> One of the outstanding characteristics of traditional socie-
> ties is the opposition that they assume between their inhab-
> ited territory and the unknown and indeterminate space
> that surrounds it. The former is the world (more precisely,
> our world), the cosmos; everything outside it is no longer a
> cosmos but a sort of "other world," a foreign, chaotic space,
> peopled by ghosts, demons, "foreigners" (who are assimi-
> lated to demons and the souls of the dead).[20]

Attempts to define and explain ordered society depend upon recognition of the unknown, and so the sacred order contrasts with an otherness often labeled demonic or chaotic. Consequently, "an attack on 'our world' is equivalent to an act of revenge by the mythical dragon, who rebels against the work of the gods, the cosmos, and struggles to annihilate it. 'Our' enemies belong to the powers of chaos."[21]

We can link the fascination with horror to the unsettled experience of encountering otherness, a phenomenon further illuminated by Sigmund Freud's notion of "uncanny strangeness." As Freud explains, the German adjective *unheimlich* means frightening, eerie, or sinister, whereas its antonym—*heimlich*—involves associations with the home (*Heim*), that which is familiar, comfortable, and safe. The positive adjective also means secret. For Freud, this is significant because the term can hold in tension the positive idea of things friendly and comfortable (*heimlich*, associated with home and domesticity) and the more sinister resonance of something hidden from sight, potentially deceitful and malicious (*heimlich* as secret).

Significantly, there is a close link between the terms *heimlich* and *unheimlich*; in the former, "the familiar and intimate are reversed into their opposites, brought together with the contrary meaning of 'uncanny strangeness' harbored in *unheimlich*."[22] This semantic observation—the presence of the strange within the familiar—provides Freud with support for "the psychoanalytic hypothesis according to which 'the uncanny is that class of the frightening which leads back to what is known of old and long familiar' . . . 'everything is *unheimlich* that ought to have remained secret and hidden but has come to light.' "[23] In these terms, Freud found a linguistic basis to articulate his concept of "uncanny strangeness"— that which is vaguely familiar and yet strange and terrifying. Encounters with people who differ from us, those perceived as frightening, eerie, or sinister (*unheimlich*), involve that mix of the familiar yet strange (*heimlich*).

Closely related to this idea is the fascination with monsters, from ancient times to the present. Timothy K. Beal explores this phenomenon in his analysis of a long lineage of monstrous villains—a list that includes such infamous figures as the Babylonian Tiamat, the Hebrew Leviathan, the Sanskrit Vṛtra, the Ugaritic Yamm and Mot, Frankenstein's Creature, Dracula, and the flying monkeys of Oz. He links this culturally diverse tradition with the need to personify "that which is of the world but not of it," that "ambiguous [edge] of the conceptual landscape, where the right order of things touches on a wholly other chaos, where inside and outside, self and other intertwine."[24] Beal also finds in Freud's idea of the "unhomely" or "uncanny" the key to explaining the universal need to give otherness a monstrous face.[25] Horror films, literature, and songs articulate fears of that which is only vaguely familiar, something outside that may invade our settled, ordered world. For this reason, many turn to music (and films and literature) that introduces fright, terror, and macabre subject matter, both lyrically and visually. They find in it a means of confronting the frightening unknown.

Facing Fear and Dread in Music

Following the remarkable success of his 1972 album *Harvest*, Neil Young entered what William Echard describes as a "darker, oppositional period."[26] In the years following *Harvest*, Young gave few interviews but he finally discussed this evident shift in music and attitude in 1975, the year he released the album *Tonight's the Night* with his band Crazy Horse after a lengthy delay. He explained that the band recorded the album in 1973 following the deaths of Crazy Horse guitarist Danny Whitten and roadie Bruce Berry. According to Echard, they recorded most of the songs in one night, "at a session marked by extreme alcohol and drug use which Young and others described as a wake for Whitten and Berry." The record label did not like the results because the album appeared "sloppy, dark, cathartic, and . . . unsuitable for commercial release."[27] I mention Young's *Tonight's the Night* in this context because it illustrates how music can serve the needs of people in distress, in this case the musicians themselves. I also mention this album because it illustrates how horror and music can meet. Echard continues:

> Aside from a lack of technical polish, the recordings [on *Tonight's the Night*] displayed a level of emotional distress foreign to most rock music. In [an interview] Young says that the band felt "spooked," and characterizes the album as "the first horror record." Young also notes that for much of the material he was consciously playing a role, adopting an extreme persona as a way of dealing with his grief.[28]

This is only one example of many. Horror-influenced music, especially heavy metal and hard rock, deals with a variety of fears and anxieties, such as violence, death, lack of independence, and marginalization. This music provides audiences with a way of confronting these fears, through a medium that is both transgressive and provocative.

Heavy Metal, Hard Rock, Heavy Rock, Death Metal, Thrash, Industrial . . . there is a bewildering list of related genre categories associated with fast-paced, guitar-driven styles of rock music falling under or related to the umbrella category heavy metal. Efforts to organize this music around key labels are remarkably complex.[29] Such considerations as musical form (rhythm, beat, virtuosity, instrumentation, amplification), the sociological makeup of audiences (region, gender, socioeconomic location, education), and associated ideologies are all relevant.[30] Exploring the audiences of religion-influenced heavy metal is particularly interesting for our purposes. Hard rock music often parodies religion, which is a form of resistance to authority. We might describe heavy metal's incorporation of religion as, borrowing Linda Hutcheon's term, "authorized transgression."[31] Though it is not true that only the disenfranchised listen to metal, it remains than many find in this genre a forum to confront and express their frustrations and fears.

The terms hard rock and heavy metal do have definitions that are more precise. Heavy metal tends to indicate music that is "louder, 'harder,' and faster-paced than conventional rock music, and remains predominantly guitar-oriented."[32] The audience subculture associated with heavy metal is "predominantly working class, white, young and male, identifying with the phallic imagery of guitars and the general muscularity and oppositional orientation of the form."[33] The music also attracts audiences who are disenfranchised in different ways. Citing Jeffrey Arnett's study of heavy metal music fans, in which he determined that fans display a tendency toward dissatisfaction with family relationships and education, and a profound sense of alienation, Sylvan concludes that the "dark themes" of heavy metal music "accurately reflect the grim reality of their contemporary situation."[34] One study of Ozzy Osbourne focusing on sociological factors bears this out.

> Black Sabbath, emerging from the poor, working class of Birmingham . . . infused common rock and roll with an aggressive sense of frustration known only to the silent working classes of the time. This sense of frustration would eventually catch on with a vast population that connected with Black Sabbath at an emotional level. . . . Black Sabbath catered to the emotions of the disenfranchised.[35]

This approach emphasizes the artist's need to act out against the status quo, the establishment, of which religious authorities are a part. Similarly, punk and other forms of rock music are typically working class in origin.

In the context of the United Kingdom, the link between class and musical preferences is particularly visible when contrasting rock, heavy metal, and punk with progressive rock groups. The latter "were formed and nurtured in universities or the British equivalent of private schools" and made "no effort to conceal their upper-middle-class background, an attitude critics condemned as elitist." By contrast, punk and other rock styles have roots in the working class.[36] John J. Scheinbaum describes the original audience for progressive rock (late 1960s, early 1970s, southern England) as privileged, white, educated, and upper middle class.[37] At the risk of oversimplifying, just as progressive rock reflects its environments, interests, and privileges, the same is true of heavy metal for the most part. Again, the audience tends to be largely white males with working class, blue-collar backgrounds.[38] For many in this music's audience, heavy metal is reactionary, providing an outlet for frustration and a form of expression.

What is true of audiences is no doubt true for many performers of heavy metal music (cf. Moreman's comments about Black Sabbath above), but a word of caution is in order. Beware making the jump from song content to biographical reconstruction too quickly. The music may provide an outlet for aggression and articulating frustration but this does not necessarily mean the songs provide an unambiguous insight into a musician's worldview or religious beliefs. Indeed, some hard rock musicians view their work with some levity. They avoid taking themselves too seriously and are careful to distinguish their real lives from their public personae. Vincent Furnier, aka Alice Cooper, looks back on his career and distinguishes what he did from contemporary artists like Marilyn Manson: "The difference was that Alice Cooper had a sense of humor. I mean, the things that I did, they were never political. They were never religious. They were never anything. Mine was all pure schlock horror, comedy, and rock 'n' roll. It was pretty harmless compared to what's going on now."[39] It is best to avoid pressing stage antics and lyrical content too hard for clues about an artist's personal beliefs.

It seems unlikely that the mere use of this religious material indicates much about what songwriters and audiences believe or do not believe. Walser points out, for instance, with reference to alleged connections between forms of violence and religious practice, that "The vast majority of heavy metal fans don't worship Satan and don't commit suicide; yet many fans enjoy that fraction of heavy metal songs that deals with such things."[40] While some bands employ a great deal of imagery related to religious subject matter, they deny there is any direct connection to religious activity. This language often serves purposes other than expressing theological opinions. Further comments by Alice Cooper fit this discussion:

> Heavy metal doesn't automatically have to be Satan's music—only if the lyrics go that way. Does a chord progression necessarily constitute music that's evil? I don't think so. People talk about diminished-fifth chords supposedly being the devil's music, but I think it all depends on the lyrics you put in there. If you're saying "Worship Satan"! then sure, that's Satanic—though most rock and heavy-metal musicians don't believe in that anyway, not even most of the guys playing so-called black metal.[41]

We have another example of the distance between persona and personal belief in Ozzy Osbourne, who denies that he or members of Black Sabbath have any interest in or involvement with the occult. This leads Pete Ward to conclude that religious elements in their music operate "almost entirely at the level of representation":

> They form a part of the act rather than a part of the lived reality of the band or their audience. So the symbolic function of the occult in heavy metal operates in a way that is possibly more akin to the use of the occult by Shakespeare in a play such as *The Tempest*. In other words, the occult

forms part of the artistic context in which audiences and artists are working symbolically with a range of issues and concerns.[42]

Sacred imagery provides artists with a rich lexicon of symbolic and thematic terms to help articulate a wide variety of attitudes, beliefs, anxieties, and experiences.

Furthermore, as Sylvan points out, part of the appeal of satanic imagery is that it offers a form of resistance to religion, which many view with suspicion as a dubious form of authority. He points out that while most metalheads are not practicing Satanists, "they are obviously drawn to Satanic imagery for other reasons. I would argue that these reasons include heavy metal's individualistic philosophy, its rebellion against normative authority, and its connection with the supernatural."[43]

A further characteristic of heavy metal relevant for our purposes is its tendency to incorporate imagery and symbols associated with religion and the Bible. My adolescent introduction to the book of Revelation through Iron Maiden's "The Number of the Beast" points to a typical quality of this style of music. With reference to Iron Maiden in particular, Robert Walser notes they are "among the most mystical and philosophical heavy metal bands; many of their lyrics, taking inspiration from the Bible, Romantic poetry, and various other mythologies."[44] Deena Weinstein adds, "Heavy metal's major source for its imagery and rhetoric of chaos is religion, particularly the Judeo-Christian tradition. Although other religions speak to chaos, Judeo-Christian culture nourished the creators of heavy metal and their core audience. The Book of Revelations [sic], that unique apocalyptic vision in the New Testament, is a particularly rich source of imagery for heavy metal lyrics."[45] Another formative religious tradition for the genre, Weinstein observes, is paganism, "the aggregate of the pre-Christian religions of Northern Europe."[46]

This fascination with the religiously spooky is obvious from a random selection of song and album titles. References to the devil or the beast, for instance, are commonplace: Alice Cooper, "Devil's

Food," *Welcome to My Nightmare* (1975); Iron Maiden, "The Number of the Beast," *The Number of the Beast* (1982); Mötley Crüe, "Shout At the Devil," *Shout At the Devil* (1983); Twisted Sister, "The Beast," *Stay Hungry* (1984); Rob Zombie, "The Devil's Rejects," *Educated Horses* (2006). Similarly, the term "hell" is often heard in hard rock songs: AC/DC, "Highway to Hell," *Highway to Hell* (1979); Alice Cooper, "Go to Hell," *Goes to Hell* (1976); Black Sabbath, "Heaven and Hell," *Heaven and Hell* (1980); KISS, "Hotter Than Hell," *Hotter Than Hell* (1974); Megadeth, "Go To Hell," *Hidden Treasures* (1995). The use of terms like "devil" and "hell" does not necessarily have a clear religious sense in the context of such songs. AC/DC's "Highway to Hell" (*Highway to Hell*, 1979) describes life on the road for a rock and roll band: "Hey Satan / Paid my dues / Playin' in a rockin' band." This song, like most others using the term, is not an endorsement of Satanism or a theological statement.

Songwriters do not limit themselves to terms from the dark side of religion, of course. Marilyn Manson has songs titled "Cruci- fiction in Space," "Lamb of God," and "Born Again," on the album *Holy Wood (In the Shadow of the Valley of Death)* (2000), each one alluding to a story about Jesus in the Gospels. Other positive images widely represented in song include heaven and prayer: Led Zeppelin, "Stairway to Heaven," *Led Zeppelin IV* (1971); Meat Loaf, "Heaven Can Wait," *Bat Out of Hell* (1977); The Rolling Stones, "Heaven," *Tattoo You* (1981); Slayer, "South of Heaven," *South of Heaven* (1988); Disturbed, "Prayer," *Believe* (2002). Although sing- ers use these terms in a wide variety of ways, in each case the terms lend an emotive force, making the lyrics provocative simply by the introduction of sacred language in this setting.

I am particularly interested in artists who use religious sym- bols self-consciously, particularly when they introduce these symbols with an unexpected twist. We often hear such subver- sions of religious values in songs that surprise the listener by plac- ing emphases on certain concepts over others (the devil instead of God, and so forth). We also find forms of subversion in this music when musicians engage in parodies of religious rituals. We see this, for example, in Mötley Crüe's "Wild Side" (*Girls, Girls, Girls*, 1987), which includes a recognizable structure for prayer, beginning with a call to kneel before "streetwise religion" and ending appropriately with an "Amen."[47] Another example is Jim Steinman's "Seize the Night" (on Meat Loaf's *Bat Out Of Hell III: The Monster Is Loose*, 2006), which includes Latin text sung by a boy soprano, and elements of a Requiem Mass such as the phrases *dies irae* (day of wrath) and *libera me, Domine* (deliver me, Lord). In this song, though the language creates the atmosphere of a Catholic religious service, most of the song's lyrics are ironic: darkness provides salvation; there are no taboos or inhibitions; there is celebration because devils are falling; everything is permissible. Steinman mimics a sacred space and ritual (a church choir at a church service) only to shift the values of this ecclesial setting in the direction of mock parody. There is a similar use of Latin liturgy in Rob Zombie's "Super Charger Heaven" (*Astro Creep: 2000—Songs of Love, Destruction, and Other Synthetic Delusions of the Electric Head*, 1995). As we will see in the examples that follow, readings of the New Testament book of Revelation with unexpected twists often provide inspiration for horror-influenced hard-rock songs.

Ozzy Osbourne's Armageddon

Religious imagery helps songwriters express fear or anger over issues that are not religious, as a song from Ozzy Osbourne's later work illustrates. If Osbourne has no personal interest in the occult or any other religious perspective as he claims, we can observe other motives behind his use of sacred terminology. Osbourne's "Countdown's Begun" (written with Zakk Wylde and Kevin Churko) from the album *Black Rain* (2007) shows how a religious concept is reworked to express concern over a human-generated political and possibly environmental disaster. The song refers to "armageddon" and a man-made "doomsday clock."[48] In most instances, a religious understanding of the concept of doomsday would involve a divinely initiated cataclysm, God's judgment on a sinful world (for example, "Then I heard a loud voice from the temple telling the seven angels, 'Go and pour out on the earth the seven bowls of *the wrath of God*'" [Rev 16:1; emphasis added]). In

Osbourne's song, however, there is no mention of a divine initiative. He credits the apocalyptic scenario to human activity entirely. This doomsday "was made by mankind."

Of course, there is nothing remarkable about expressing concern over nuclear holocaust, but what is interesting about Osbourne's description of this feared eventuality is the inclusion of a religious image in his lyric. He introduces a Christian concept—the term "armageddon" is biblical in origin (Rev 16:16)—but reinterprets the word and its original sense to accommodate the song's political agenda. The ancient term armageddon is the location where "the kings of the whole world . . . assemble for battle on the great day of God the Almighty" (Rev 16:14; and again, note the divine initiative in the wider context [16:1, cited above]). Whatever the first-century seer John intended by the image, clearly it was not the nuclear holocaust it becomes in Osbourne's song.

The reference to Armageddon (usually capitalized because it is a proper name—Har [mountain] Megiddo) in the Apocalypse appears in a section in which God vents "the fury of his wrath" (Rev 16:19). Osbourne's armageddon is man-made. Here again we see the clear dependence on, and misreading of, a religious precursor in popular music. To use Harold Bloom's terminology, we have here an instance of a poet completing a precursor "by so reading the parent-poem as to retain its terms but to mean them in another sense, as though the precursor had failed to go far enough."[49] The term armageddon is widely used in the English language, of course, so there is no need to posit a careful, deliberate reworking of that text. At the same time, the fact that the songwriters specifically mention human responsibility for doomsday implies awareness that most assume God initiates world conflagration (the Armageddon). The songwriters deliberately misread this commonplace religious notion to give the lyric's antinuclear-arms message a clever twist and emotive force.

Meat Loaf and the Lake of Fire

More often than not, subversions of biblical or sacred material provide a vehicle to assert youthful rebellion and independence. I will mention here another song involving an unexpected use of a text from the Apocalypse. In 2006, Meat Loaf released the third album in the *Bat Out of Hell* trilogy (though only seven of the fourteen songs are Jim Steinman compositions), titled *Bat Out of Hell III: The Monster Is Loose*. The album's title track is an intriguing rewrite of a rather obscure scene in the New Testament found in Revelation 20:1-10:

> Then I saw an angel coming down from heaven, holding in his hand the key to the bottomless pit and a great chain. He seized the dragon, that ancient serpent, who is the Devil and Satan, and bound him for a thousand years, and threw him into the pit, and locked and sealed it over him, so that he would deceive the nations no more, until the thousand years were ended. After that *he must be let out for a little while.* (Rev 20:1-3; emphasis added)

"The Monster Is Loose," written by Desmond Child (the album's producer), Nikki Sixx (of Mötley Crüe), and guitarist John 5, retells this mysterious story of the devil's capture and short-term release, emphasizing that brief moment of freedom mentioned in the italicized portion of the above citation. The connection to the biblical millennium or thousand-year period of peace is explicit in the song. The devilish narrator claims he was banished for a thousand years, which corresponds with Revelation 20:2 (cf. 20:3, 4, 7). This narrator also mentions the chains that bound him, language echoing the reference to a great chain in Revelation 20:1 (cf. "his prison" [20:7]). That the biblical devil's story is intended here is further supported by the album's artwork; the liner notes include two pictures of devils or fallen angels, sinister figures with wings and a tail (regarding the devil's tail, see Rev 12:4).

This presentation of the millennium story is as interesting for what it omits as for what it includes. The Apocalypse and the song both make it clear that the devil/"Monster" roams the earth full of rage now that it is loose (see Rev 12:12, 17), and in this respect the songwriters follow the biblical precursor. To great effect, however, the song subtly obscures the sense of the ancient story by omitting any reference to Satan's ultimate fate. Listeners not aware of the conclusion of the narrative in Revelation 20 might assume that the monster will remain loose indefinitely. This is not the case, however, in the story told by John the Seer in the Apocalypse:

> Then I saw thrones, and those seated on them were given authority to judge. I also saw the souls of those who had been beheaded for their testimony to Jesus and for the word of God. They had not worshipped the beast or its image and had not received its mark on their foreheads or their hands. They came to life and reigned with Christ for a thousand years. [I.e., during the time the devil is in chains] . . . When the thousand years are ended, Satan will be released from his prison and will come out to deceive the nations at the four corners of the earth . . . in order to gather them for battle; they are as numerous as the sands of the sea. They marched up over the breadth of the earth and surrounded the camp of the saints and the beloved city. And fire came down from heaven and consumed them. And *the devil who had deceived them was thrown into the lake of fire and sulphur, where the beast and the false prophet were, and they will be tormented day and night for ever and ever.* (Rev 20:4, 7-10; emphasis added)

The songwriters' familiarity with Revelation is clear, and so their omission of this second capture of the devil (the italicized portion), and his ultimate destruction, is conspicuous. It is a willful retelling of that apocalyptic story that involves what Bloom calls a deliberate misreading, one in which the poets swerve from their precursor in a way suggesting a correction of the source. There is no destruction for the Monster/Devil in the song.

The song "The Monster Is Loose" describes the moment when the devilish narrator is just emerging from his cage. Having lost his freedom, having experienced abuse and disgrace, he is now dangerous and hate-filled. Here too there is a clear biblical echo: "woe to the earth and the sea, for the devil has come down to you with great wrath, because he knows that his time is short!" (Rev 12:12;

cf. Iron Maiden's use of this passage in "The Number of the Beast" noted earlier). This warning of inevitable chaos on earth refers to an emerging force; a previously suppressed, dominated, and contained spirit is now on the cusp of freedom, now liberated by its own strength. He breaks his own chains, thus capturing a revolutionary outburst directed at those in authority, giving voice to a sense of profound injustice. This cluster of ideas signifies what we might call the traditional gestalt of rock and roll music. The song is ultimately about youthful rebellion. It encapsulates a coming of age, and the longing for independence and self-expression and even tendencies toward violence and self-destruction. These are recurring tropes in Meat Loaf albums, particularly in some of the earlier Jim Steinman lyrics. In "Wasted Youth" (*Bat Out of Hell II: Back Into Hell*, 1993), Steinman himself narrates the part of an angry young man, threatening to smash his parents with a guitar, who cries out, "you've gotta helluva lot to learn about rock and roll!"

Alice Cooper's Satanic Tempter

This pattern of identification with dark characters and themes (the devil, violence, antisocial behavior, resistance to authority, and so on) is widespread in heavy metal and hard rock music. One interesting exception deserves notice in this context because of its dialogue with biblical narratives and religious subject matter. Alice Cooper released *The Last Temptation* in 1994.[50] This concept album opens with the story of a bored young man speaking in the first person who longs for some kind of diversion to bring thrills into his life ("Sideshow"). The excitement of a circus-like life, with its freaks and creep shows, intrigues him. As the song closes, we hear a new speaker, a clichéd step-right-up "ring master," or carnival worker with an unmistakably sinister tone. This ringmaster invites the timid narrator/spectator to enter the sideshows, even if he is afraid.

The story continues in "Nothing's Free," but the ringmaster becomes far more menacing. We hear his voice now, offering to enter into a contract with the young man that involves the shake of a hand and "30 pieces of silver." This unambiguous allusion to

the story of Jesus' betrayer Judas Iscariot (Matt 26:15), along with
several other terms and phrases, introduces a religious overtone to
the story. The thrill-seeking youth now has an opportunity to gain
what he wants, but the choices before him are moral ones with dire
consequences. He must agree to Faustian terms with the devilish
circus showman by signing on "the dotted line" with his blood if
he wants to be free from moral restraints. However, this is freedom
with an ironic twist: "free to take your fill / free from your own
free will / Nothing's free." This is an insightful remark. Absolute
liberty, uninhibited behavior, is another form of bondage. The happiness on offer from the circus master is illusory and ultimately
leads to a different kind of emptiness.

The allusion to Judas Iscariot is simultaneously an allusion
to the devil who, the Gospel writer tells us, directs the betrayer's
actions: "After he received the piece of bread, Satan entered into
[Judas Iscariot]" (John 13:27). Cooper's *The Last Temptation* depicts a
drama that operates on more than one level. Thrill-seekers will find
all kinds of opportunities available in the sideshows of the world,
but what is occurring, Cooper asserts, is a cosmic battle. We can
get whatever we want, but ultimately nothing is free. There is a
devilish tempter who wants the souls of those willing to give them
in exchange for sideshow experiences. All one needs to do is "sign
upon the dotted line" and "*bow to me* [the circus master / show-
man] if you wanna be free" ("Nothing's Free"; emphasis added).
The latter phrase is an allusion to the biblical story about the devil
tempting Jesus in the wilderness:

> Then Jesus was led up by the Spirit into the wilderness to
> be tempted by the devil. . . . the devil took him to a very
> high mountain and showed him all the kingdoms of the
> world and their splendor; and he said to him, "All these I
> will give you, *if you will fall down and worship me*." (Matt 4:1,
> 8-9 [emphasis added])

Everything a person could want is available and easily attainable.
All that is required is devotion to the devil (or the circus master).

Surprisingly, Cooper's *The Last Temptation* does not embrace the alignment with the devilish character that occurs so often in hard rock music (compare, for example, the celebration of the devil's temporary freedom in Meat Loaf's "The Monster Is Loose"). Instead, the young man recognizes how dangerous the offers put on the table by the devil/ringmaster really are, and chooses to turn away from them. It is clear that *The Last Temptation* narrates Alice Cooper's personal journey toward the Christian faith. When he describes making the album in his autobiography, he even hints at the notion of divine influence on his work:

> When I finally wrote *Last Temptation*, I saw a way of doing something clever, making a rock record that was as good as any rock record I'd ever made . . . but with Alice talking about morality. For people who aren't paying attention to the lyrics, they'll give the album a thumbs-up when normally they might not be into religious music. It's one of the best records I've ever made. Sure, I was walking on thin ice using Alice as the medium, but I felt like I was being guided through the process.[51]

This album gave notice of Alice Cooper's conversion, something that did not go over well with his fan base: "My commitment to Christianity hit the newswires. I was now officially off the fence, intellectually, spiritually, and publicly. I immediately lost sales and bookings."[52] Cooper describes this embrace of faith in an unusual way in the song "You're My Temptation," where he describes his greatest temptation as Christ, not the devil (though the songwriter does not name Christ explicitly). He succumbs to the temptation of religion, ultimately abandoning the ringmaster/devil. By the end of the album, his struggle with the ringmaster/devil is complete. In "Cleansed By Fire," the narrator refers back to all that the circus offered, alluding to the temptation narratives of the New Testament Gospels in the process: "You offer me the world and all its wealth" (cf. Matt 4:8-9: "the world and their splendor. . . . All these I will give you, if you fall down and worship me"). His reply to this offer is an unambiguous rejection of the ringmaster/devil and shift in his allegiance. He tells the ringmaster to go to hell. Again, the contrast between this Alice Cooper album—one of the first shock-rock artists—and others by similar artists is remarkable.[53]

Velvet Revolver's Fallen Angel

I include one final illustration of a song introducing an unexpected twist of a biblical narrative, again drawing on the book of Revelation. On April 1, 2008, the founding members of super-group Velvet Revolver announced a parting of the ways with singer Scott Weiland (of the Stone Temple Pilots).[54] Weiland fronted former members of Guns N' Roses (Slash, Duff McKagan, Matt Sorum), and guitarist Dave Kushner of Wasted Youth. Though the band's career in this particular formation proved shortlived, they put out two excellent albums (*Contraband*, 2003; *Libertad*, 2007).

The song "She Builds Quick Machines" on Velvet Revolver's second album offers another interesting example of ironic reversal of biblical and religious values. The song describes a female who dances across the country at "all night sex shows" after leaving home and burning through her inheritance. The video for the song portrays this girl as an angel, complete with wings, dropping from the sky. As the band members look on, she crashes to the ground. She is literally a fallen angel. The song's lyrics make no mention of the girl as an angel, and they are ambiguous about the reasons why she acts the way she does. They do not indicate whether she is an erotic dancer by choice, perhaps expressing her independence in doing so, or a victim in some way. As the video presents the story, the first option seems most likely.

After the angel of the video crashes to earth, residents from a nearby town capture and imprison her, and then band members storm the town and rescue the winged damsel in distress. The video locates the song's action in what looks like a quasi-western movie set with all the essential clichés (gunfighting, hats, saloons, dusty streets) but with various anachronisms as well (cars, motorcycle, electric guitar, and so forth).

We learn more about the angel's identity when the townspeople capture the winged girl. A man compares her face to the visage on a 1 Onza Mexican Libertad series coin. The picture on these coins is the Independence Angel, El Ángel de la Independencia, the symbol of Mexico City. A statue of this angelic symbol rests on a monument in Paseo de la Reforma. Libertad is of course the name of the album and, presumably, the name of the winged girl/angel (though the name does not appear in the lyrics). This is a provocative image in the context of the video. This symbol of independence comes crashing to the ground, suggesting lost freedom. The band comes to the rescue, entering the town with guns blazing to rescue Libertad (liberty). Music, by inference, protects, rescues, and embodies freedom. On some level, *Libertad* and the "She Builds Quick Machines" video are making a political statement. They are also asserting the power of music to secure freedom. Slash plays away on his guitar as his bandmates shoot up the town and release the girl from the chains of her oppressors.

At the same time, the image of a winged figure falling from heaven to the earth has religious overtones that are hard to miss. The image of this beautiful girl crashing down in a ball of fire brings to mind the story of Lucifer's demise, known from both biblical and literary sources. "How you are fallen from heaven, O Day Star, son of Dawn!" the prophet Isaiah exclaims (14:12). Christian readers, especially since the publication of John Milton's *Paradise Lost* (1667), tend to read this and other biblical passages as an account of the angel Lucifer's fall (that is, Satan's fall) from grace.

Th' infernal serpent; he it was, whose guile,
Stirred up with envy and revenge, deceived
The mother of mankind, what time his pride
Had cast him out from Heav'n, with all his host
Of rebel angels, by whose aid aspiring
To set himself in glory above his peers,
He trusted to have equaled the Most High,
If he opposed; and with ambitious aim
Against the throne and monarchy of God

Raised impious war in Heav'n and battle proud
With vain attempt. Him the Almighty Power
Hurled headlong flaming from th' ethereal sky
With hideous ruin and combustion down
To bottomless perdition, there to dwell
In adamantine chains and penal fire,
Who durst defy th' Omnipotent to arms.

                    (*Paradise Lost* 1.34-49)[55]

Like the fallen angel in Milton's epic poem, Libertad in the "She Builds Quick Machines" video falls "headlong flaming" from the sky to earth, only to be put in penal chains by the townspeople who capture her. If we press this reading further, we can identify her rescuers, the members of Velvet Revolver, as the "rebel angels" aiding her cause.

Milton found much of his imagery in the Bible, where we also read of the devil's fall from heaven. The clearest statement appears in the Apocalypse: "The great dragon was thrown down, that ancient serpent, who is called the Devil and Satan, the deceiver of the whole world—he was thrown down to earth, and his angels were thrown down with him" (Rev 12:9; cf. Luke 10:18). Though the song lyrics do not include explicit reference to the Lucifer myth, the presentation of the girl as a fallen angelic figure carries those associations into the narrative told in the song's lyrics. (It is likely that many familiar with the song would also be familiar with the video. The deluxe edition of Velvet Revolver's CD *Libertad* includes it). The song's lyrics highlight the girl's drug use and sexuality, and the video models her story on the biblical/Miltonian villain. The band in the video associates with Libertad, indeed they rescue the girl from her imprisonment, and by doing so they subvert traditional values (the fallen angels in the Bible are bad, but the band celebrates her). Why do they do this?

Obviously, the members of Velvet Revolver are the heroes of their own music video, and it follows that the Lucifer/Libertad angel they rescue must be a hero as well in this context. The townspeople, therefore, necessarily become the villains of the story. It is interesting to note that the video includes brief glimpses of the townspeople's church, casting this Christian sacred site in a negative light because it is associated with the cruel town that opposes the story's heroes. Like Meat Loaf's "The Monster Is Loose," Velvet Revolver's "She Builds Quick Machines" casts a biblical villain (the same one in fact) as a hero. Here too, it is doubtful the songwriters are making a religious/theological statement. Rather, this song is an expression of defiance in the face of authority and convention more generally (Satan defied God; the rebellious band members defy the town and its church; Libertad defies societal expectations and dances across America). Like "The Monster Is Loose," this song expresses the longing to be free from restraints.

TWO MINUTES TO MIDNIGHT: LAST THOUGHTS ON ROCK AND THE DARK SIDE OF RELIGION

Whereas some artists explicitly identify with dark themes, others introduce them to their music with clearly satiric intent as a way of rejecting the very things they invoke (evil, the devil, etc.). Alice Cooper describes his onstage persona and antics as "satirizing villainy." He claims the band never takes itself too seriously, that the act involves humor.[56] The U2 tours of the early 1990s involved a similar satirizing of villainy. Bono would wear makeup and devil's horns as part of his Mister Macphisto persona, something that left some audience members a little confused, as Bill Flanagan reports. Bono typically pulls a girl up on stage during concerts to dance, and during the Zoo TV stop in Cardiff, Wales, the girl he happened to choose surprised him with an impromptu scolding about his devil-horned Macphisto character. It turns out she was a Christian who found the impersonation of a devilish character offensive. While they slow danced, the angry woman tried to wipe off the makeup and questioned the singer about his reasons for dressing this way. By way of explanation, says Flanagan, Bono referred to C. S. Lewis' *The Screwtape Letters* in support (all of this in the middle of a rock concert!).

The Screwtape Letters by the Christian writer C. S. Lewis pretends to be a series of instructions about how to corrupt mortals sent by a senior devil to a young demon-in-training. Lewis described his devil this way: "Screwtape's outlook is like a photographic negative; his whites are our blacks and whatever he welcomes we ought to dread." While waltzing with the angry evangelical Bono invoked Screwtape and told her, "That's what this is." "Oh." She thought about it and then nodded, put her arm on his shoulder, and gave in to the dance.[57]

By playing the role of an evil, dangerous Other, artists can uphold an entirely different set of values or beliefs than the one portrayed in song or on stage.[58]

What fears does horror-influenced music confront? Why do we characterize Otherness as monstrous? Musicians confront several anxieties, among them violence, death, lack of independence, and perceived alienation. This music provides audiences with a way of coping with these fears through a medium that is transgressive and provocative. These artists frequently draw on sacred subject matter and reinterpret that material in shocking ways, reversing the received wisdom about appropriate valuations (what is bad and evil is now good) and acceptable behavior (license and inhibition replace more familiar moral codes).

Through music, lyrics, dress, and behavior, musicians and fans idealize and romanticize freedom from convention. "I'm not a prisoner, I'm a free man, / And my blood is my own now," as Iron Maiden puts it.[59] My blood is my own *now*, hinting here at the assertion of independence so typical of youth music, with its appeal to adolescents struggling to escape parental, educational, and societal expectations and restrictions. In Alice Cooper's "Nothing's Free," independence includes freedom to flout moral expectations, control one's own destiny, and ignore both conscience and authority.[60] Celebrations of individuality and freedom from restraint may be shocking (as in The Sex Pistols' "Anarchy in the U.K.": "I am an antichrist / I am an anarchist")[61] or humorous (AC/DC's Angus

Young performing in a schoolboy outfit, gradually losing pieces of this uniform as concerts proceed). Whatever form such celebrations take, as long as the music is too loud, the clothes inappropriate, the behavior lacking in decorum, or the values promoted questionable, then it will appeal to the one longing for autonomy. If you do not like my music, then it truly is my music.

LOOKING BEYOND THE STEEPLE AND MENORAH

On April 12, 1996, Peter Gzowski of the Canadian Broadcasting Corporation interviewed Burton Cummings on his radio show *Morningside*. When asked about his song "I'm Scared" (*Burton Cummings*, 1976), Cummings described an occasion in 1974 or 1975 when he was walking past the Cathedral of St. Thomas in downtown New York City. It was a particularly cold day, and he was not wearing gloves, something that concerned the piano player who was anxious to protect his hands from arthritis. After noticing the door to the church was open, he explains, he went in "primarily to warm [his] hands." The church was deserted, and while sitting on a pew at the back of the sanctuary, Cummings adds,

> I got spooked . . . I felt a presence of some type there, and I said, "oh boy, I'm getting out of here," and I ran back to the hotel and scribbled down the lyrics [to "I'm Scared"].[1]

The song "I'm Scared" is one of the ex-Guess Who member's best-known solo works. As these interview comments and the song itself indicate, his brief encounter with this indefinable presence turned the songwriter's mind toward an unknown but clearly sacred Other. The song is in fact an unusual confession and invitation to that unknown entity. The singer admits in "I'm Scared" that he never paid religion much attention before but now he is curious and wants to hear its call. The lyrics even include the admission that he "fell down on his knees" in response to the experience at the Cathedral of St. Thomas. The song does not appear to be ironic or disingenuous. On the contrary, it suggests an act of obeisance that is sincere, even if lacking clear direction. There is genuflection, but the singer directs this act of submission to a mysterious and ambiguous presence that he does not, indeed cannot, explain. Many songs explore spiritualities lacking in clear definition. For Cummings in "I'm Scared," there was "something in the air" rare and indefinable, and this is as far as his explanation can go. Of course, many other songwriters comment on spiritual encounters associated with recognizable religious traditions.

The dominance of Judeo-Christian influences in the popular music of the Western world is obvious from examples found throughout this book, but this stream of religiosity is certainly not the only one. For instance, various scholars trace the roots of popular music generally back to West African possession religion,[2] and the list of individual artists turning to spiritualities outside the Judeo-Christian traditions is long and varied. Leonard Cohen, for one, credits various religious influences behind his work. On his official Web site, we find the following remarks about his song "The Future," in which the singer describes himself as "the little Jew who wrote the Bible": "his immersion in Jewish culture, obsession with Christian imagery, and deep commitment to Buddhist detachment rendered him an ideal commentator on the approaching millennium and the apocalyptic fears it generated."[3] Deena Weinstein observes the influence of paganist Rupert Brooke on Roger Waters' songwriting (including elements of Pink Floyd's *Dark Side of the Moon*, 1973). Brooke's interest in ancient Egyptian religion contributed to his writing, and this in turn had a trickle-down effect on Waters' work.[4]

Some obscure religious influences figure prominently in the rave and heavy metal subcultures. In the case of the latter, Sylvan notes "a fascination with the religious symbolism, mythology, and practices of pre-Christian European folk traditions like the Vikings or the Druids. This fascination can . . . be traced back to Led Zeppelin, whose music, lyrics, and cover art contained numerous folk allusions."[5] With reference to the former, he notes that many raves include altars "containing fabric, figurines, paintings, candles, incense, and various assorted sacred objects" and that these altars and decorations "are sometimes organized around particular spiritual themes." He gives the example of a subgenre of electronic dance music called Goa Trance. The raves associated with this particular kind of music "include images of various Hindu deities like Vishnu, Krishna, Ganesha, Kali, and others."[6]

Of course, not all musicians and songwriters with religious convictions articulate their faith through art. Randy Bachman, formerly of The Guess Who (best known for the song "American Woman") and Bachman Turner Overdrive (best known for "Takin' Care of Business" and an appearance on *The Simpsons*), and now a solo artist and radio host with the Canadian Broadcasting Corporation, converted to Mormonism at an early stage in his career. According to biographer John Einarson, Bachman took his faith seriously: "Like all recent converts embarking on a life-affirming transformation coupled with his own compulsive nature, Randy embraced the tenets of the Mormon faith with fervent missionary zeal."[7] It does not appear that Bachman's religious convictions influenced his music in any way, though apparently his conversion contributed to tensions among members of The Guess Who. Bachman defended his chosen lifestyle to his musical colleagues, including Burton Cummings, claiming his decisions could only help the band: "I kept saying to them . . . 'I don't cheat, I don't lie, I don't smoke, I don't drink, I don't drink coffee or tea, I don't do drugs. I write songs and play guitar and will always do that to my fullest capacity, one hundred percent heart and soul.' What else can you ask of a musician?" Despite his best apology, his convictions still created friction: "I no longer partied all night, and I went to church on Sundays. I know the guys in the band found this distancing us."[8]

GEORGE HARRISON AND LORD KRISHNA: "BOW TO GOD
AND CALL HIM SIR"

Perhaps the best-known example of a popular music artist embracing a non-Western religious tradition is George Harrison, whose zeal for and joy in his Hindu spirituality is obvious from the music of his solo career.[9] To discuss ways Harrison articulates his faith, I offer a few reflections on his final album *Brainwashed*, posthumously released in 2002.[10]

While not a specialist in Eastern religion, I make the following observations as a curious fan with an interest in the religious dimensions in Harrison's work. I approach the subject as an outsider. George Harrison, as most music fans are aware, was a devout Hindu, and the primary inspiration for his final album is the *Bhagavad Gita*. My own introduction to Hinduism and the *Bhagavad Gita* has come largely through George Harrison's music and writing, and a few books known to Harrison or having some connection to him (see notes below). This is not, then, a scholarly study of the *Bhagavad Gita* or Hinduism but rather an illustration of how religion can be "heard" in popular music by an audience member.

George Harrison's posthumous album *Brainwashed* was his final gift to music fans. One immediately senses how intensely personal this album is, with the inclusion of his signature on the front cover and his handwritten song titles. George even speaks at the beginning of the CD, telling those in the studio, "Give me plenty of that guitar." These small gestures make the album accessible and give the impression that in *Brainwashed* Harrison offers a sincere attempt to communicate with his audience.

The most intriguing of these personal touches is a sketch found on the back cover of the liner notes. It is simple enough. At its base we find a paraphrase of the biblical expression: "A Voice Cry's [*sic*] in the Wilderness" (cf. Isa 40:3; Matt 3:3; Mark 1:3; Luke 3:4), and above that a sign giving directions to "Bullshit Avenue," which apparently can be found in the city toward which the sign points. Moreover, looking over the whole scene, there is a crudely drawn head, with eyes closed, and a cartoon thought bubble with the chant "God-God-God."

All the words appearing in the picture are from the album's closing song. "Brainwashed" is a prayer. The mess referred to in the song appears to be the state we find ourselves in when living on Bullshit Avenue, those cities of concrete where individuals and institutions brainwash the unwary. Harrison once wrote about the dangers of missing spiritual realities:

> As a single drop of water has the same qualities as an ocean of water, so has our consciousness the qualities of GOD'S consciousness . . . but through our identification and attachment with material energy (physical body, sense pleasures, material possessions, ego, etc.) our true TRANSCENDENTAL CONSCIOUSNESS has been polluted, and like a dirty mirror it is unable to reflect a pure image.[11]

Brainwashed warns of the pitfalls that lie before us in our modern world, namely the risk of losing sight of ultimate truths. It also offers advice on how to avoid these pitfalls.

On the album's cover are five crash test dummies, perhaps indicating a traditionally sized family. They are holding a television and appear repeatedly throughout the liner notes. In one picture, they are looking directly at the television on which the word "Brainwashed" appears. How do we avoid being brainwashed ourselves? The doodle of the closed-eyed man meditating may be the answer because, as the *Bhagavad Gita* states, there is no peace without meditation (2.66). Turning to the *Bhagavad Gita* for clues regarding the album's intent is a logical step, since references to Harrison's Hindu spirituality are explicit. In addition to his thanks to "The Yogis of the Himalayas,"[12] there is a quotation from the *Bhagavad Gita* provided in the album's liner notes: "There never was a time when you or I did not exist. Nor will there be any future when we shall cease to be" (Krishna to Arjuna; compare the citation of 2.19-20 below]).[13]

Furthermore, there are numerous clear allusions to the *Gita* in the album, particularly "Any Road" and "Brainwashed," the opening and closing songs. To be sure, the religious imagery in the songs is not exclusively Eastern, though it certainly dominates. The song "P.2. Vatican Blues" refers to Roman Catholicism in an entirely negative way (recalling for this reason "Awaiting On You All" from *All Things Must Pass*, 1970). Harrison's mother was Roman Catholic, and he attended Mass regularly as a child.[14]

Harrison fans first learned of his interest in Eastern spirituality when he was still part of The Beatles, and it is widely acknowledged that his religious interests influenced the band's later work.[15] In 1968 all four members of the band spent time in India with Maharishi Mahesh Yogi, founder of Transcendental Meditation.[16] Harrison also had ties with the Hare Krishna movement (the International Society for the Krishna Consciousness [ISKCON]). He donated a mansion to the organization and further endorsed the movement by writing the preface for *KRSNA: The Supreme Personality of Godhead* (1970) by founder Abhay Charan De Bhaktivedanta Swami Prabhupāda. Harrison credits Prabhupāda for inspiring his song "Material World," namely the insight that "'we are not these bodies,' we are *in* these material bodies in the physical world." Prabhupāda is also the inspiration behind "The Lord Loves the One."[17]

A Sacred Text and a "Secular" Album

The *Bhagavad Gita* is a poem within a poem. The long *Mahabharata* is an epic that tells the story of an actual war. This context is evident in the *Gita* (see, e.g., 1.2-20), and its principal characters (Arjuna and Krishna) appear elsewhere in the *Mahabharata*. However, the war and these characters are not the same between the two poems. The smaller poem begins with the words "On the field of Truth, on the battle-field of life" (1.1), suggesting a shift from the literal/historical to the metaphorical.[18] The war becomes spiritual in nature (see previous note), and Arjuna comes to represent the human archetype and Krishna the cosmic one.[19] The *Gita* and *Brainwashed* identify the enemies of the human spirit, and they point the reader/listener to the appropriate responses. Harrison thus "translates" the ancient *Gita* for a modern audience in this album, presenting its message in an entirely new medium (cf. the diagram in track 5, illustrating this process). In a way, Harrison the musician resembles Krishna (spiritual guide) and the audience member resembles Arjuna (spiritual quester). Like the charioteer Krishna, Harrison begins the album as a traveler (by boat, plane, car, bike, bus, train, etc. ["Any Road"]), and the album's intimate nature resembles Krishna's relationship with Arjuna; the former reveals "this Yoga eternal, this secret supreme" because of Arjuna's "love for me, and because I am thy friend" (4.4). We can observe three related themes in *Brainwashed* that, I suggest, Harrison draws out of the *Bhagavad Gita*. For Harrison, this ancient Hindu text is a significant precursor that he rewrites in this creative work.

Theme One: The True Nature of Humanity

As seen, the album and the song "Any Road" begins with the songwriter's claim to have been traveling. The song describes a journey with no beginning and no end because there is something in the songwriter that was never born and never dies, a clear allusion to Krishna's teaching in the *Gita*:

> If any man thinks he slays, and if another thinks he is slain, neither knows the ways of truth. The Eternal in man cannot kill: the Eternal in man cannot die. He is never born, and he never dies. He is in Eternity: he is for evermore. Never-born and eternal, beyond times gone or to come, he does not die when the body dies (2.19-20; cf. various phrases in 2.11-30).

Arjuna is troubled early on in the *Bhagavad Gita* because his participation in a war will require him to kill: "I see forebodings of evil, Krishna. I cannot foresee any glory if I kill my own kinsmen" (1.31). In response, Krishna introduces the concept of *dehin*, "the 'one in the body' ('spirit,' 'soul'), which cannot be killed, and which will repeatedly take another body after the death of the current one."[20] As Prabhupāda's puts it in comments on 2.12, "It is not that they did not exist as individuals in the past, and it is not that they will not remain as eternal persons. Their individuality existed in the past, and their individuality will continue in the future without interruption. Therefore, there is no cause for lamentation for any one of the individual living entities."[21]

People may not be aware of their eternal natures, however, and indeed might mistakenly conclude there is nothing beyond the experiences of this life. "Rising Sun" speaks to this lack of understanding and the deception to which individuals are prone in this world. The song begins on a street full of criminals where one will find the devil is available to serve as guide. Boundaries and guilt hinder those foolish enough to trust the devil to lead them on their way. The narrator of the song, a clearly biographical use of the first-person singular, looks into mirrors but finds only disguises, suggesting some greater reality lies hidden beneath. He too was a victim of the devil's deception, working on this avenue of sinners until he was "near destroyed." However, the song speaks of a spiritual awakening, a "rising sun" that comes from within. What he discovers is the eternal nature, a universe within. Not to be aware of this is to fall prey to the devil, villains, and sinners mentioned in the song, to be brainwashed. In his book *I Me Mine*, Harrison describes this differently:

> Reality is a concept. Everybody has their own reality. . . . Most people's reality is an illusion, a great big illusion. You automatically have to succumb to the illusion that "I am this body." I am not George. I am not really George. I am this living thing that goes on, always has been, always will be, but at this time I happen to be in "this" body. The body has changed; was a baby, was a young man, will soon be an old man, and I'll be dead. The physical body will pass but this bit in the middle, that's the only reality. All the rest is the illusion.[22]

Prabhupāda explains this further in his commentary on the *Gita* (which I cite because Harrison himself endorsed this writer). The *Gita* "is meant to deliver one from the nescience of material entanglement. Everyone is in difficulty, just as Arjuna was on the

Battlefield of Kuruksetra. Not only Arjuna, but each of us is full of anxieties because of this material entanglement. Our existence is eternal, but somehow we are put into this position which is *asat*. *Asat* means unreal."[23]

Harrison states his views on reincarnation quite clearly in comments on the song "The Art of Dying" in *I Me Mine*. The song acknowledges that the time will come when we will all face death, and further, that most will return to this world, the result of our desire *"to be a perfect entity."*[24] Karma, he explains, is the law of action and reaction. Every thought, word, and deed acts like a pebble thrown in water, sending ripples across the universe that eventually return: "Whatever you do, it comes right back on you."[25] Switching metaphors, he adds that these actions-reactions are like knots on a piece of string. From the moment of birth on, we try to undo all the knots from previous lives (past Karma), but most people end up adding more along the way. If we get ourselves entangled in the affairs of this life, chances are our last thought or desire will be on matters of this world and not God, and such thoughts or desires provide "the motivation for rebirth." The point of the song is that unless we want to experience a million years of crying we need to practice the art of dying—which involves detachment from the world while living. To illustrate, Harrison adds, "I mean *I* don't want to be lying there as I'm dying thinking 'Oh shit, I forgot to put the cat out,' or 'I didn't get a Rolls-Royce' because then you may have to come right back just to do those things, and then you have got more knots on your piece of string."[26]

Theme Two: The Search for Truth

The lyrics to the opening song on *Brainwashed* ("Any Road") are mostly in the first person, using the familiar metaphor describing life as a journey. This journey has no beginning and no end, presents many unresolved questions, and involves a search for truth. The chorus shifts to the second person, and there we find the songwriter, after describing his own experiences, offering advice and assurance for those on a spiritual quest: "if you don't know where you're going / Any road will take you there." There are two ways to take this statement. Positively it might offer assurance to those on a sincere spiritual quest since Krishna, in the *Gita*, teaches that even those "who in faith worship other gods, because of their love they worship me, although not in the right way. For I accept every sacrifice, and I am their Lord supreme" (9.23-24a). Negatively it warns those who have not stepped out in this journey toward spiritual enlightenment that inaction has consequences. If you do not have a spiritual destination or goal in mind, you will get nowhere.

According to the songs on *Brainwashed*, the biggest obstacle to spiritual discovery is distraction. Misplaced priorities and passions clutter the mind and turn our attentions away from that which is of ultimate importance. The singer refers to losing his concentration when in fact the only thing that matters to him is touching "your lotus feet" ("Stuck Inside a Cloud"). As described earlier, the doodle found in the liner notes includes a smiling man meditating on the words "God-God-God." The *Bhagavad Gita* speaks of meditation/contemplation as a necessary spiritual exercise. "Without contemplation," we are told, "there cannot be peace, and without peace can there be joy?" (2.66). The man in the diagram—Harrison himself perhaps—appears to have both. The message conveyed by the voice that "Cry's [sic] in the Wilderness" is don't be distracted or brainwashed by all that happens in the great cities of the world (Brussels, Bonn, Washington, London) or by their leaders and teachers. God alone can "stop the rot" and lead us out of ignorance.

Harrison and the *Gita* speak of the importance of meditation (6.10-14; 12.8-10, 12; 13.24, and so forth) and chanting (9.13-14).[27] In fact, the album closes with a Sanskrit chant ("Namah Parvarti") performed by George and his son Dhani Harrison. Prior to this, the recurring "God-God-God" in the song "Brainwashed" functions as a chant, perhaps in a form more accessible to the majority of listeners (that is, an English term repeating as part of a pop song's chorus).

Theme Three: The Pleasure-Seeking Life Brings Pain and Darkness

Harrison's "Living in the Material World" (*Living in the Material World*, 1973) illustrates his wonderful sense of humor and his religious convictions regarding attachment to worldly possessions. This song refers to meeting John and Paul. They (The Beatles) started out poor but soon "got 'Richie' on a tour" and "caught up" in all that the material world offered.[28] There is an unmistakable humility in this song. He does not claim to be everything he should be, stating in the same song that his desire to escape the material world, his salvation, requires Krishna's grace. Harrison's ironically titled book *I Me Mine* points to his recognition that attachment with possessions lies at the heart of many sorrows and is something that one must escape. His wife Olivia Harrison explained the title in her lovely and informative introduction to the 2002 edition of this book:

> During our life together the issues of possessions, attachment and identification with the ego were in the forefront of our awareness and George was always quick to point out that in reality there is no I, Me or Mine. George was relentless at keeping our spiritual aim true. We were only humans walking a long road towards our shared goal of enlightenment. . . . [He would remind himself and me] that we are pure Spirit, and that the Spirit is in "every grain of sand," belonging to everyone and no one; that nothing is "mine" and that "I" we all refer to must be recognized as the little "i" in the larger scheme of the Universe. George was tired of the I Me Mines of this world, including his own. . . . When searching for a title to this book, he was well aware that the lyrics to these songs would always be tied to his name and considered *his* songs, even though he knew the creativity bestowed upon him was a divine gift. So rather than conjuring a book title that might try to explain away the gift of songwriting with, "Well, I wrote them but they don't really belong to me," he took the opposite approach and the risk of claiming this book in a slightly cynical trinity of pronouns.[29]

This concern with detachment is prominent in "Brainwashed," the closing song on the album. Like Krishna, who warns that dwelling on the pleasures of the senses leads to desire, the lust of possession, passion and anger (2.62), Harrison finds that such symbols of the pursuit of wealth as the Nikkei, Dow Jones, FTSE, and Nasdaq do no more than stifle spirituality. Wealth and noble birth are no guarantee of happiness and peace, according to the *Gita*: "Led astray by many wrong thoughts, entangled in the net of delusion, enchained to the pleasures of their cravings, they fall down into a foul hell" (16.16). "Brainwashed" includes recurring prayers addressed to God, who is at one point defined as "Bliss." Krishna directs devotees to a different kind of happiness: "When a man surrenders all desires that come to the heart and by the grace of God finds the joy of God, then his soul has indeed found peace" (2.55).

George Harrison's *Brainwashed* is distinct from other "secular" pop music in three respects. First, Harrison is explicit in his lyrics about his own spiritual journey. The presence of religious themes in popular music is not remarkable in itself, as I hope this book makes clear. What is unusual is to find songwriters charting their own spiritual experiences in the sort of detail found in Harrison's *Brainwashed*.

Second, Harrison brings his spirituality into the mainstream to an extent that few, if any, have been able to match. Others release explicit statements of personal faith in their music (such as Alice Cooper, Bob Dylan, Yusuf Islam, Sinéad O'Connor), but in terms of quantity, Harrison is unmatched. His Hinduism is plain for all to hear throughout the music of his thirty-year solo career. And some of this work has critical and mass appeal. For instance, *All Things Must Pass* (1970) quickly reached number one on U.S. and British charts. The single "My Sweet Lord," described by David Fricke as "a psalm to Krishna," was number one in the U.K.[30] When the album was re-released in 2001 to mark the thirtieth anniversary, "My Sweet Lord" returned to number one on the charts in the U.K. *Brainwashed* also proved to be a successful album. In February 2004, Harrison won a Grammy (posthumously) for "Mawra Blues" in the Best Pop Instrumental Performance category. He also earned a nomination for Best Male Pop Vocal Performance for the song "Any Road."

A third distinctive quality of Harrison's religious lyrics is accessibility. The theology is challenging for neophytes, but Harrison has a wonderful way of introducing a disarming touch of humor with lofty themes (e.g., the cartoon included with the album *Brainwashed*). As suggested throughout this study, attention to the ways in which musicians dialogue with influential religious precursors provides important clues for understanding contemporary song lyrics. *Brainwashed* offering an exposition of its literary/religious precursor, the *Bhagavad Gita*, is a compelling illustration of the potential of a popular medium to communicate religious content with imagination and surprising beauty.

THE MUSLIM MUSICIAN YUSUF ISLAM
(AKA CAT STEVENS)

If George Harrison is the most famous devotee to a non-Western religious tradition among musicians, Cat Stevens comes in a close second. Stevens, now known by the name Yusuf Islam, converted to Islam in 1978, much to the surprise of fans the world over. "I came to the Koran," he explains in a 2007 interview on National Public Radio, "and quite literally it seemed to be speaking everything I needed to hear."[31] His conversion to Islam surprised audiences, but even more startling was Stevens' decision to leave his music career behind because of this momentous transformation. After the release of *Back to Earth* in 1978, Cat Stevens announced his retirement. This decision to leave his art while at the height of his creative powers was a huge disappointment to his fans.

C. S. Lewis once observed that the closest of friendships experience strain when one of the two discovers new interests.

> Change is a threat to Affection. A brother or sister, or two brothers . . . grow to a certain age sharing everything. They have read the same comics, climbed the same trees, been pirates or spacemen together, taken up and abandoned stamp-collecting at the same moment. Then a dreadful thing happens. One of them flashes ahead—discovers poetry or science or serious music or perhaps undergoes a religious

conversion. His life is flooded with the new interest. The other cannot share it; he is left behind. I doubt whether even the infidelity of a wife or husband raises a more miserable sense of desertion or a fiercer jealousy than this can sometimes do.[32]

Though maybe a little overstated, this seems like a reasonable way of thinking about the reaction of fans to the news of Stevens' conversion and retirement. The fact that most Westerners understand so little of the Islamic faith makes it even truer that Stevens' fans would feel a sense of abandonment: "The other cannot share [the new interest]; he is left behind." Next to George Harrison and Bob Dylan, no other musician's personal religious journey dominates public thinking as much as Cat Stevens. All three artists turned to religion while at the height of their professional careers. Furthermore, all three artists turned to religious traditions far removed from their family roots (Harrison from Catholicism to Hinduism; Dylan from Judaism to fundamentalist Christianity; Stevens from Greek Orthodoxy to Islam). Arguably, the dramatic and sudden changes in Stevens' life startled his fans more because of his retirement. His religious transformation was so complete that, in addition to his name change, he entered into an arranged Muslim marriage and thoroughly committed himself to the community, something evident in his decision to open a Muslim school in London.[33] Yusuf Islam even wrote about Mohammed in a short book entitled *The Life of the Last Prophet*, in which he describes the prophet as "a mercy to the universe" and "a symbol of light and guidance for all time and for all people."[34]

With the release of Islam's *An Other Cup* in 2006 and *Roadsinger* in 2009—his first mainstream albums of new material in thirty years—the singer provides audiences with a musical glimpse inside his religious tradition. In some ways, the first of these albums is analogous to George Harrison's *All Things Must Pass* (1970) and Bob Dylan's *Slow Train Coming* (1979), even Alice Cooper's *The Last Temptation* (1994), in that it is the first musical confession of new belief. At the same time, Islam's *An Other Cup* is arguably a more mature articulation of religious faith than the other three albums; whereas Harrison, Dylan, and Cooper released their albums soon after their embrace of a new spirituality, Islam's album follows nearly thirty years of adherence to his beliefs.

Islam wrote all the songs on *An Other Cup* save one. His cover of the Bennie Benjamin, Gloria Caldwell, and Sol Marcus song "Don't Let Me Be Misunderstood" stands out as a result (a song best known to pop audiences from The Animal's 1965 recording). To hear Islam sing "I'm just a soul whose intentions are good / Oh Lord, please don't let me be misunderstood" sounds like an attempt to reach out to listeners. He is aware, of course, that many in the Western world misunderstand, even fear, the Muslim faith. He is also aware that many view him personally with suspicion. Reports in 1989 claimed he supported the infamous *fatwa* against writer Salman Rushdie, and in 2004, authorities pulled the singer off a flight after his name appeared on a United States terrorism watch list. In light of the general misconceptions about the Islamic religion in general, and these incidents in particular, this song is a superb fit for Islam's return to the recording studio. He says himself that the song is "tailor-made" for the album.[35]

Islam makes another gesture towards those with questions in his article "Chinese Whiskers," posted at the Mountain of Light Web site.[36] This Web site includes a lengthy question-and-answer section, suggesting the singer's interest in reaching out to those who misunderstand him. He begins this particular article with the following words of explanation:

> Over the years, since becoming a Muslim, I have been accused of saying and doing things I have neither said nor done. Stories spread from person to person, whether intentionally or not, the result is that some people are led into thinking I am connected to causes I don't believe in or subscribe to. Now that I've decided to sing again, I'm sure it will attract a whole new wave of articles and allegations to diminish my work for peace and better understanding. So to avoid relying on whispers or hearsay, here's a chance to

glance at what I have to say first-hand about some of those *controversial* issues people tried to tag me with—past and present—as well as a chance to reprise some of my old lyrics.[37]

This excerpt makes clear the tendency to misunderstand Islam's conversion and his awareness that he needs to take particular care in explaining his beliefs and activities. Like his recording of "Don't Let Me Be Misunderstood," this article is an attempt at bridge-building.

At the same time, *An Other Cup* is an explicit articulation of his cherished Muslim faith. He opens his acknowledgments in the liner notes with the words "All praise to God," and he cites, among other inspirations, the Prophet Muhammad, and the thirteenth-century Persian poet Rumi. Two qualities about Islam's writing in this album deserve note. For one thing, *An Other Cup* is an intensely personal album, and he repeatedly articulates his dependence on divine favor. He thanks God for all he has in "Midday (Avoid City after Dark)"[38]; he acknowledges that his search for spiritual meaning is complete now that God has entered his life ("Heaven / Where True Love Goes"); and he is able to love others now because God softened his stone heart ("I Think I See the Light"). The album is a bare confession of faith, expressing joy and confidence in his God, largely using the first-person singular. There are no songs addressing nonreligious subjects (assuming the reading of "Don't Let Me Be Misunderstood" suggested above).[39]

The writing on this album also directs the celebration of divine grace outward. The album has moments of introspection as the artist considers his own spiritual state, but much of it is unabashedly evangelistic in tone, explicitly urging listeners to consider their own spiritual condition in terms few other mainstream artists use. Islam's prophetic address is unambiguous but still gentle and well meaning (consider, for example, "In The End" and "The Beloved"). Yusuf Islam also looks outward in another sense. He signals his interest in social justice and charitable causes, calling attention to the plight of those in need. He encourages his audience to "support the orphans" and directs them to his charity's Web site www.small-kindness.org. He dedicates his album "to all those long suffering people, praying to return to their land in peace and security," inevitably a political statement, even if an oblique one, coming as it does from a Muslim.

CLOSING THOUGHTS ON POP MUSIC PREACHERS

If the writings and activities of the Hindu George Harrison and Muslim Yusuf Islam, along with Christian musicians like Alice Cooper and members of U2, teach us anything, it is that mainstream music provides a powerful medium to articulate genuine, serious religious conviction. These presentations of a religious worldview may be unconventional, given that they appear outside official venues of religious proclamation (temple, mosque, synagogue, church), but this in itself is not reason to question their sincerity. Attempts to articulate religious belief through mainstream music are not usually systematic in any sense; songs and albums tend to be highly selective regarding the issues addressed, and they usually emphasize emotional engagement with the faith traditions in question. Unlike other songwriters who draw on religious terminology for other purposes (politics, humor, hyperbole, irony, criticism), these artists introduce the same language while accepting the relevant presuppositions these faith traditions require (there is a God, he speaks through his prophets, and so so). By using mainstream music to articulate their beliefs, they are able to bring religious discourse into the public sphere in ways other representatives of these traditions cannot.

FADE OUT
STEALING FROM THE SACRED
AND REWRITING RELIGION

I begin this closing chapter with a heuristic illustrating the relationship between religion and popular songwriting described in this book. It offers a way of thinking about songwriters' habit of introducing religious content into their work. They pick up terms and phrases, names and storylines, recurring themes and ideas from religious discourse, and bring that material into their own creative compositions. They do not choose to stay in the official spaces of formal religion and they write songs for wide audiences that are not self-consciously religious as a whole (compared to the contemporary Christian music industry, for instance), and in this way there is a kind of subversion at work. They leave sacred spaces (artistically) for secular ones, but remain under the influence of that rich body of religious source material.

The diagram below presents one way of imagining this dance between religious subject matter and artistic rewritings intended for mass consumption. Songwriters repeat sacred terms, taking them out of one realm, which inevitably results in new meanings when they appear in another. The left side of the diagram indicates the proper, official places of religious language, broadly speaking. The place could be textual (such as the Jewish and Christian Bibles, the Koran, or the *Bhagavad Gita*) or a more natural environment

for discussion of religious subjects (such as a mosque, synagogue, church, or temple; theological treatises or sermons). Songwriters carry sacred terms and themes out from official spaces of religious discourse for many different reasons: irony, humor, criticism, entertainment. In some cases, this use of sacred material is unwitting (for example, phrases from the Bible that are commonplace expressions in the English language).

The diagram offers a visual metaphor illustrating how popular music returns constantly to sacred subject matter. Post-1960s popular culture often assumes an anti-establishment / anti-tradition / anti-religion stance, claiming independence from all authority, yet there remains a persistent tendency to push religion away while simultaneously pulling it back. The diagram pictures an old-fashioned turntable, a long play record player. (Imagine a CD player if you prefer.) Vinyl albums rotate clockwise on a stereo. The left side of the page represents the realm of the sacred: traditional religious beliefs and ethical codes, the Bible, institutional faith, and the like. The right side of the page indicates the secular space assumed by popular songwriters: counterculture, artistic independence, freedom from restraint, creativity, and so on. Record players rotate in a clockwise direction, and here this movement illustrates two distinct tendencies in popular music. First, it indicates *continuous movement away from* religious precursors, and the restrictions organized religion imposes. Imagine the record spinning, say, from 10 o'clock to 2 o'clock, out of the sacred sphere into a space beyond the confines of institutional religion. They produce a nonreligious religion of sorts, because as they move out of the sacred contexts, songwriters bring some of that discourse with them (the inescapable influence of religion).

Popular music is either unable or unwilling to let go of the sacred entirely. Artists and audiences may have left the confinements and structures of narrowly defined spirituality with the 1960s counterculture, but they have not left religion/spirituality itself. So second, there is *constant movement back to* sacred themes, the Bible, and other religious content. Imagine the record spinning, say, from 4 o'clock to 8 o'clock. Artists' motives for doing so vary

widely. They may introduce this material to criticize religion, their
language may be ironic, or they may wish to articulate genuine
faith. Regardless of their intent, this mainstream musical return
to sacred space is recurrent and unmistakable. The rotation of a
record represents this inevitable return to all that the sacred realm
provides (a myth, a story, a vocabulary, a basis of authority, a body
of symbols and metaphors from which to draw).

The continual return of artists to the left side of the page (6
o'clock to 12 o'clock) followed by escape back to the independence
of the right (12 o'clock to 6 o'clock), provides a way of imagining
several arguments in the book. By returning to those old stories and
beliefs (left side), and then bringing them back out and retelling them
(right side), they are in a position to subvert those stories, assert
their artistic independence, and claim liberation from authority
and influence. Artists also have freedom to articulate their genuine
spiritual experiences apart from the narrowly defined terms and
rituals of the more official, sanctioned venues.

The uppercase terms on the outer edges represent general
qualities of the sacred discourse and popular music, respectively.
The indented, lowercase terms are examples of recurring, more
specific thematic elements in each category.

Many songwriters are explicit about their influences, acknowledging dependence on other musicians and recognizing their root-
edness in a long musical tradition. There is no escaping the influence
of other performers and songwriters, and indeed, drawing on one's
peers and predecessors is often brazen and deliberate. As Dan Zanes
(of The Del Fuegos, and Dan Zanes and Friends) puts it, "A great
songwriter borrows; a genius steals."[1] According to Elvis Costello,
"Every pop musician is a thief and a magpie. I have an emotional
affinity for certain styles, but none of them belong to me."[2] Quite
often, acknowledging one's influences is a point of pride and a way
of identifying with recognized masters. In the liner notes to his 2006
album *Continuum*, John Mayer confesses, "Eric Clapton knows I
steal from him and is still cool with it." Musicians constantly offer
tributes to, cover the songs of, and speak about other musicians.
Though all strong writers experience anxiety because of influence,

this is, according to Harold Bloom, a "liberating burden." "It is only by repressing 'creative freedom,' through the initial fixation of influence," he explains, "that a person can be reborn as a poet. And only by revising that repression can a poet become and remain strong."[3] This constant emphasis on musical precursors makes sense if we think of this process in Bloom's terms. It also provides a model for reflecting on religious influences on pop music.

We hear traces of and responses to this paradoxical "liberating burden" in the work of many songwriters of the post-1960s. Artists experience an "initial fixation of influence" stemming from ubiquitous and therefore inescapable religious traditions, but in their work they revise those precursors. Songwriters do so to articulate their own unique visions, to demonstrate that they too are strong poets, visionaries, and prophets. They take religious concepts and shape them to suit their own purposes.

Paul Simon admits to a modest ambition in one of his later albums: "I'm trying to tap into some wisdom. Even a little drop will do."[4] Along with him, we direct a great deal of mental energy toward this vaguely defined objective, this longing to know what we do not know now, to express what we lack words to say, to find *it*! For many of us, expressing emotions, articulating questions or fears, or communicating deep longings is no easy thing. Fortunately there are artists in the world who can, and if we are lucky, we will find one or more who can speak for us, who can serve, as Northrop Frye puts it, as "a kind of spiritual preceptor," a writer with a mind and imagination so large "that one has no sense of claustrophobia within it."[5] Through diverse media, artists celebrate and lament, confront and examine humanity's endlessly diverse experiences.

When writing about musical sounds, Susanne K. Langer refers to its "wealth of wordless knowledge, its whole knowledge of emotional and organic experience, of vital impulse, balance, conflict, the *ways* of living and dying and feeling. Because no assignment of meaning is conventional, none is permanent beyond the sound that passes; yet the brief association was a flash of understanding."[6] Jennifer Rycenga makes the interesting jump from Langer's analysis of *musical sound*, bringing her observations to the *lyrics* of songwriter

Jon Anderson of the band Yes. Langer's description "fits what he is doing *with words*: a transient, shifting kaleidoscopic play of meanings, tinged with physical and dreamt affect, but concerned with vital meanings, creating flashes of understanding but nothing denotative enough to be static or permanent."[7] Expanding Langer and Rycenga's observations to songwriting more widely, this approach allows for reading music and words as a striving toward insight, understanding, or God. It may not be systematic, but it is earnest, engaging the emotions as much as the intellect. In their efforts to find the ineffable, to tap into some wisdom, to find *it*, these artists teach and provoke their audiences, often questioning our values and assumptions in the process. They force us to reconsider, rethink, and reevaluate our views of religion and spirituality.

For many, the urge to categorize forms of art into high and low, serious and frivolous remains. Consequently, many overlook prophetic voices heard on their radios, never thinking these artists can speak meaningfully to their reflections on spiritual matters. Simon Frith maintains as "a matter of analytic strategy" that criticism should operate with the principle that there is no difference between high and low culture. As we engage high and low artistic productions, we are in fact "employing the same evaluative principles." Audiences and critics bring "similar questions to high and low art . . . their pleasures and satisfactions are rooted in similar analytic issues, similar ways of relating what they see or hear to how they think and feel." The questions and expectations we bring to cultural productions are in fact consequences of our "historical and material circumstances."[8] This approach to cultural artifacts allows us to listen to music expectantly, open to the possibility of finding insight in unlikely sources. This does not necessitate abandoning a creedal fixed point, if indeed the music fan holds to one. It is a matter of how long a tether we use to keep us fixed to that theological center. To be sure, not everyone will agree that we see the words of the prophets written on the subway wall, or hear them on the radio.

Popular music is unique among the arts as a medium for introspection and reflection on the spiritual side of our being. For one, it is widely accessible to its audiences. Music is ubiquitous in the modern world, available for private or collective consumption in many formats. Furthermore, unlike association with an organized religion, or alignment with any developed theology or ideology, the spirituality on offer in popular song is not systematic and makes no demands on the listener. We can select what we hear, and when we hear it; we can choose to reflect on lyrics or not; we can choose to participate in musical subcultures or not; we can choose to incorporate our favorite music into our philosophies and theologies, our personal belief systems, or not. This implies that individuals will experience popular songs as spiritually relevant to different degrees, and some not at all.

There is endless diversity in the music available to audiences. The small sampling touched on in this book is hardly representative of the diversity available in the English language, and regarding the singers and bands mentioned, my few remarks do not reflect their work as a whole. Songwriters change and develop over time, and commenting on one or two songs or albums does not do justice to a writer's body of work. My aim is to call attention to certain songwriting *tendencies*, habits of writing and reflection evident in the music. Religious language provides artists with linguistic and metaphoric resources that are simply not available to them otherwise. Regardless of their oppositional stance, their belief or unbelief, their ideology or motive, songwriters tend to borrow and rewrite sacred stories.[9] Though this book mentions only a random selection of songs and albums, the tendencies identified in the preceding chapters would apply to many more.

Some musicians are aware that musicmaking is in some sense a spiritual or mystical act. Paul McCartney claims he and his touring band "hugged and prayed and gave thanks" moments before the start of shows,[10] and Adam Clayton of U2, who does not claim to be a Christian, once made the following observation about the band's concerts: "I don't know what it is . . . but I definitely know when it's there. It doesn't happen every night, but some nights, there's a sense of community and fellowship. And people have said there's a spiritual aspect to what's happening in the house."[11] According to Echard, summarizing the views of Stan W. Denski, "many rock musicians take a mystical view of composition, feeling that the song is not a product of their own ideas and work but something for which they are only a conduit."[12] This kind of religious or mystical experience defies clear explanation. It is highly experiential, but it appears to relate to such things as artistic inspiration, pleasure in good music, and the experience of community in performing that music (with band mates, with audiences). An analogy may be helpful here. Psychedelic music in particular illustrates well what is true of music more generally. This habit of associating a vague mysticism with music indicates openness to spirituality like that evident in psychedelic rock. The term formally applies to music that is either inspired by or somehow related to drug-induced experiences, and by extension, to the mind-expanding potential of drug use.[13] Jim DeRogatis opens up the terms somewhat, defining psychedelic rock as music "inspired by a philosophical approach implied by the literal meaning of 'psychedelic' as 'mind-revealing' and 'soul-manifesting.'" Music fans of the 1960s and later, seeking some form of encounter with transcendence and an enhanced sense of awareness, looked to rock and roll as a way of accessing these elusive experiences. Psychedelic rock is, DeRogatis continues, "open to spirituality, whether it's in the forms of Eastern religions, nature worship, or Christianity."[14]

I suspect that musicians and audiences searching for some form of spirituality in music rather than organized religion are ultimately searching for spirituality without boundaries. The settings of formal religious practice—churches, synagogues, mosques, temples—and the activities and authorities associated with these places introduce rigid definitions that some would find limiting. Adherence to a fixed creed, compliance with rituals of worship, and conformity of behavior to a mandated morality codifies and regulates how one may experience the divine. Some might conclude there is little room for individuality in organized religion. Through popular music, many catch glimpses of something transcendent, something bigger than themselves that approximates an encounter with a spiritual Other. When artists and fans attempt to explain their encounters with *it*, to return to Dean Moriarty's term, they typically turn to the reservoir of language and imagery available to them from traditional religious discourse to articulate the experience. The distance between this spiritually inclined music and organized religion varies considerably.

Of course, we must also be careful not to assume that every reference to a religious practice, and every use of a term associated with sacred subject matter, is serious, deliberate, or self-conscious.[15] Indeed, there is always a risk of imposing a particular logic on song lyrics when either none exists, or a different one exists. Authors use words in many ways. Certainly, some songs have a recognizable linear development, telling a story proceeding from something approximating a beginning through to an end, but this is not always the case. As noted elsewhere, resistance to conformity and expectations is typical of much popular songwriting, and even in the use of language, artists (rappers, for instance) make language their own, finding ways to give expression to their resistance and individuality through forms of speech.[16] By defying rules of grammar, introducing slang or expletives, or disturbing the usual rhythms of the English language, artists can make political statements.

At other times, apparent nonsequiturs involve creative decisions. Those who study Bob Dylan's lyrics, for instance, observe ways he breaks free of rigid narrative sequence. Stephen Scobie writes of Dylan's tendency to heap images and "produce a rather loose, nonlinear structure. Image piles on image, and verse follows verse, without a great deal of consecutive necessity." The effect of this style of writing is to "de-emphasize the linear progression of the song and to see its structure more in spatial terms, as if all the images were laid out alongside each other in a continuous present tense. Or as if each verse were a separable unit in a modular, nonlinear structure."[17] In 1974 Dylan studied painting with artist Norman Raeben, whose insights shaped the way the songwriter constructed lyrics. Raeben "brought Dylan to a more fruitful understanding of time, enabling him to view narrative not in such strictly linear terms, but to telescope past, present, and future together," an effect evident in *Blood On The Tracks* (1975) that was released about the same time. In "Tangled Up in Blue," for instance, "temporality, location, and viewpoint shift back and forth from verse to verse, rather in the manner of montaged jump cuts in a movie . . . allowing him to reveal underlying truths about the song's characters while letting them remain shadowy, secretive figures."[18] The point is that interpreters are always at risk of imposing order on the language of pop songs that is ultimately not the songwriter's, but the listener's own invention. Ambiguities and disruptions to narrative and linguistic logic may in fact be intentional, even at times nonsensical.

In other instances still, the phrasings of song lyrics might defy expectations because they try to capture the intensity of experiences like rebellion, sex, or drug use. Many take Jefferson Airplane's "White Rabbit" (*Surrealistic Pillow*, 1967), with its allusions to Lewis Carroll's *Alice's Adventures in Wonderland* and *Through the Looking Glass*, as an example of the latter. The same is true of Jimi Hendrix's "Purple Haze" (*Are You Experienced*, 1967), and The Beatles' "A Day in the Life" (*Sgt. Pepper's Lonely Hearts Club Band*, 1967). Naturally, if in fact these songs attempt to document something analogous to drug-induced disruptions of the mind's usual activities, then some language in the song may appear disjointed and incoherent to those who are sober.

In other songs, perhaps even most songs, far simpler explanations account for the particular choices about terms and phrases. When lyrics are cryptic, there is always a temptation to read some deeper meaning into them. However, word choices may involve no more than accommodations to rhyme schemes, or attempts to introduce humor, or simply provide satisfying sounds that work with musical accompaniment. By focusing on narrative logic, listeners may end up asking the wrong questions about songs. For The Beatles' song "Lucy in the Sky with Diamonds" (*Sgt. Pepper's Lonely Hearts Club Band*, 1967), and Van Halen's album *For Unlawful Carnal Knowledge* (1991), for instance, the resulting acronyms of these titles may account for the particular choice of words, as much as anything else. Similarly, we cannot assume that every reference to religion and its texts and practices in popular music are theologically significant. Listeners beware.

Such challenges for interpretation notwithstanding, it remains that popular song lyrics offer a world of compelling texts rich with religious speculation. It is an art form easily overlooked by both the academy and organized religion as a site of serious spiritual reflection. Popular music is often antiauthoritarian in its posturing, limiting by its very nature dialogue with institutions like the church or university. Overt ethical libertinism is often on display by performers and their audiences, which likely offends some and makes it hard for others to take this art form seriously. Also, a typical four-to-six minute song will lack the sophistication and detail possible in, say, a movie or novel. Since brief pop songs often rewrite religious precursors, introducing irony or humor, the brevity of this engagement can appear as irreverent trivializing of something serious and sacred, or simple misunderstanding. For these and many other reasons, popular songs present unique challenges to those listening for religious insights over the airwaves, and yet despite the difficulties, the study of this informal theologizing provides clues about the religious thinking of both songwriters and their enormous audiences. As this is a generation increasingly removed from organized religion, such clues—however vague—help us see ways in which the arts provide a surrogate spirituality and a venue to explore, express, and experience transcendent possibilities.

NOTES

Preface

1 Bono, "Introduction," *Selections from the Book of Psalms*, The Pocket Canon (New York: Grove, 1999), x–xi (ellipses in original).

2 For some of the issues involved in defining the label popular music, see, e.g., Roy Shuker, *Popular Music: The Key Concepts*, 2nd ed. (London: Routledge, 2005), 203–5. Attempts to distinguish the term from other musical categories often emphasize such things as the commercialization of the music in question, audience size, and the nature of the music's preservation and distribution (i.e., recordings as opposed to oral transmission and musical notations).

3 Larry Starr and Christopher Waterman, *American Popular Music: From Minstrelsy to MP3*, 2nd ed. (Oxford: Oxford University Press, 2007), 2.

4 For analysis of the quasi-religious overtones of fan idolization of celebrities, see, e.g., Ellis Cashmore, *Celebrity/Culture* (New York: Routledge, 2006). Cashmore notes a spectrum in the fascination with celebrity that runs from a normal developmental process in children who adore their heroes—a form of "parasocial interaction" (254)—to the psychologically abnormal state of adult obsession. He adds that "the intensity of emotional involvement, the impact on the life of the believer, the pattern of engagement with the rest of the world (from sociability to withdrawal) are all features of celebrity worship that have religious counterparts" (254). One of the most famous examples of this near reverence for musicians occurs in Don McLean's ode to American music, which weaves the

theological language of religious devotion into a song celebrating rock and roll. "American Pie" (*American Pie*, 1971) decries the day the music died, usually taken as a reference to February 3, 1959, when the world lost The Big Bopper (Jiles Perry Richardson Jr.), Ritchie Valens, and Buddy Holly in a plane crash. I suspect the song involves a synecdoche; the allusion to these specific pioneers of rock and roll represents the genre more broadly. The singer celebrates music in the most exalted terms imaginable. Not only does he admire these musicians above all others, he even refers to them as "Father, Son, and Holy Ghost."

5   For reflections on religious dimensions in Harrison's life and music, see, e.g., Dale C. Allison Jr., *The Love There That's Sleeping: The Art and Spirituality of George Harrison* (New York: Continuum, 2006) and Joshua M. Greene, *Here Comes the Sun: The Spiritual and Musical Journey of George Harrison* (Hoboken, N.J.: John Wiley & Sons, 2006).

6   On literary dimensions in Dylan's writing, see, e.g., Christopher Ricks, *Dylan's Visions of Sin* (New York: HarperCollins, 2003) and Michael Gray, *Song and Dance Man III: The Art of Bob Dylan* (London: Continuum, 2000).

7   Reinhold Niebuhr, *The Essential Reinhold Niebuhr: Selected Essays and Addresses*, ed. Robert McAfee Brown (New Haven: Yale University Press, 1986), 251.

8   Niebuhr, *The Essential Reinhold Niebuhr*, 251.

9   Taken from the Alcoholics Anonymous Web site, www.aa.org.

10 Linda Hutcheon, *A Theory of Adaptation* (London: Routledge, 2006), xvi; cf. 173.

11 Hutcheon, *A Theory of Adaptation*, xvi.

12 Robert Alter, *Canon and Creativity: Modern Writing and the Authority of Scripture* (New Haven: Yale University Press, 2000), 5–6.

13 Umberto Eco, *On Literature*, trans. Martin McLaughlin (Orlando: Harcourt, 2004), 157.

14 Eco, *On Literature*, 159, 160.

Introduction

1   Kerouac likely based this character on the Beat playwright and poet, Alan Ansen.

2   Jack Kerouac, *On the Road* (New York: Penguin, 1991 [original publication, 1957]), 115.

3   Kerouac, *On the Road*, 115 (ellipses not in brackets are original).

4   I take the term, and this particular sense of it, from Northrop Frye: "I think it advisable for every critic proposing to devote his life to literary scholarship to pick a major writer of literature as a kind of spiritual preceptor for himself, whatever the subject of his thesis. I am not speaking,

of course, of any sort of moral model, but it seems to me that growing up inside a mind so large that one has no sense of claustrophobia within it is an irreplaceable experience in humane studies" (*Spiritus Mundi: Essays on Literature, Myth, and Society* [Bloomington: Indiana University Press, 1976], 15).

5 Kerouac, *On the Road*, 187–88 (italics original). Dean is referring here to an alto horn player in a San Francisco club (182–83).

6 Kerouac, *On the Road*, 116.

7 Kerouac, *On the Road*, 219, 159, 160.

8 Kerouac, *On the Road*, 242.

9 Kerouac, *On the Road*, 115.

10 Sam Shepard, *The Rolling Thunder Logbook* (Cambridge, Mass.: Da Capo, 2004), 115.

11 The program originally aired December 5, 2004. Citations are taken from excerpts and transcripts of the interview available at the CBS Web site. See "Dylan Looks Back: Music Legend Talks to Ed Bradley in His First TV Interview in 19 Years."

12 Bob Dylan, *Chronicles: Volume One* (New York: Simon & Schuster, 2004), 9.

13 Dylan, *Chronicles*, 34.

14 From the song "Where Are You Tonight? (Journey through Dark Heat)," *Street Legal*, 1978. I take these words from Bob Dylan's *Lyrics: 1962–2001* (New York: Simon & Schuster, 2004), 394–95. As much as possible, I cite song lyrics from album liner notes, official artist Web sites, or separately published sources (as in the case of Dylan's *Lyrics*), and I indicate this in notes. When these are not available, I offer my own transcriptions but do not identify them as such.

15 "Every Grain of Sand," *Shot of Love*, 1981. See Dylan, *Lyrics*, 451.

16 Cole Porter and Robert Fletcher, "Don't Fence Me In" (1934). There are many recordings of this song. For an outstanding example, reference the performance by Canadian jazz singer Holly Cole on her album *Romantically Helpless* (2000).

17 Salman Rushdie, *The Ground Beneath Her Feet* (Toronto: Alfred A. Knopf, 1999), 19–20.

18 Harold Bloom, *The Anxiety of Influence: A Theory of Poetry*, 2nd ed. (Oxford: Oxford University Press, 1997), 26 (emphasis in original). Graham Allen provides helpful introductions to Bloom's thought in *Harold Bloom: A Poetics of Conflict* (New York: Harvester Wheatsheaf, 1994) and *Intertextuality: The New Critical Idiom* (London: Routledge, 2000), 133–44. For a succinct discussion of Bloom's concept of "the anxiety of influence," see also M. H. Abrams, with Geoffrey Galt Harpham, *A Glossary of Literary Terms*, 8th ed. (Toronto: Thomas Nelson, 2005), 132–34.

19 Bloom describes six "revisionary ratios," the first two of which I have in mind in this context. Clinamen involves poetic "misreading or misprision" and describes a poet swerving away from a literary precursor in what appears as a "corrective movement" in the later work. Tessera involves completion and antithesis, as the later poet uses the terms of an earlier work but "in another sense, as though the precursor had failed to go far enough" (*The Anxiety of Influence*, 14; for short summaries of all six revisionary ratios, see 14–16).

20 I return to and elaborate on connections to Rushdie's *The Ground Beneath Her Feet* and Bloom's *The Anxiety of Influence* below.

21 Daniel Lanois, spoken preface to "Sacred and Secular," *Here Is What Is* (2008). This CD is the soundtrack to Lanois' film of the same name.

22 Keith Urban, "God's Been Good to Me," *Be Here* (2004).

23 See, for example, the videos "Demonoid Phenomenon" and "Spookshow Baby," both included in Rob Zombie, *Past, Present & Future* (2003; a package that includes a CD and a DVD).

24 See the DVD *Vertigo 2005: U2 Live from Chicago* (2005). This concert also includes Bono giving a mini-sermon on Abraham, a figure of importance in Judaism, Christianity, and Islam.

25 See the Martin Scorsese film of that name (1978; 2002).

26 Mark D. Hulsether, "Like a Sermon: Popular Religion in Madonna Videos," in *Religion and Popular Culture in America*, ed. Bruce David Forbes and Jeffrey H. Mahan (Berkeley: University of California Press, 2000), 77. Not everyone welcomes the attention scholars give to pop-culture media, something Hulsether knows all too well. After stating his thesis, he anticipates some readers will launch into "a jeremiad about the nihilism and vacuity of scholars these days," and begins his apology of the project in light of this anticipated response.

27 Paul Martens, "Metallica and the God that Failed: An Unfinished Tragedy in Three Acts," in *Call Me the Seeker: Listening to Religion in Popular Music*, ed. Michael J. Gilmour (New York: Continuum, 2005), 95.

28 Robin Sylvan, *Traces of the Spirit: The Religious Dimensions of Popular Music* (New York: New York University Press, 2002), 114.

29 Jeremy S. Begbie, *Resounding Truth: Christian Wisdom in the World of Music*, Engaging Culture (Grand Rapids: Baker, 2007), 24.

30 Begbie, *Resounding Truth*, 24–25.

31 Keith Negus, "Living, Breathing Songs: Singing Along with Bob Dylan," *Oral Tradition* 22.1 (2007): 72.

32 I referred to Bob Dylan's *Lyrics* already. Other examples include Nick Cave, *The Complete Lyrics: 1978–2006* (London: Penguin Books, 2007); Leonard Cohen, *Book of Longing* (Toronto: McClelland & Stewart, 2006); Ani DiFranco, *Verses* (New York: Seven Stories Press, 2007); Alicia Keys,

Tears for Water: Songbook of Poems and Lyrics (New York: Penguin, 2004); Gordon Downie (of the Tragically Hip), *Coke Machine Glow* (Toronto: Vintage Canada, 2001); Metallica, *Metallica: The Complete Lyrics* (New York: Cherry Lane Music, 2002); Sting, *Lyrics* (New York: The Dial Press, 2007); Tom Waits, *The Lyrics of Tom Waits: The Early Years* (New York: HarperCollins, 2007).

33 See, e.g., B. P. Nichol, *An H in the Heart: A Reader*, selected by George Bowering and Michael Ondaatje, The Modern Canadian Poets Series (Toronto: M & S, 1994). I mention Nichol as an example because many of his works are handwritten and include doodles/pictures alongside words.

34 See also comments about the liner notes to George Harrison's 2002 album *Brainwashed* in track four.

35 The line of argument presented here presupposes music buyers have access to album art and liner notes available with CDs. Many download their music now, of course, and this changes the dynamics. Though some downloads available from Web sites such as iTunes include "digital booklets," with lyrics and photos, most do not. I thank my friend Joey Royal for this observation.

36 Taken from *The Norton Anthology of English Literature: The Major Authors*, ed. Stephen Greenblatt, M. H. Abrams, et al., 8th ed. (New York: Norton, 2006), 629.

37 There are further allusions to Donne's tolling bell image on Meat Loaf's *Bat Out of Hell III: The Monster Is Loose* (2006), the third album in the *Bat* trilogy. Note the songs "Cry to Heaven" ("toll a bell") and "The Future Ain't What It Used to Be" ("toll a bell for the brokenhearted").

38 Colin Larkin describes Nine Inch Nails' album *The Downward Spiral* as "a fascinating soundscape for [Trent] Reznor's exploration of human degradation through sex, drugs, violence, depression and suicide, closing with personal emotional pain on 'Hurt'" (compiler and ed., *The Encyclopedia of Popular Music*, 5th concise ed. [London: Omnibus Press, 2007], 1037).

39 Simon Frith, *Performing Rites: On the Value of Popular Music* (Cambridge: Harvard University Press, 1996), 164.

40 Frith, *Performing Rites*, 165. For his full discussion, see chap. 8, "Songs as Texts."

41 Hutcheon makes a similar observation about Springsteen's song in *Adaptation*, 145.

42 Frith, *Performing Rites*, 166 (emphasis in original).

43 See, e.g., Steve Stockman, *Walk On: The Spiritual Journey of U2*, updated and expanded ed. (Orlando: Relevant Books, 2005), 2, 63–64. Frith mentions an interesting misreading of Beethoven in *Performing Rites*, 109 (with n. 25).

44 Gordon Lynch reminds us that studies of religion in media and popular culture often assume that defining religion is a straightforward task, lacking in nuance. He observes the tendency in these studies to define religion in one of three ways. The first are substantive models of religion that focus on the identification of "core elements" in the sociocultural systems recognized as religious practice and belief. The second is an emphasis on phenomenological dimensions of religion, and attention to "the lived experience and perceptions of people in relation to religion and the sacred." As Lynch notes, a phenomenological approach is a middle position between the substantive and his third category, a functionalist approach. The emphasis here is on what religion does. This allows for "the possibility that any sociocultural system which serves . . . basic 'religious' needs for community, identity and meaning could be defined as religious, even though it may fall far outside the conventional canon of religions" (Gordon Lynch, "What Is This 'Religion' in the Study of Religion and Popular Culture?" in *Between the Sacred and Profane: Research Religion and Popular Culture*, ed. Gordon Lynch [London: I.B. Tauris, 2007], 125, 126–28). The present study tends to discuss religion in this third sense, though as Lynch points out, a functionalist approach is not without its problems (131–32).

45 "There is a realization that strikes one sometimes while surfing the net late at night as you come to understand that someone out there has written a detailed synopsis of every episode of *The Simpsons*, that someone has catalogued Bob Dylan's every concert performance for the last forty years. . . . It really is a strange world out there, there really are a lot of different people, with a lot of different points of view and a lot of different beliefs and concerns and cares and worries. Some of those people have a lot to say about Elvis Presley. . . . What the internet makes clear is that interest in Elvis, both religious and non-religious, is not really an aberration, but instead part of the incredible variety of phenomena, religious and secular, that make up everyday life in this weird world of democratic and technological individualism that many of us call home" (Gregory L. Reece, *Elvis Religion: The Cult of the King* [London: I.B. Tauris, 2006], 135, 136).

46 Compare, e.g., Deena Weinstein on this point: "The experience of the concert is charismatic. The artists on stage are rock-and-roll heroes to their fans, who adore and identify with them. The power of the band's music and the allure of its members' life-style are an inseparable unity for the fan who aspires to become like them" (Deena Weinstein, *Heavy Metal: A Cultural Sociology* [New York: Lexington Books, 1991], 59).

47 Townshend's comments about "Jools and Jim" appear in the liner notes to the greatest hits package, *Pete Townshend Gold* (2005).

48 Allison, *The Love There That's Sleeping*, 14–15. There are in fact some interesting examples of prominent musicians with academic credentials. Art Garfunkel has a master's degree in mathematics (Larkin, *Encyclopedia*, 580). Sterling Morrison of The Velvet Underground earned a doctorate in medieval literature (Wayne Robins, *A Brief History of Rock, Off the Record* [London: Routledge, 2008], 143). Milo Aukerman of the punk band Descendents has a doctorate in biochemistry (Larkin, *Encyclopedia*, 423). Greg Graffin of Bad Religion has a doctorate from Cornell in zoology, and lectures at UCLA (see the UCLA Web site for details). Brian May of Queen completed a doctorate in astrophysics at London's Imperial College in 2007.

49 On the "accumulation of knowledge" and "cultural capital" by fans, see Frith, *Performing Rites*, 9. Frith makes the interesting observation in this context that music critics annoy fans not because they have different opinions at times but because they have "sanction to state them" and a forum to do so. The same is true of academics.

50 Susan Fast, *In the Houses of the Holy: Led Zeppelin and the Power of Rock Music* (Oxford: Oxford University Press, 2001), 203. For her questionnaire, see 203–6.

51 Robert Walser, *Running With the Devil: Power, Gender and Madness in Heavy Metal Music* (Hanover and London: Wesleyan University Press / University Press of New England, 1993).

52 Robert Hunter, "Foreword," in *The Complete Annotated Grateful Dead Lyrics*, ed. Alan Trist and David Dodd, annotations by David Dodd (New York: Free Press, 2005), xi.

53 William Echard, *Neil Young and the Poetics of Energy* (Bloomington: Indiana University Press, 2005), 2–3. Echard takes the term "scholar-fan" from Richard Middleton's "Popular Music Analysis and Musicology: Bridging the Gap," *Popular Music* 12.2 (1993): 177–90.

54 Echard, *Neil Young*, 3.

55 Paul Nonnekes, *Three Moments of Love in Leonard Cohen and Bruce Cockburn* (Montreal: Black Rose Books, 2001), 179 (emphasis added).

56 Sylvan, *Traces of the Spirit*, 3. For reasons why religionists should take an interest in popular culture generally, see, e.g., Bruce David Forbes, "Introduction: Finding Religion in Unexpected Places," in *Religion and Popular Culture in America*, ed. Bruce David Forbes and Jeffrey H. Mahan (Berkeley: University of California Press, 2000), 1–20; and Lynn Schofield Clark, "Why Study Popular Culture?: Or, How to Build a Case for Your Thesis in a Religious Studies or Theology Department," in *Between Sacred and Profane: Researching Religion and Popular Culture*, ed. Gordon Lynch (London: I. B. Tauris, 2007). For reflections from a Christian theological perspective, see, e.g., William D. Romanowski, *Eyes Wide Open: Looking*

for God in Popular Culture, rev. and expanded ed. (Grand Rapids: Brazos, 2007).

57 Don E. Saliers, *Music and Theology*, Horizons in Theology (Nashville: Abingdon, 2007), xi, 55.

58 Saliers, *Music and Theology*, 60.

59 Saliers, *Music and Theology*, ix; cf. 61.

60 Mark Allan Powell, *Encyclopedia of Contemporary Christian Music* (Peabody, Mass.: Hendrickson, 2002), 8 (emphasis in original).

61 Allison, *The Love There That's Sleeping*, 3.

62 Allison, *The Love There That's Sleeping*, 133.

63 After all, our cultural judgments can be "self-revealing." For discussion, see Frith, *Performing Rites*, 5.

64 Jennifer Rycenga, "Tales of Change within the Sound: Form, Lyrics, and Philosophy in the Music of Yes," in *Progressive Rock Reconsidered*, ed. Kevin Holm-Hudson (London: Routledge, 2002), 148. See full comments on this point, 147–50.

65 *Rolling Stone* 986 (November 2005): 20.

66 David B. Knight, *Landscapes in Music: Space, Place, and Time in the World's Great Music* (Lanham, Md.: Rowman & Littlefield, 2006), 210, vii.

67 For my full argument, see "Going Back to the Prairies: Neil Young's Heterotopia in the Post-9/11 World," in *West of Eden: New Approaches in Canadian Prairie Literature*, ed. Sue Sorensen (Winnipeg: Canadian Mennonite University Press, 2008), 205–18.

68 Echard, *Neil Young*, 205.

69 Young's song about his sentimental attachment to an old musical instrument is consistent with his preference for vintage musical equipment. Echard suggests old instruments provide a way of "sonically encoding nostalgia" (*Neil Young*, 79; cf. 51–52). Young prefaces his performance of "This Old Guitar" on *Neil Young: Heart of Gold* by noting that the instrument he plays is one that belonged to Hank Williams. There is also a picture of that guitar on the *Prairie Wind* liner notes.

70 Kelton Cobb, *The Blackwell Guide to Theology and Popular Culture*, Blackwell Guides to Theology (Malden, Mass.: Blackwell, 2005), 211.

71 My friend Gary Conway kindly directed me to this concert featuring Neil Young and Willie Nelson, and I am grateful to him for this and for his many other tips and suggestions.

72 Taken from the official Willie Nelson Web site (www.willienelson.com). Nelson wrote these lines on Christmas Day 2003, first performed "Whatever Happened to Peace on Earth" in 2004, but did not release the song until 2006.

73 Other singers refer to the government's questionable evidence about weapons of mass destruction in Iraq. Consider, e.g., Tom Morello's

phrase "Colin Powell's lies" in the song "House Gone Up in Flames" (*One Man Revolution*, 2007; he sings under the name The Nightwatchman for this album). Sheryl Crow refers to a war based on lies in "God Bless this Mess" (*Detours*, 2008).

Track 1

1 Rushdie, *The Ground Beneath Her Feet*, 390.
2 Rushdie, *The Ground Beneath Her Feet*, 390.
3 Rushdie, *The Ground Beneath Her Feet*, 391.
4 Roger Y. Clark, *Stranger Gods: Salman Rushdie's Other Worlds* (Montreal and Kingston: McGill-Queen's University Press, 2001), 198.
5 Salman Rushdie, *Step Across This Line: Collected Nonfiction 1992–2002* (Toronto: Alfred A. Knopf Canada, 2002), 95.
6 Rushdie, *Step Across This Line*, 89, 91. Rushdie first published this essay in 1995.
7 Salman Rushdie, *The Satanic Verses* (New York: Picador, 1988), 4; cf. 10. The Rolling Stones' song "Sympathy for the Devil" appears on the album *Beggars Banquet* (1968). On the echoes of "Sympathy for the Devil" in *The Satanic Verses*, see Clark, *Stranger Gods*, 146, 164, 174–75.
8 Rushdie, *Satanic Verses*, 10.
9 Larry Norman, "Why Should the Devil (Have All the Good Music)," *Only Visiting This Planet*, 1972. Cliff Richard's well-known cover of this song appears on *Small Corners*, 1978.
10 Rushdie, *Step Across This Line*, 93.
11 The poem appears in the novel on p. 475.
12 For Rushdie's comments about this, see his article "U2" in *Step Across This Line*, 94–98.
13 Rushdie, *Step Across This Line*, 95.
14 Taken from www.u2.com.
15 Graham Allen and Roy Sellars, "Harold Bloom and Critical Responsibility," in *The Salt Companion to Harold Bloom*, ed. Graham Allen and Roy Sellars (Cambridge: Salt, 2007), xiii.
16 Bloom, *The Anxiety of Influence*, xxiv.
17 Harold Bloom, *Genius: A Mosaic of One Hundred Exemplary Creative Minds* (New York: Warner, 2002), 476.
18 Again, I am aware that defining songwriters as poets, and song lyrics as poetry, is a contested matter, but I will persist in using these terms interchangeably just the same. For a clear, concise argument for the view that lyrics are not poetry, see Frith, *Performing Rites*, 181–82. For another perspective, consider, for example, the serious analyses of poetic qualities in Bob Dylan's lyrics by Aidan Day (*Jokerman: Reading the Lyrics of Bob Dylan* [Oxford: Basil Blackwell, 1988]), Christopher Ricks (*Dylan's Visions*

of Sin), and Stephen Scobie (in *Alias Bob Dylan Revisited* [Calgary: Red Deer Press, 2003]).

19 Harold Bloom, *The Western Canon: The Books and School of the Ages* (New York: Riverhead, 1994), 7.

20 Bob Dylan, "It's Alright, Ma (I'm Only Bleeding)," *Bringing It All Back Home* (1965). Taken from Dylan, *Lyrics*, 157.

21 Cf. Bob Dylan, "Trust Yourself," *Empire Burlesque* (1985). Taken from Dylan, *Lyrics*, 497.

22 Consider, e.g., the impressive solo acoustic performance at Madison Square Garden released on *Bob Dylan: The 30th Anniversary Concert Celebration* (1993; CD and DVD formats).

23 Nor is the use of music as a vehicle for social commentary and critique unique to the 1960s.

24 Don Lattin, *Following Our Bliss: How the Spiritual Ideals of the Sixties Shape Our Lives Today* (New York: HarperCollins, 2003), 3.

25 Lattin, *Following Our Bliss*, 29–44 (Catholicism), Eastern spiritualities (63–110), rock and roll as a vehicle for transcendence (114, 173–83), Sun Myung Moon (189–204), Jim Jones (95–97).

26 Mark Oppenheimer, *Knocking on Heaven's Door: American Religion in the Age of Counterculture* (New Haven: Yale University Press, 2003), 26. On his rationale for focusing on mainstream religion, see further, 11–14.

27 Oppenheimer, *Knocking on Heaven's Door*, 7.

28 Sylvan, *Traces of the Spirit*, 3, 5 (emphasis added). Sylvan examines the musical subcultures associated with The Grateful Dead (Deadheads), club/dance music (raves), heavy metal, and rap/hip-hop culture, tracing the roots of American popular music back to West African possession religion.

29 Robert Detweiler and David Jasper, editorial introduction, *Religion and Literature: A Reader* (Louisville, Ky.: Westminster John Knox, 2000), xiii–iv (emphasis added).

30 Sylvan, *Traces of the Spirit*, 78, 81. In support of this point, he cites, among others, Andrew Greeley, *God in Popular Culture* (Chicago: Thomas More, 1988); and Jon Wiley Nelson, *Your God Is Alive and Well and Appearing in Popular Culture* (Philadelphia: Westminster Press, 1976).

31 Bruce David Forbes and Jeffrey H. Mahan, eds., *Religion and Popular Culture in America* (Berkeley: University of California Press, 2000), 163. See also the four essays in part 3 of this book.

32 Taken from the album liner notes.

33 Larkin, *Encyclopedia of Popular Music*, 1047.

34 Sinéad O'Connor made these remarks on the television program "The Hour," in conversation with interviewer George Stroumboulopoulos, January 22, 2008. See the Canadian Broadcasting Corporation Web site,

cbc.ca/thehour. O'Connor stole the Bible, she explains, because logically "it should be free" since God "isn't getting the royalties." Makes sense.

35 Peter Gzowski interviewed Burton Cummings on April 12, 1996 on the radio program *Morningside* (Canadian Broadcasting Corporation). I discuss this interview further at a later point.

36 The Who, "The Seeker," *Meaty Beaty Big and Bouncy* (1971).

37 Consider, for instance, the lyrics to John Lennon, "God" (*John Lennon/Plastic Ono Band*, 1970); Pantera, "Slaughtered" (*Far Beyond Driven*, 1994); and Bad Religion, "Atheist Peace" (*The Empire Strikes First*, 2004), to name but a few.

38 Stephen H. Webb, *Dylan Redeemed: From* Highway 61 *to* Saved (London: Continuum, 2006), 16 and 17, n. 11.

39 Oppenheimer, *Knocking on Heaven's Door*, 2 and 4.

40 Oppenheimer, *Knocking on Heaven's Door*, 4 (emphasis in original).

41 Rushdie, *The Ground Beneath Her Feet*, 20.

42 Sylvan, *Traces of the Spirit*, 67.

43 Robbie Fulks, "God Isn't Real," *Let's Kill Saturday Night* (1998). Lyrics taken from robbiefulks.com. It is a little unusual to find such an explicit denial of the existence of God in the context of country music.

44 Larkin, *Encyclopedia*, 98.

45 Nine Inch Nails, "Heresy," *The Downward Spiral* (1994); Gary Numan, "A Prayer for the Unborn," *Hybrid* (2003); Gary Numan, "The Angel Wars," *Exile* (1998).

46 These comments appear at the band's official Web site, http://www.billytalent.com.

47 There are numerous books examining U2's Christian worldview, among them Christian Scharen, *One Step Closer: Why U2 Matters to Those Seeking God* (Grand Rapids: Brazos, 2006); and Stockman, *Walk On*.

48 Bob Dylan, "Dignity," from *Bob Dylan's Greatest Hits,* vol. 3 (1994); *Unplugged* (1995); and *Tell Tale Signs,* The Bootleg Series, vol. 8 (2008). See *Lyrics*, 540–41.

49 West engages religion in other songs and albums, most famously in "Jesus Walks" (*The College Dropout*, 2004).

50 For an earlier version of the following argument, see my article "Arcade Fire's Parodic Bible," *Journal of Religion and Popular Culture* 20 (forthcoming).

51 Arcade Fire won a Juno (Canadian equivalent of a Grammy Award) in 2008 for *Neon Bible* in the category Alternative Album of the Year.

52 Mikhail Bakhtin, *Rabelais and His World*, trans. Helene Iswolsky (Bloomington: Indiana University Press, 1984), 6.

53 Cobb, *The Blackwell Guide to Theology and Popular Culture*, esp. 213–20.

54 Abrams, *Glossary of Literary Terms*, 145.

55 Cobb, *The Blackwell Guide to Theology and Popular Culture*, 220, 227.

56 Cobb, *The Blackwell Guide to Theology and Popular Culture*, 227–28.

57 "The official feasts of the Middle Ages, whether ecclesiastic, feudal, or sponsored by the state, did not lead the people out of the existing world order and created no second life. On the contrary, they sanctioned the existing pattern of things and reinforced it" (Bakhtin, *Rabelais and His World*, 9).

58 According to Bakhtin, sacred parody was common in medieval times (*Rabelais and His World*, 14).

59 Linda Hutcheon, *A Theory of Parody: The Teachings of Twentieth-Century Art Forms* (Urbana: University of Illinois Press, 2000), 5, 20.

60 Linda Hutcheon, *A Poetics of Postmodernism: History, Theory, Fiction* (New York: Routledge, 1988), 26 (emphasis in original).

61 Hutcheon, *Poetics of Postmodernism*, 210–11.

62 I will use lower case for the word *bible* as a category. I will use upper case when referring to the Christian Scriptures or the album and song titles that include the term.

63 Sean Michaels reports that, "while touring the world on the heels of their debut full-length, *Funeral*—Arcade Fire bought and renovated [a] church in the middle of nowhere [the Petite Église church in Farnham, a town about 80 kilometres outside of Montréal]. And they began working on some new songs" ("Arcade Fire: Inside the Church of Arcade Fire," *Paste Magazine* 30, published online April 11, 2007, http://www.pastemaga zine.com/action/article/4047/feature/music/arcade_fire).

64 This was not the band's first experience performing their music in churches. They launched their earlier album *Funeral* (2004) in one. When asked about this, Win Butler offered the following: "We wanted to play in a different space, and my friend Anita, who used to play harp with us, told me that when she was younger she saw Petra play at a church—they're this shitty Christian rock band. So that got me thinking about finding a local church we could play" (from an interview conducted by Lorraine Carpenter, "Hot Property: Montreal's Next Big Thing, The Arcade Fire, Channel Familial Grief and Internal Upheaval into an Ecstatic Debut Album," *Montreal Mirror* 20.13, September 16–22, 2004, http://www .montrealmirror.com/2004/091604/cover_music.html).

65 The band acknowledges that the name *Neon Bible* is the title of a John Kennedy Toole novel and they use it with the publisher's permission. However, Win Butler denies any connection, claiming the album's concept is independent of the book: "I had that image in my mind before" (taken from Ryan Adams, "Arcade Fire," *Interview* 37.7 [2007]: 101).

66 Gavin Edwards, "The Magnificent Seven," *Rolling Stone* 1027 (2007): 63–64, 66–67.

67 Carpenter, "Hot Property." Larkin reports the same thing: "Butler relocated to Montreal, Canada to study religion and Russian literature at McGill University, where he began working with Régine Chassagne . . . a student of medieval music" (*Encyclopedia of Popular Music*, 66).

68 Taken from Adams, "Arcade Fire," 101. Butler does not define what he means by counterculture in this context, and the band does not offer any clear alternative to the religious expressions they criticize in *Neon Bible*.

69 Are these the "salesmen" mentioned in the song "Windowsill," included on the same album?

70 A nun forced Régine Chassagne of Arcade Fire—Win Butler's wife—to play organ when she was a child. She says of the experience, "the sister was really intense, like she was going to have a heart attack any minute. I wanted to sing so bad—I love singing!—but she made me replace the organ player, and I was only 10 or 12" (Carpenter, "Hot Property"). Her experience resembles the plight of characters in the *Neon Bible* songs who encounter religious authority figures who force them into situations they would rather avoid, most obviously the thirteen-year-old "mocking bird" mentioned in "(Antichrist Television Blues)."

71 See, e.g., Allison Stewart, "Arcade Fire's 'Bible': A Searing Success," Special to *The Washington Post*, Sunday, March 11, 2007, http://www.washingtonpost.com/wp-dyn/content/article/2007/03/09/AR2007030900480.html: "The sprawling, masterly '(Antichrist Television Blues)' somehow conflates 9/11, God, television and Joe Simpson—the father of Ashlee and Jessica—into a tale of a struggling father who sees his talented daughter as a ticket out of downtown Manhattan, where planes might crash at any minute."

72 In the song immediately following "(Antichrist Television Blues)," the narrator wonders what MTV has done to him ("Windowsill"). This song appears to continue the story told in "(Antichrist Television Blues)" with its ongoing interest in television. If so, the narrator of "Windowsill" could be the voice of a now repentant father no longer wanting to hear the noise the television makes. The TV screen/MTV presents him with a world of temptations that include easy money, and he seems to blame this commercial/entertainment culture for destroying his values: "MTV, what have you done to me?"

An impending judgment frightens the narrator of "Windowsill" (though he is not sure whether it will be fire or water [cf. 2 Pet 3:5-7] or "World War III"), and he may even be suicidal because he wonders why he swallowed a pill. He longs to escape the noise, the "salesmen," and the debt in his father's house and does not want to live "in America no more," which seems to be a criticism of the American entertainment industry and consumer culture more than a political statement. With reference to Bakhtin, it is noteworthy that Butler does not allow this voice of conscience to disappear. The song presents a dialogue between these two (commercial and genuine) forms of religion.

73 Cf. the previous note. The idea of a future calamity appears also in "Black Mirror," where the singer refers to a future time when "words will lose their meaning."

74 Remarks by Win Butler fit well in this connection: "There are two kinds of fear: The Bible talks a lot about fear of God—fear in the face of something awesome. That kind of fear is the type of fear that makes someone want to change. But a fear of other people makes you want to stay the same, to protect what you have. It's a stagnant fear; and it's paralyzing" (Win Butler, interview with Michaels, "Arcade Fire").

75 This song reminds me of anecdotes I have heard about the traumatic experiences of those who watched Donald W. Thompson's rapture movie *A Thief in the Night* (1972) as children. Undoubtedly, a new generation of children is experiencing similar anxieties because of the books and movies in the Left Behind franchise. In both of these examples, religious teachers emphasize aspects of a future judgment.

76 As in the hymn, "Onward Christian Soldier" (words by Sabine Baring-Gould, music by Arthur Sullivan, 1871).

77 Hutcheon, *Parody*, 115.

Track 2

1 Rushdie, *The Ground Beneath Her Feet*, 19.

2 For instance, J. R. C. Cousland argues that the sometimes-disturbing lyrics of Nick Cave and P. J. Harvey "aim to shock and discomfit their listeners," and in the process of adopting what he calls an aesthetic of the grotesque, "the unrighteous and the unlovely are dwelt upon to evoke their alternatives." By concentrating on evil and violence, these songwriters call attention "to the need for redemption in the actual lives that humans lead." Furthermore, the "focus of both artists upon the evil, the grotesque, and the unlovely in human experience has led both to consider what is implicit in the other side of the grotesque—the beautiful, the divine, and the lovely" ("God, the Bad, and the Ugly: The *Vi(t)a Negativa* of Nick Cave and P. J. Harvey," in *Call Me the Seeker: Listening to Religion in Popular Music*, ed. Michael J. Gilmour [New York: Continuum, 2005], 129, 152).

3 John Lennon, "Imagine" (*Imagine*, 1971).

4 Several other songs in the John Lennon catalogue present this antireligion sentiment, among them "I Found Out" (*John Lennon/Plastic Ono Band*, 1970), "Serve Yourself," "The Great Wok," and "The Rishi Kesh Song" (*John Lennon Anthology*, 1998). The contrast between John Lennon's

cynicism and George Harrison's devout Hinduism in the early 1970s is striking. For comments on their "complex relationship," see Allison, *The Love There That's Sleeping*, 50–54 (50).

5   Taken from the official U2 Web site (www.u2.com).

6   David Chidester, "The Church of Baseball, the Fetish of Coca-Cola, and the Potlach of Rock 'n' Roll," in *Religion and Popular Culture in America*, ed. Bruce David Forbes and Jeffrey H. Mahan (Berkeley: University of California Press, 2000), 228.

7   Chidester, "The Church of Baseball," 228.

8   Lyrics are available at the artist's Web site, www.paulsimon.com.

9   Frith, *Performing Rites*, 168.

10 National Public Radio program World Café. The interview first aired November 23, 2006. See http://www.npr.org/templates/story/story .php?storyId=6533879.

11 Presumably, the songwriters had in mind stories about Jesus multiplying bread for crowds of four and five thousand hungry people (Matt 14:13-21, 15:32-39; Mark 6:30-44, 8:1-10; Luke 9:10-17; John 6:1-14). However, it was Satan, not God, who urged Jesus to turn stones to bread (Matt 4:3; Luke 4:3), something that he chose not to do. This does not change the emotive force of the overall argument or the poignancy of the metaphor.

12 John Milton, *The Poetical Works of John Milton*, ed. Charles Dexter Cleveland (Ann Arbor: University of Michigan Library, 2006), 500.

13 Fast, *In the Houses of the Holy*, 60. Fast is here citing Edward Macan, *Rocking the Classics: English Progressive Rock and the Counterculture* (New York: Oxford University Press, 1997), 73.

14 E.g., allusions to J. R. R. Tolkien's *Lord of the Rings* trilogy appear in various songs, including "Battle of Evermore," "Misty Mountain Hop," "Over the Hills and Far Away," and "Ramble On."

15 Fast, *In the Houses of the Holy*, 60. Fast's citation of Jimmy Page is from a 1970 interview, quoted in Robert Godwin, *Led Zeppelin: The Press Reports* (Burlington, Ontario: CG, 1997), 96.

16 For the words to the song, see Dylan, *Lyrics*, 75. Dylan recorded "Seven Curses" in 1963 but did not release it until 1991 (*The Bootleg Series, Volumes 1–3, Rare and Unreleased 1961–1991*). For the most thorough and significant commentary on "Seven Curses," see Ricks, *Dylan's Visions of Sin*, 233–46.

17 See liner notes for lyrics.

18 Frith, *Performing Rites*, 112.

19 Frith, *Performing Rites*, 303n38. See also pp. 224–25.

20 Bill Flanagan, *U2 at the End of the World* (New York: Delta, 1995), 427. Eamon Dunphy adds the details that "Greg had been with the band eighteen months. He looked after Bono, on stage and off. They were friends" (*Unforgettable Fire: The Story of U2* [London: Penguin, 1987], 346).

21 Robbie Robertson, with Martin Page, "Fallen Angel," *Robbie Robertson*, 1987.

22 For his account of the story, see Eric Clapton, *Clapton: The Autobiography* (New York: Broadway Books, 2007), 229–46.

23 For lyrics, see the artist's Web site, www.davidgray.com. The imagery in this song is not unique. Compare, e.g., The Doors' "Break On Through (To the Other Side)" (*The Doors*, 1967) and Ozzy Osbourne's "See You On the Other Side" (*Ozzmosis*, 1995).

24 Comment made on the artist's Web site.

25 Andrew Dansby, "David Gray's 'New Day': Death and Success Share Spotlight on New Album," *Rolling Stone* (www.rollingstone.com).

26 Saliers, *Music and Theology*, x.

27 See Calvin Klein and Bryan Adams, *American Woman* (Brooklyn: Powerhouse Books, 2005).

28 Bob Geldof, *Geldof in Africa* (London: Arrow Books, 2005).

29 Geldof offers this striking description of the event that celebrates the potential of musicians and music to mobilize humanitarian efforts: "We were led [to efforts on behalf of Africa] by our bands, by musicians who articulate us better than we can ourselves. They talk a global language of understanding understood by all humanity, and they have led us on this long twenty-year journey from Live Aid [July 13, 1985]. In their music is the sum of our longing for a universal decency. They communicate dismay and disgust at the daily carnival of dying that parades across our television screens. In the nightly pornography of poverty vast hundreds of thousands die annually simply because they are too poor to stay alive. What a glorious, magnificent day [Live 8, July 2, 2005]. What a rejection of the defeat of cynicism, I thought as I watched the TV monitor side stage showing me four continents, nine countries and their greatest artists, nine cities and their greatest sites, millions physically present and thousands of millions spiritually there as they watched this one concert, one moment, one idea winding itself around what was truly one world that afternoon" (Geldof, *Africa*, 295).

30 There is a link to video of this speech at www.georgeharrison.com.

31 Allison, *The Love There That's Sleeping*, 68.

32 Allison, *The Love There That's Sleeping*, 69.

33 George Harrison, *I Me Mine* (San Francisco: Chronicle Books, 2002), 224.

34 For this detail, and some of the logistics involved in organizing the event, see Harrison, *I Me Mine*, 59–61.

35 Aung San Suu Kyi and Alan Clements, *The Voice of Hope: Conversations with Alan Clements* (New York: Seven Stories, 1997), 132–33.

36 The lyrics to this song are included in the liner notes for *All That You Can't Leave Behind*. All of U2's song lyrics are also available at www.u2.com.

I develop more fully the argument put forward here in "The Prophet Jeremiah, Aung San Suu Kyi, and U2's *All That You Can't Leave Behind*: On Listening to Bono's Jeremiad," in *Call Me the Seeker: Listening to Religion in Popular Music*, ed. Michael J. Gilmour, 34–43 (London: Continuum, 2005), 34–43.

37 Aung San Suu Kyi, *Letters From Burma* (London: Penguin, 1997), 25.

38 For comments on this symbol, see, e.g., Robert Vagacs, *Religious Nuts, Political Fanatics: U2 in Theological Perspective* (Eugene, Ore.: Cascade Books, 2005), 59n2; Stockman, *Walk On*, 157.

39 Clements, in Suu Kyi and Clements, *The Voice of Hope*, 10.

40 Sylvan, *Traces of the Spirit*, 3–4, 4.

Track 3

1 On the oppositional tendency in popular music, see, e.g., Sylvan, *Traces of the Spirit*, 67.

2 John Lennon, "God," *John Lennon / Plastic Ono Band*, 1970.

3 Taken from Greene, *Here Comes the Sun*, 142. See too Allison, *The Love There That's Sleeping*, 155.

4 Lyrics taken from www.u2.com.

5 Taken from Flanagan, *U2 at the End of the World*, 270 (emphasis in original).

6 For other uses of the term "angel," consider Sarah McLachlan's beautiful "Angel" (*Surfacing*, 1997), and U2's "Angel of Harlem" (*Rattle and Hum*, 1988). The great jazz singer Billie Holiday is the inspiration for the latter (see the album liner notes).

7 See the liner notes to Sinéad O'Connor's *Theology* (2007).

8 Keys, "Lilly of the Valley," in *Tears for Water*, 21–22. Keys' comments about the poem appear on p. 23.

9 Keys, "Cosmopolitan Woman," in *Tears for Water*, 54; full text, 53–55.

10 Keys, "A Woman's Worth," in *Tears for Water*, 109–12.

11 Keys, "Slow Down," in *Tears for Water*, 163–64.

12 Keys, "Still Water," in *Tears for Water*, 57–58.

13 Keys, "Is It Insane?," in *Tears for Water*, 59–61.

14 For discussion of the biblical contexts and developments in later interpretation linking these women with sexual sin, see, e.g., Gail Corrington Streete, *The Strange Woman: Sex and Power in the Bible* (Louisville, Ky.: Westminster John Knox, 1997), esp. 62–65 on Jezebel and 161–64 on Mary Magdalene.

15 For an introduction, see Frances Finnegan, *Do Penance or Perish: Magdalen Asylums in Ireland* (New York: Oxford University Press, 2004).

16 From the "rockumentary" film *This Is Spinal Tap* (1984). The cover of the

album referred to features pictures of band members as part of stained glass windows, hands together in postures of prayer.

17 Taken from the liner notes to Iron Maiden, *The Number of the Beast* (1982).

18 Regarding the latter, see, e.g., Douglas E. Cowan, *Sacred Terror: Religion and Horror on the Silver Screen* (Waco, Tex.: Baylor University Press, 2008).

19 Mircea Eliade, *The Sacred and the Profane: The Nature of Religion*, trans. Willard R. Trask (New York: Harcourt Brace & World, 1959), 20–24.

20 Eliade, *The Sacred and the Profane*, 29.

21 Eliade, *The Sacred and the Profane*, 48.

22 Julia Kristeva, *The Portable Kristeva*, ed. Kelly Oliver, updated edition (New York: Columbia University Press, 2002), 283.

23 Kristeva, *The Portable Kristeva*, 283; cf. Sigmund Freud, "The Uncanny," *The Standard Edition of the Complete Psychological Works of Sigmund Freud*, vol. 17, trans. James Strachey et al. (1919; London: Hogarth, 1955), 220, 225.

24 Timothy K. Beal, *Religion and Its Monsters* (London: Routledge, 2002), 195.

25 Beal, *Religion and Its Monsters*, 4–5.

26 Echard, *Neil Young*, 26.

27 Echard, *Neil Young*, 26.

28 Echard, *Neil Young*, 26.

29 For a convenient introduction to individual bands—more than 270 of them—organized by subgenre, see Garry Sharpe-Young, *Metal: The Definitive Guide* (London: Jawbone Press, 2007). The categorization distinguishes bands using such terms as Heavy Metal (e.g., Black Sabbath and Judas Priest), NWOBHM (New Wave of British Heavy Metal; e.g., Grim Reaper and Iron Maiden), Thrash, Death, Grindcore, Black, and so on, divided further by various geographical regions (Swedish, Norwegian, Finnish, South and Central American, Japanese, etc.). The author of the foreword is Rob Halford of Judas Priest.

30 For a general introduction to some of the relevant considerations regarding genre classifications, see Frith, *Performing Rites*, 75–95. With reference to heavy metal music specifically, see Weinstein, *Heavy Metal*. Weinstein approaches this music through the makeup of its audiences. Robert Walser, on the other hand, analyzes heavy metal through conventions of performance (*Running with the Devil*, 1993). For discussion of the heavy metal subculture, see Sylvan, *Traces of the Spirit*, chap. 5.

31 Hutcheon, *A Theory of Parody*, 26.

32 Shuker, *Popular Music*, 132–33.

33 Shuker, *Popular Music*, 133.

34 Sylvan, *Traces of the Spirit*, 158, with reference to Jeffrey Jensen Arnett, *Metalheads: Heavy Metal Music and Adolescent Alienation* (Boulder: Westview Press, 1996), 97–98.

35 Christopher M. Moreman, "Devil Music and the Great Beast: Ozzy

Osbourne, Aleister Crowley, and the Christian Right," *Journal of Religion and Popular Culture* 5 (Fall 2003), http://www.usask.ca/relst/jrpc/art5-devilmusic.html.

36 Kevin Holm-Hudson, "Introduction," in *Progressive Rock Reconsidered*, ed. Kevin Holm-Hudson (London: Routledge, 2002), 15, drawing in part on Macan, *Rocking the Classics*.

37 John J. Sheinbaum, "Progressive Rock and the Inversion of Musical Values," in *Progressive Rock Reconsidered*, ed. Kevin Holm-Hudson (London: Routledge, 2002), 25, and in the same volume, Deena Weinstein, "Progressive Rock as Text: The Lyrics of Roger Waters," 92–93.

38 Sylvan, *Traces of the Spirit*, 158.

39 Taken from Doug Van Pelt, *Rock Stars On God: 20 Artists Speak Their Mind about Faith* (Orlando: Relevant Books, 2004), 151.

40 Walser, *Running with the Devil*, 151.

41 Alice Cooper, with Keith and Kent Zimmerman, *Alice Cooper, Golf Monster: A Rock 'N' Roller's 12 Steps to Becoming a Golf Addict* (New York: Crown, 2007), 197.

42 Pete Ward, "The Eucharist and the Turn to Culture," in *Between Sacred and Profane: Researching Religion and Popular Culture*, ed. Gordon Lynch (London: I. B. Tauris, 2007), 91.

43 Sylvan, *Traces of the Spirit*, 178.

44 Walser, *Running with the Devil*, 151.

45 Weinstein, *Heavy Metal*, 39. She adds later, "A significant part of metal's mythology revolves around the more apocalyptic strain of Christianity, especially the Book of Revelations [*sic*]" (129).

46 In addition to religious influences, Weinstein argues that the second major source for metal is secular entertainment: "Literature, especially the gothic horror stories of Edgar Allen [*sic*] Poe and the fantasy of H. P. Lovecourt and J. R. R. Tolkien, has inspired songs. Iron Maiden's 'Murder in the Rue Morgue,' for example, is a liberal and literal borrowing from Poe's story of that name. Sword and sorcery and horror movies, from *Conan the Barbarian* to *Friday the 13th*, have also inspired heavy metal lyrics. Heavy metal's debt to these movie genres, which themselves increasingly use heavy metal songs on their sound tracks, is particularly noticeable on album covers, posters, and stage sets" (40). It is interesting that Weinstein names Tolkien as an influence. Tolkien drew much from religious traditions in developing his stories. Some religious elements in heavy metal music, it follows, arrive indirectly, mediated through the stories that inform the artists. They do not indicate direct engagement with religious traditions.

47 Taken from the liner notes to Mötley Crüe's *Red, White & Crüe*, 2005.

48 Taken from the album liner notes.

49 Bloom, *Anxiety of Influence*, 14.

50 I take the lyrics from the album's liner notes.

51 Cooper, *Golf Monster*, 198.

52 Cooper, *Golf Monster*, 198.

53 As a point of interest, Cooper developed the concept found in this album in a three-part comic book series by Marvel Comics (written by The Sandman, created by Neil Gaiman, and drawn by Michael Zulli). According to *The Last Temptation* liner notes, these comics are "essential companion pieces to this Alice Cooper album." The CD includes a short sample.

54 www.velvetrevolver.com.

55 Taken from Greenblatt, Abrams, et al, eds., *Norton Anthology*, 8th ed., 727.

56 Cooper, *Golf Monster*, 205; cf. 82, 84, 94, 99–100, 198.

57 Flanagan, *U2 at the End of the World*, 434.

58 Cf. Cousland's remarks about Nick Cave and P. J. Harvey, cited in track 2.

59 Iron Maiden, "The Prisoner," *The Number of the Beast* (1982).

60 Alice Cooper, "Nothing's Free," *The Last Temptation* (1994). This description of freedom is ironic. As noted, this album explores Cooper's conversion to Christianity, and the one promoting this freedom is in fact a devilish figure. The story told in this song is analogous to the serpent in the garden, or the devil tempting Jesus during his time in the wilderness. It is still a fine description of the independence celebrated by hard rock music, even if Cooper is ultimately casting it in a negative light on this album.

61 The Sex Pistols, "Anarchy in the U.K.," *Never Mind the Bollocks, Here's the Sex Pistols* (1977). Mötley Crüe's cover of the song (with slight adaptation of the lyrics accommodating "U.S.A." for "U.K.") first appeared on the album *Decade of Decadence* (1991), and more recently on the compilation album *Red, White & Crüe* (2005).

Track 4

1 Burton Cummings, *Morningside*, with Peter Gzowski (Canadian Broadcasting Corporation, April 12, 1996). Cited with permission.

2 See, e.g., John Storm Roberts, *Black Music of Two Worlds: African, Caribbean, Latin, and African American Traditions*, 2nd rev. ed. (New York: Schirmer, 1998).

3 www.leonardcohen.com.

4 Weinstein, "Progressive Rock as Text," 102.

5 Sylvan, *Traces of the Spirit*, 178–79. See also 177.

6 Sylvan, *Traces of the Spirit*, 141.

7   John Einarson and Randy Bachman, *Randy Bachman: Takin' Care of Business* (Toronto: McArthur, 2000), 118.
8   Einarson and Bachman, *Randy Bachman*, 169.
9   The subitle for this section is a line from George Harrison's "Any Road," *Brainwashed* (2002). I take all citations of lyrics from the album's liner notes.
10   For an earlier version of the following discussion, see my short online article, *"Brainwashed*, by George Harrison and the *Bhagavad Gita*," *Journal of Religion and Popular Culture* 8 (2004), http://www.usask.ca/relst/jrpc.
11   "Words from Apple," introductory note to His Divine Grace A. C. Bhaktivedanta Swami Prabhupāda, *KRSNA: The Supreme Personality of Godhead* (New York: The Bhaktivedanta Book Trust, 1970). This note appears in volumes 1 and 2. Cf. *Bhagavad Gita* 2.70.
12   In the *Bhagavad Gita*, Krishna speaks of the positive influences his devotees have on one another: "Their thoughts are on me, their life is in me, and they give light to each other. For ever they speak of my glory; and they find peace and joy" (10.9). Prabhupāda says of such people, "Their minds cannot be diverted from the lotus feet of K[rishna]. Their talks are solely transcendental" (His Divine Grace A. C. Bhaktivedanta Swami Prabhupāda, *Bhagavad-Gītā As It Is* [New York: The Bhaktivedanta Book Trust, 1972], 167). The latter expression appears also in *Brainwashed* (in "Stuck Inside a Cloud"). This metaphor speaks of a student's devotion to a teacher. Swami Prabhupāda's name means "One at whose feet many masters sit" (F. Daner, *The American Children of Krsna* [New York: Holt, Rinehart and Winston, 1976], 17). He was one of a series of spiritual masters extending back to Lord Krishna himself (as stated in his publications, as on the book jacket to *Bhagavad-Gītā*).
13   His album *Dark Horse* (1974) includes the dedication "All Glories to Sri Krishna."
14   Adam Clayson, *The Quiet One: A Life of George Harrison* (London: Sidgwick & Jackson, 1990), 8.
15   See, e.g., Steve Turner, *The Gospel According to the Beatles* (Louisville Ky.: Westminster John Knox, 2006), esp. chaps. 8–10.
16   For various details, see, e.g., Kenneth Womack, *Long and Winding Roads: The Evolving Artistry of the Beatles* (London: Continuum, 2007), 216–17.
17   Harrison, *I Me Mine*, 258 (emphasis in original), 254, 256.
18   Juan Mascaró reads it this way (see his introduction to *The Bhagavad Gita*, trans. Juan Mascaró with updated introduction by Simon Brodbeck [London: Penguin, 2003], xlvi–xlvii; Mascaró's comments were originally published in the 1962 edition and reprinted in the 2003 edition). After seeing Harrison and John Lennon interviewed with Maharishi Mahesh Yogi, Mascaró wrote a letter to Harrison encouraging him in his spiritual quest.

Mascaró also sent a book (*Lamps of Fire*) that served as an inspiration for Harrison's song "The Inner Light." Harrison says this song "was written especially for Juan Mascaró because he sent me the book and is a sweet old man. It was nice, the words said everything. AMEN" (Harrison, *I Me Mine*, 118; the lyrics for "The Inner Light," Harrison's comments, and a copy of Mascaró's letter are found in pp.117–19). Mascaró summarizes: "We find in the *Gita* that there is going to be a great battle for the rule of a Kingdom; and how can we doubt that this is the Kingdom of Heaven, the kingdom of the soul? Are we going to allow the forces of light in us or the forces of darkness to win? And yet, how easy not to fight, and to find reasons to withdraw from the battle! In the *Bhagavad Gita* Arjuna becomes the soul of man and Krishna the charioteer of the soul" (Mascaró, *Bhagavad Gita*, xlvii). All citations from the *Bhagavad Gita* are taken from the Mascaró translation unless otherwise noted. On Harrison's relationship with Mascaró see also Clayson, *The Quiet One*, 149; Turner, *The Gospel According to the Beatles*, 143–44; Womack, *Long and Winding Roads*, 214.

19   Simon Brodbeck, introduction to Mascaró, *Bhagavad Gita*, xxiii.

20   Brodbeck, introduction to Mascaró, *Bhagavad Gita*, xiv.

21   Prabhupāda, *Bhagavad-Gītā*, 23.

22   Harrison, *I Me Mine*, 44.

23   Prabhupāda, *Bhagavad-Gita*, xxi.

24   Harrison, *I Me Mine*, 181. Emphasis in original.

25   Harrison, *I Me Mine*, 180.

26   *I Me Mine*, 181 (emphasis in original). Following his death on November 29, 2001, Harrison was cremated within hours and Hindu rites were performed by members of the Hare Krishna. His family immersed Harrison's ashes in the Ganges River. "According to Hindu religion, this final act would allow for the final separation of George Harrison's soul from his body and his spirit to avoid the cycle of reincarnation and to travel straight to heaven" (Marc Shapiro, *Behind Sad Eyes: The Life of George Harrison* [New York: St. Martin's, 2002], 205).

27   Prabhupāda: "when people in general are short-living, slow in spiritual realization and always disturbed by various anxieties, the best means of spiritual realization is to chant the holy name of the Lord" (*Bhagavad-Gītā*, 107). See also his comments on 10.9 (167).

28   Harrison, "Living in the Material World," taken from *I Me Mine*, 262.

29   Olivia Harrison, introduction to George Harrison, *I Me Mine*, 1–2 (emphasis in original).

30   David Fricke, "The Stories behind the Songs," in *Rolling Stone Special Edition: George Harrison* (New York: Rolling Stone, 2001), 61.

31   National Public Radio program World Café. The interview first aired

January 5, 2007, http://www.npr.org/templates/story/story.php?story
Id=6730507.

32 C. S. Lewis, *The Four Loves* (Glasgow: Collins, 1960), 45–46.

33 Larkin, *Encyclopedia of Popular Music*, 1331.

34 Yusuf Islam, *The Life of the Last Prophet* (London: Mountain of Light, 1996),
1.

35 He uses the phrase during a National Public Radio interview, posted at
www.npr.org.

36 See www.mountainoflight.co.uk. According to *Islam for Today* (islamfor
today.com), Mountain of Light is a company started by Yusuf Islam
providing various religious educational materials. Islam's personal Web
site (yusufislam.com) includes a link to the site.

37 The emphasis is original.

38 For lyrics, see the album's liner notes.

39 Listeners will recognize some lyrics from earlier albums. For instance, lines
from "Foreigner Suite" (*Foreigner*, 1973) reappear in "Heaven/Where True
Love Goes" (*An Other Cup*). There are phrases from "(I Never Wanted) To
Be a Star" (*Izitso*, 1977) in "I Think I See the Light" (*An Other Cup*).

Track 5

1 Taken from Tom Russell and Sylvia Tyson, eds., *And Then I Wrote: The
Songwriter Speaks* (Vancouver: Arsenal Pulp Press, 1995), 119.

2 Taken from Russell and Tyson, *And Then I Wrote*, 121.

3 From Harold Bloom, *The Ringers in the Tower: Studies in Romantic Tradition*
(Chicago: University of Chicago Press, 1971), 9–10, and *Poetry and
Repression: Revisionism from Blake to Stevens* (New Haven: Yale University
Press, 1976), 27, respectively. I take both citations from Graham Allen,
"The Anxiety of Choice, the Western Canon and the Future of Literature,"
in *The Salt Companion to Harold Bloom*, ed. Roy Sellars and Graham Allen
(Cambridge: Salt, 2007), 52.

4 Paul Simon, "Wartime Prayers," *Surprise* (2006). Lyrics taken from www
.paulsimon.com.

5 Frye, *Spiritus Mundi*, 15.

6 Susanne K. Langer, *Philosophy in a New Key: A Study in the Symbolism of
Reason, Rite, and Art*, 2nd ed. (New York: New American Library, 1951),
206–7 (emphasis in original). I take this quote from Rycenga, "Tales of
Change within the Sound," 146.

7 Rycenga, "Tales of Change within the Sound," 146 (emphasis in
original).

8 Frith, *Performing Rites*, 18–19.

9 As we consider the ways religious content appears in mainstream popular music, we must not overlook the subgenre of songs associated

with sacred seasons, particularly Christmas. The tremendous success of Bing Crosby's recording of "White Christmas" by Irving Berlin (first introduced in the film *Holiday Inn* in 1942), and the 1957 album *Elvis' Christmas Album*, no doubt gave impetus for the ongoing proliferation of holiday-themed albums. Few of these albums address the sacred stories behind these festivals in any detail. Adam Sandler's various versions of his "Chanukah Song" (first released on his comedy album, *What the Hell Happened?* [1996]) and AC/DC's "Mistress for Christmas" (*The Razors Edge*, 1990) are radio-play favorites, but little more than vehicles for good music and good humor. However, it remains striking that many artists record songs that explicitly engage theological implications of the Christmas story.

Christmas songs appear in most genres, as even a few examples show: The Barenaked Ladies (*Barenaked for the Holidays*, 2004; mix of Hanukkah and Christmas songs); Michael Bublé, *Let It Snow!* (2003, 2007); Mariah Carey, *Merry Christmas* (1994); The Carpenters, *Christmas Collection* (1984); Sarah McLachlan, *Wintersong* (2006); James Taylor, *At Christmas* (2006); and Twisted Sister (*A Twisted Christmas*, 2006; including "Oh Come All Ye Faithful"!). Other songs mention aspects of Christmas but do not fall under the category of seasonal music (e.g., The Who's "Christmas," in the rock opera *Tommy* [1969]; John Lennon and the Plastic Ono Band, "Happy Xmas (War Is Over)," [1971]). There is no equivalent to the fascination with Christmas music for other seasons of the religious calendars (Easter, Yom Kippur, etc.). My friend Chris Banman kindly reminded me of the relevance of seasonal songs for a discussion of religion and popular music.

10　Liner notes to Paul McCartney, *Back In the U.S.: Live 2002* (2002). In the same notes, Abe Laboriel Jr. also mentions "Five men embracing, praying and feeling the warmth and the calm before the storm."

11　Cited in Stockman, *Walk On*, 28 (ellipses original).

12　Echard, *Neil Young*, 97, referring to Stan W. Denski, "Music, Musicians, and Communication: The Personal Voice in a Common Language," in *Popular Music and Communication*, ed. J. Lull, 2nd ed. (London: Sage, 1992), 33–48.

13　Shuker, *Popular Music*, 211.

14　Jim DeRogatis, *Kaleidoscope Eyes: Psychedelic Rock from the '60s to the '90s* (Secaucus, N.J.: Carol, 1996), 12, 14. I take these citations from Fast, *Houses of the Holy*, 35–36.

15　Cf. Richard Middleton on this point: "Unfortunately, most study of lyrics has taken the form of content analysis—which tends to oversimplify the relationship between words and 'reality,' and to ignore the structural specificity of the verbal and musical signifying systems" (*Studying*

Popular Music [Milton Keynes and Philadelphia: Open University Press, 1990], 227–28).

16 With reference to rap and resistance, including comments on rap lyrics, see, e.g., Anthony Pinn, "Rap Music and Its Message: On Interpreting the Contact between Religion and Popular Culture," in *Religion and Popular Culture in America*, ed. Bruce David Forbes and Jeffrey H. Mahan (Berkeley: University of California Press, 2000), 258–75. In outlining the history of rap music, Pinn observes that when faced with "declining opportunities for socioeconomic mobility, and the accompanying marginality, young artists made use of their creative resources to establish an alternative 'way of being' in the world, complete with a vocabulary, style of dress, visual artistic expression (graffiti art emerges as early as 1971), and dance (breakdancing is present as early as 1973) uniquely their own" (263). Pinn finds some of the roots of rap music in the blues, songs that "connote a shift to an individualized and personal accounting of existence within a hostile society" (260).

17 Scobie, *Alias Bob Dylan Revisited*, 97.

18 Andy Gill and Kevin Odegard, *A Simple Twist of Fate: Bob Dylan and the Making of* Blood on the Tracks (Cambridge, Mass.: Da Capo Press, 2004), 39. See full discussion about Raeben, 37–39.

BIBLIOGRAPHY

Abrams, M. H., with Geoffrey Galt Harpham. *A Glossary of Literary Terms*, 8th ed. Toronto: Thomas Nelson, 2005.

Adams, Ryan. "Arcade Fire." *Interview* 37.7 (2007): 98–101.

Allen, Graham. "The Anxiety of Choice, the Western Canon and the Future of Literature." In *The Salt Companion to Harold Bloom*, edited by Roy Sellars and Graham Allen, 52–65. Cambridge: Salt, 2007.

———. *Harold Bloom: A Poetics of Conflict*. New York: Harvester Wheatsheaf, 1994.

———. *Intertextuality*. The New Critical Idiom. London: Routledge, 2000.

Allen, Graham, and Roy Sellars. "Harold Bloom and Critical Responsibility." In *The Salt Companion to Harold Bloom*, edited by Graham Allen and Roy Sellars, xiii–xxiv. Cambridge: Salt, 2007.

Allison Jr., Dale C. *The Love There That's Sleeping: The Art and Spirituality of George Harrison*. New York: Continuum, 2006.

Alter, Robert. *Canon and Creativity: Modern Writing and the Authority of Scripture*. New Haven: Yale University Press, 2000.

Aristotle. *Poetics*. In *Aristotle's Poetics: A Translation and Commentary for Students of Literature*, edited by Leon Golden and O. B. Hardison Jr. Gainesville, Fla.: University Press of Florida, 1982.

———. *Politics*. In *The Politics of Aristotle*. Translated by Ernest Barker. London: Oxford University Press, 1958.

Arnett, Jeffrey Jensen. *Metalheads: Heavy Metal Music and Adolescent Alienation*. Boulder: Westview Press, 1996.

Bakhtin, Mikhail. *Rabelais and His World*. Translated by Helene Iswolsky. Bloomington: Indiana University Press, 1984.

Beal, Timothy K. *Religion and Its Monsters*. London: Routledge, 2002.

Begbie, Jeremy S. *Resounding Truth: Christian Wisdom in the World of Music*. Engaging Culture. Grand Rapids: Baker, 2007.

Bloom, Harold. *The Anxiety of Influence: A Theory of Poetry*. 2nd ed. New York: Oxford University Press, 1997.

———. *Genius: A Mosaic of One Hundred Exemplary Creative Minds*. New York: Warner, 2002.

———. *Poetry and Repression: Revisionism from Blake to Stevens*. New Haven: Yale University Press, 1976.

———. *The Ringers in the Tower: Studies in Romantic Tradition*. Chicago: University of Chicago Press, 1971.

———. *The Western Canon: The Books and School of the Ages*. New York: Riverhead, 1994.

Bono. "Introduction." *Selections from the Book of Psalms*. The Pocket Canon, vii–xii. New York: Grove, 1999.

Carpenter, Lorraine. "Hot Property: Montreal's Next Big Thing, The Arcade Fire, Channel Familial Grief and Internal Upheaval into an Ecstatic Debut Album." *Montreal Mirror* 20.13, September 16–22, 2004. http://www.montrealmirror.com/2004/091604/cover_music.html.

Cashmore, Ellis. *Celebrity/Culture*. New York: Routledge, 2006.

Cave, Nick. *The Complete Lyrics: 1978–2006*. London: Penguin Books, 2007.

Chidester, David. "The Church of Baseball, the Fetish of Coca-Cola, and the Potlach of Rock 'n' Roll." In *Religion and Popular Culture in America*, edited by Bruce David Forbes and Jeffrey H. Mahan, 219–38. Berkeley: University of California Press, 2000.

Clapton, Eric. *Clapton: The Autobiography*. New York: Broadway Books, 2007.

Clark, Lynn Schofield. "Why Study Popular Culture?: Or, How to Build a Case for Your Thesis in a Religious Studies or Theology Department." In *Between Sacred and Profane: Researching Religion and Popular Culture*, edited by Gordon Lynch, 5–20. London: I. B. Tauris, 2007.

Clark, Roger Y. *Stranger Gods: Salman Rushdie's Other Worlds*. Montreal and Kingston: McGill-Queen's University Press, 2001.

Clayson, Adam. *The Quiet One: A Life of George Harrison*. London: Sidgwick & Jackson, 1990.

Cobb, Kelton. *The Blackwell Guide to Theology and Popular Culture*. Blackwell Guides to Theology Malden, Mass.: Blackwell, 2005.

Cohen, Leonard. *Book of Longing*. Toronto: McClelland & Stewart, 2006.

Cooper, Alice, with Keith and Kent Zimmerman. *Alice Cooper, Golf Monster: A Rock 'N' Roller's 12 Steps to Becoming a Golf Addict*. New York: Crown, 2007.

Cousland, J. R. C. "God, the Bad, and the Ugly: The *Vi(t)a Negativa* of Nick Cave and P. J. Harvey." In *Call Me the Seeker: Listening to Religion in Popular Music*, edited by Michael J. Gilmour, 129–57. New York: Continuum, 2005.

Cowan, Douglas E. *Sacred Terror: Religion and Horror on the Silver Screen*. Waco, Tex.: Baylor, 2008.

Cummings, Burton. Interview on *Morningside*, with Peter Gzowski. Canadian Broadcasting Corporation, April 12, 1996.

Daner, F. *The American Children of Krsna*. New York: Holt, Rinehart & Winston, 1976.

Dansby, Andrew. "David Gray's 'New Day': Death and Success Share Spotlight on New Album." *Rolling Stone*, posted November 1, 2002. http://www.rollingstone.com/artists/davidgray/articles/story/593 4587/david_grays_new_day.

Day, Aidan. *Jokerman: Reading the Lyrics of Bob Dylan*. Oxford: Basil Blackwell, 1988.

Denski, Stan W. "Music, Musicians, and Communication: The Personal Voice in a Common Language." In *Popular Music and Communication*, edited by J. Lull, 33–48. 2nd ed. London: Sage, 1992.

DeRogatis, Jim. *Kaleidoscope Eyes: Psychedelic Rock from the '60s to the '90s*. Secaucus, N.J.: Carol, 1996.

Detweiler, Robert, and David Jasper, eds. *Religion and Literature: A Reader*. Louisville, Ky.: Westminster John Knox, 2000.

DiFranco, Ani. *Verses*. New York: Seven Stories Press, 2007.

Downie, Gordon. *Coke Machine Glow*. Toronto: Vintage Canada, 2001.

Dunphy, Eamon. *Unforgettable Fire: The Story of U2*. London: Penguin, 1987.

Dylan, Bob. *Chronicles: Volume One*. New York: Simon & Schuster, 2004.

———. *Lyrics: 1962–2001*. New York: Simon & Schuster, 2004.

Echard, William. *Neil Young and the Poetics of Energy*. Bloomington: Indiana University Press, 2005.

Eco, Umberto. *On Literature*. Translated by Martin McLaughlin. Orlando: Harcourt, 2004.

Edwards, Gavin. "The Magnificent Seven." *Rolling Stone* 1027 (2007): 63–64, 66–67.

Einarson, John, and Randy Bachman. *Randy Bachman: Takin' Care of Business*. Toronto: McArthur, 2000.

Eliade, Mircea. *The Sacred and the Profane: The Nature of Religion*. Translated by Willard R. Trask. New York: Harcourt Brace & World, 1959.

Fast, Susan. *In the Houses of the Holy: Led Zeppelin and the Power of Rock Music*. New York: Oxford University Press, 2001.

Finnegan, Frances. *Do Penance or Perish: Magdalen Aylums in Ireland*. New York: Oxford University Press, 2004.

Flanagan, Bill. *U2 at the End of the World*. New York: Delta, 1995.

Forbes, Bruce David. "Introduction: Finding Religion in Unexpected Places." In *Religion and Popular Culture in America*, edited by Bruce David Forbes and Jeffrey H. Mahan, 1–20. Berkeley: University of California Press, 2000.

Forbes, Bruce David, and Jeffrey H. Mahan, eds. *Religion and Popular Culture in America*. Berkeley: University of California Press, 2000.

Freud, Sigmund. "The Uncanny." 1919. *The Standard Edition of the Complete Psychological Works of Sigmund Freud*, vol. 17, 217–56. Translated by James Strachey et al. London: Hogarth, 1955.

Fricke, David. "The Stories behind the Songs." In *Rolling Stone Special Edition: George Harrison*. New York: Rolling Stone, 2001.

Frith, Simon. *Performing Rites: On the Value of Popular Music*. Cambridge: Harvard University Press, 1996.

Frye, Northrop. *Spiritus Mundi: Essays on Literature, Myth, and Society*. Bloomington: Indiana University Press, 1976.

Geldof, Bob. *Geldof in Africa*. London: Arrow Books, 2005.

Gill, Andy, and Kevin Odegard. *A Simple Twist of Fate: Bob Dylan and the Making of* Blood On The Tracks. Cambridge, Mass.: Da Capo Press, 2004.

Gilmour, Michael J. "Arcade Fire's Parodic Bible." *Journal of Religion and Popular Culture* (forthcoming).

———. "*Brainwashed*, by George Harrison and the *Bhagavad Gita*." *Journal of Religion and Popular Culture* 8 (2004). http://www.usask.ca/relst/jrpc/art8-georgeharrison.html.

———. "Going Back to the Prairies: Neil Young's Heterotopia in the Post-9/11 World." In *West of Eden: New Approaches in Canadian Prairie Literature*, edited by Sue Sorensen, 205–18. Winnipeg: Canadian Mennonite University Press, 2008.

———. "The Prophet Jeremiah, Aung San Suu Kyi, and U2's *All That You Can't Leave Behind*." In *Call Me the Seeker: Listening to Religion in Popular*

Music, edited by Michael J. Gilmour, 34–43. New York: Continuum, 2005.

Godwin, Robert. *Led Zeppelin: The Press Reports*. Burlington, Ontario: CG, 1997.

Gray, Michael. *Song and Dance Man III: The Art of Bob Dylan*. London: Continuum, 2000.

Greeley, Andrew. *God in Popular Culture*. Chicago: Thomas More, 1988.

Greenblatt, Stephen, M. H. Abrams, et al., eds. *The Norton Anthology of English Literature: The Major Authors*. 8th ed. New York: Norton, 2006.

Greene, Joshua M. *Here Comes the Sun: The Spiritual and Musical Journey of George Harrison*. Hoboken, N.J.: John Wiley & Sons, 2006.

Harrison, George. *I Me Mine*. San Francisco: Chronicle Books, 2002.

Holm-Hudson, Kevin. "Introduction." In *Progressive Rock Reconsidered*, edited by Kevin Holm-Hudson, 1–18. London: Routledge, 2002.

Hulsether, Mark D. "Like a Sermon: Popular Religion in Madonna Videos." In *Religion and Popular Culture in America*, edited by Bruce David Forbes and Jeffrey H. Mahan, 77–100. Berkeley: University of California Press, 2000.

Hunter, Robert. "Foreword." In *The Complete Annotated Grateful Dead Lyrics*, edited by Alan Trist and David Dodd, annotations by David Dodd, xi–xxvi. New York: Free Press, 2005.

Hutcheon, Linda. *A Poetics of Postmodernism: History, Theory, Fiction*. London: Routledge, 1988.

———. *A Theory of Adaptation*. London: Routledge, 2006.

———. *A Theory of Parody: The Teachings of Twentieth-Century Art Forms*. Urbana: University of Illinois Press, 2000.

Islam, Yusuf. *The Life of the Last Prophet*. London: Mountain of Light, 1996.

Kerouac, Jack. 1957. *On the Road*. New York: Penguin, 1991.

Keys, Alicia. *Tears for Water: Songbook of Poems and Lyrics*. New York: Penguin, 2004.

Klein, Calvin, and Bryan Adams. *American Woman*. Brooklyn: Powerhouse Books, 2005.

Knight, David B. *Landscapes in Music: Space, Place, and Time in the World's Great Music*. Lanham, Md.: Rowman & Littlefield, 2006.

Kristeva, Julia. *The Portable Kristeva*. Edited by Kelly Oliver. Updated edition. New York: Columbia University Press, 2002.

Langer, Susanne K. *Philosophy in a New Key: A Study in the Symbolism of Reason, Rite, and Art*. 2nd ed. New York: New American Library, 1951.

Larkin, Colin, compiler and ed. *The Encyclopedia of Popular Music*. 5th concise ed. London: Omnibus Press, 2007.

Lattin, Don. *Following Our Bliss: How the Spiritual Ideals of the Sixties Shape Our Lives Today*. New York: HarperCollins, 2003.

Lewis, C. S. *The Four Loves*. Glasgow: Collins, 1960.

Lynch, Gordon. "What Is This 'Religion' in the Study of Religion and Popular Culture?" In *Between the Sacred and Profane: Research Religion and Popular Culture*, edited by Gordon Lynch, 125–42. London: I.B. Tauris, 2007.

Macan, Edward. *Rocking the Classics: English Progressive Rock and the Counterculture*. New York: Oxford University Press, 1997.

Martens, Paul. "Metallica and the God that Failed: An Unfinished Tragedy in Three Acts." In *Call Me the Seeker: Listening to Religion in Popular Music*, edited by Michael J. Gilmour, 95–114. New York: Continuum, 2005.

Mascaró, Juan. "Introduction." *The Bhagavad Gita*. Translated by Juan Mascaró with updated introduction by Simon Brodbeck. London: Penguin, 2003.

Metallica. *Metallica: The Complete Lyrics*. New York: Cherry Lane Music, 2002.

Michaels, Sean. "Arcade Fire: Inside the Church of Arcade Fire." *Paste Magazine* 30, published online April 11, 2007. http://www.pastemaga zine.com/action/article/4047/feature/music/arcade_fire.

Middleton, Richard. "Popular Music Analysis and Musicology: Bridging the Gap." *Popular Music* 12.2 (1993): 177–90.

———. *Studying Popular Music*. Milton Keynes and Philadelphia: Open University Press, 1990.

Milton, John. *The Poetical Works of John Milton*. Edited by Charles Dexter Cleveland. Ann Arbor: University of Michigan Library, 2006.

Moreman, Christopher M. "Devil Music and the Great Beast: Ozzy Osbourne, Aleister Crowley, and the Christian Right." *Journal of Religion and Popular Culture* 5 (2003): http://www.usask.ca/relst/jrpc/art5-devilmusic.html.

Negus, Keith. "Living, Breathing Songs: Singing Along with Bob Dylan." *Oral Tradition* 22.1 (2007): 71–83.

Nelson, Jon Wiley. *Your God Is Alive and Well and Appearing in Popular Culture*. Philadelphia: Westminster, 1976.

Nichol, B. P. *An H in the Heart: A Reader*. Selected by George Bowering and

Michael Ondaatje. The Modern Canadian Poets Series. Toronto: M & S, 1994.

Niebuhr, Reinhold. *The Essential Reinhold Niebuhr: Selected Essays and Addresses.* Edited by Robert McAfee Brown. New Haven: Yale University Press, 1986.

Nonnekes, Paul. *Three Moments of Love in Leonard Cohen and Bruce Cockburn.* Montreal: Black Rose Books, 2001.

Oppenheimer, Mark. *Knocking on Heaven's Door: American Religion in the Age of Counterculture.* New Haven: Yale University Press, 2003.

Pinn, Anthony. "Rap Music and Its Message: On Interpreting the Contact between Religion and Popular Culture." In *Religion and Popular Culture in America,* edited by Bruce David Forbes and Jeffrey H. Mahan, 258–75. Berkeley: University of California Press, 2000.

Powell, Mark Allan. *Encyclopedia of Contemporary Christian Music.* Peabody, Mass.: Hendrickson, 2002.

Prabhupāda, His Divine Grace A. C. Bhaktivedanta Swami. *Bhagavad-Gītā As It Is.* New York: The Bhaktivedanta Book Trust, 1972.

———. *KRSNA: The Supreme Personality of Godhead.* New York: The Bhaktivedanta Book Trust, 1970.

Reece, Gregory L. *Elvis Religion: The Cult of the King.* London: I.B. Tauris, 2006.

Richter, David H., ed. *The Critical Tradition: Classic Texts and Contemporary Trends.* 2nd ed. Boston: Bedford/St. Martin's, 1998.

Ricks, Christopher. *Dylan's Visions of Sin.* New York: HarperCollins, 2003.

Roberts, John Storm. *Black Music of Two Worlds: African, Caribbean, Latin, and African American Traditions.* 2nd rev. ed. New York: Schirmer, 1998.

Robins, Wayne. *A Brief History of Rock, Off the Record.* London: Routledge, 2008.

Romanowski, William D. *Eyes Wide Open: Looking for God in Popular Culture.* Rev. and exp. ed. Grand Rapids: Brazos, 2007.

Rushdie, Salman. *The Ground Beneath Her Feet.* Toronto: Alfred A. Knopf, 1999.

———. *The Satanic Verses.* New York: Picador, 1988.

———. *Step Across This Line: Collected Nonfiction 1992–2002.* Toronto: Alfred A. Knopf Canada, 2002.

Russell, Tom, and Sylvia Tyson, eds. *And Then I Wrote: The Songwriter Speaks.* Vancouver: Arsenal Pulp Press, 1995.

Rycenga, Jennifer. "Tales of Change within the Sound: Form, Lyrics, and

Philosophy in the Music of Yes." In *Progressive Rock Reconsidered*, edited by Kevin Holm-Hudson 143–66. London: Routledge, 2002.

Saliers, Don E. *Music and Theology*. Horizons in Theology. Nashville: Abingdon, 2007.

Scharen, Christian. *One Step Closer: Why U2 Matters to Those Seeking God*. Grand Rapids: Brazos, 2006.

Scobie, Stephen. *Alias Bob Dylan Revisited*. Calgary: Red Deer Press, 2003.

Shapiro, Marc. *Behind Sad Eyes: The Life of George Harrison*. New York: St. Martin's, 2002.

Sharpe-Young, Garry. *Metal: The Definitive Guide*. London: Jawbone Press, 2007.

Sheinbaum, John J. "Progressive Rock and the Inversion of Musical Values." In *Progressive Rock Reconsidered*, edited by Kevin Holm-Hudson, 21–42. London: Routledge, 2002.

Shepard, Sam. *The Rolling Thunder Logbook*. Cambridge, Mass.: Da Capo, 2004.

Shuker, Roy. *Popular Music: The Key Concepts*, 2nd ed. London: Routledge, 2005.

Starr, Larry, and Christopher Waterman. *American Popular Music: From Minstrels to MP3*. 2nd ed. Oxford: Oxford University Press, 2007.

Stewart, Allison. "Arcade Fire's 'Bible': A Searing Success." Special to *The Washington Post*, Sunday, March 11, 2007. http://www.washingtonpost .com/wp-dyn/content/article/2007/03/09/AR2007030900480.html.

Sting. *Lyrics*. New York: The Dial Press, 2007.

Stockman, Steve. *Walk On: The Spiritual Journey of U2*. Updated and expanded edition. Orlando: Relevant Books, 2005.

Streete, Gail Corrington. *The Strange Woman: Sex and Power in the Bible*. Louisville, Ky.: Westminster John Knox, 1997.

Suu Kyi, Aung San. *Letters From Burma*. London: Penguin, 1997.

Suu Kyi, Aung San, and Alan Clements, *The Voice of Hope: Conversations with Alan Clements*. New York: Seven Stories, 1997.

Sylvan, Robin. *Traces of the Spirit: The Religious Dimensions of Popular Music*. New York: New York University Press, 2002.

Turner, Steve. *The Gospel According to the Beatles*. Louisville, Ky.: Westminster John Knox, 2006.

Vagacs, Robert. *Religious Nuts, Political Fanatics: U2 in Theological Perspective*. Eugene, Oreg.: Cascade Books, 2005.

Van Pelt, Doug. *Rock Stars On God: 20 Artists Speak Their Mind about Faith*. Orlando: Relevant Books, 2004.

Waits, Tom. *The Lyrics of Tom Waits: The Early Years*. New York: Harper-Collins, 2007.

Walser, Robert. *Running with the Devil: Power, Gender and Madness in Heavy Metal Music*. Hanover: Wesleyan University Press/University Press of New England, 1993.

Ward, Pete. "The Eucharist and the Turn to Culture." In *Between Sacred and Profane: Researching Religion and Popular Culture*, edited by Gordon Lynch, 82–93. London: I. B. Tauris, 2007.

Webb, Stephen H. *Dylan Redeemed: From* Highway 61 *to* Saved. London: Continuum, 2006.

Weinstein, Deena. *Heavy Metal: A Cultural Sociology*. New York: Lexington Books, 1991.

———. "Progressive Rock as Text: The Lyrics of Roger Waters." In *Progressive Rock Reconsidered*, edited by Kevin Holm-Hudson, 91–109. London: Routledge, 2002.

Womack, Kenneth. *Long and Winding Roads: The Evolving Artistry of The Beatles*. London: Continuum, 2007.

INDEX